Hanoi

Mason Florence

LONELY PLANET PUBLICATIONS
Melbourne • Oakland • London • Paris

Hanoi
1st edition – September 1999

Published by
Lonely Planet Publications Pty Ltd A.C.N. 005 607 983
192 Burwood Rd, Hawthorn, Victoria 3122, Australia

Lonely Planet Offices
Australia PO Box 617, Hawthorn, Victoria 3122
USA 150 Linden St, Oakland, CA 94607
UK 10a Spring Place, London NW5 3BH
France 1 rue du Dahomey, 75011 Paris

Photographs
All of the images in this guide are available for licensing from
Lonely Planet Images.
email: lpi@lonelyplanet.com.au

Front cover photograph
Billboard (Bethune Carmichael)

ISBN 0 86442 799 9

Printed by Colorcraft Ltd, Hong Kong

Contents – Maps

The Author

Mason Florence

Mason gave up his budding career as a rodeo cowboy in 1990, traded in his boots and spurs for a Nikon and a laptop, and relocated from Colorado to Japan. Now a Kyoto-based photo-journalist, he spends half the year on the road in Asia, and free moments in Japan restoring an old thatched-roof farmhouse in rural Shikoku and frequenting Kyoto's finest honkytonk bars. Mason has worked on Lonely Planet's *Japan, Kyoto, South-East Asia* and *Ho Chi Minh City* guidebooks. His photographs and articles have been printed in publications around the world.

Since his first arrival in Vietnam in 1991, Mason has returned over a dozen times. He has travelled the length of the country by every conceivable means of transport; from motorbike to water buffalo to basket boat. Mason's photographs, in particular those of Vietnam's colourful ethnic minorities, appear all over the country as 'Postcards from the Edge'.

FROM THE AUTHOR

Mason would like to thank: Linh, Vinh, Thang, Tuan Anh, Tung, Nghia, Gino 'the Hammer' and Hang, Fredo, Jeff, Max and Aaron, Bobby and Simon, Digby and Marcus; plus anyone else who I've forgotten. At LP, muchas gracias to Ron Gallagher, Paul Dawson, Kristin Odijk and Russ Kerr.

This Book

From the Publisher

This book was edited and proofed in Melbourne by Ron Gallagher and Shelley Muir, and mapped, designed and laid out by Paul 'Cool Hand' Dawson. Guillaume Roux designed the cover, Quentin Frayne wrote the Vietnamese Language section and Digby Greenhalgh advised on motorbiking in Vietnam. Thanks also to the A-Team, Chris Love, Greg Alford, Kristin Odijk, Linda Suttie, Russell Kerr and Tim Uden for help and advice.

Foreword

ABOUT LONELY PLANET GUIDEBOOKS

The story begins with a classic travel adventure: Tony and Maureen Wheeler's 1972 journey across Europe and Asia to Australia. Useful information about the overland trail did not exist at that time, so Tony and Maureen published the first Lonely Planet guidebook to meet a growing need.

From a kitchen table, then from a tiny office in Melbourne (Australia), Lonely Planet has become the largest independent travel publisher in the world, an international company with offices in Melbourne, Oakland (USA), London (UK) and Paris (France).

Today Lonely Planet guidebooks cover the globe. There is an ever-growing list of books and there's information in a variety of forms and media. Some things haven't changed. The main aim is still to help make it possible for adventurous travellers to get out there – to explore and better understand the world.

At Lonely Planet we believe travellers can make a positive contribution to the countries they visit – if they respect their host communities and spend their money wisely. Since 1986 a percentage of the income from each book has been donated to aid projects and human rights campaigns.

Updates Lonely Planet thoroughly updates each guidebook as often as possible. This usually means there are around two years between editions, although for more unusual or more stable destinations the gap can be longer. Check the imprint page (following the colour map at the beginning of the book) for publication dates.

Between editions up-to-date information is available in two free newsletters – the paper *Planet Talk* and email *Comet* (to subscribe, contact any Lonely Planet office) – and on our Web site at www.lonelyplanet.com. The *Upgrades* section of the Web site covers a number of important and volatile destinations and is regularly updated by Lonely Planet authors. *Scoop* covers news and current affairs relevant to travellers. And, lastly, the *Thorn Tree* bulletin board and *Postcards* section of the site carry unverified, but fascinating, reports from travellers.

Correspondence The process of creating new editions begins with the letters, postcards and emails received from travellers. This correspondence often includes suggestions, criticisms and comments about the current editions. Interesting excerpts are immediately passed on via newsletters and the Web site, and everything goes to our authors to be verified when they're researching on the road. We're keen to get more feedback from organisations or individuals who represent communities visited by travellers.

> Lonely Planet gathers information for everyone who's curious about the planet – and especially for those who explore it first-hand. Through guidebooks, phrasebooks, activity guides, maps, literature, newsletters, image library, TV series and Web site we act as an information exchange for a worldwide community of travellers.

Research Authors aim to gather sufficient practical information to enable travellers to make informed choices and to make the mechanics of a journey run smoothly. They also research historical and cultural background to help enrich the travel experience and allow travellers to understand and respond appropriately to cultural and environmental issues.

Authors don't stay in every hotel because that would mean spending a couple of months in each medium-sized city and, no, they don't eat at every restaurant because that would mean stretching belts beyond capacity. They do visit hotels and restaurants to check standards and prices, but feedback based on readers' direct experiences can be very helpful.

Many of our authors work undercover, others aren't so secretive. None of them accept freebies in exchange for positive write-ups. And none of our guidebooks contain any advertising.

Production Authors submit their raw manuscripts and maps to offices in Australia, USA, UK or France. Editors and cartographers – all experienced travellers themselves – then begin the process of assembling the pieces. When the book finally hits the shops, some things are already out of date, we start getting feedback from readers and the process begins again …

WARNING & REQUEST

Things change – prices go up, schedules change, good places go bad and bad places go bankrupt – nothing stays the same. So, if you find things better or worse, recently opened or long since closed, please tell us and help make the next edition even more accurate and useful. We genuinely value all the feedback we receive. Julie Young coordinates a well travelled team that reads and acknowledges every letter, postcard and email and ensures that every morsel of information finds its way to the appropriate authors, editors and cartographers for verification.

Everyone who writes to us will find their name in the next edition of the appropriate guidebook. They will also receive the latest issue of *Planet Talk*, our quarterly printed newsletter, or *Comet*, our monthly email newsletter. Subscriptions to both newsletters are free. The very best contributions will be rewarded with a free guidebook.

Excerpts from your correspondence may appear in new editions of Lonely Planet guidebooks, the Lonely Planet Web site, *Planet Talk* or *Comet*, so please let us know if you *don't* want your letter published or your name acknowledged.

Send all correspondence to the Lonely Planet office closest to you:

Australia: PO Box 617, Hawthorn, Victoria 3122
USA: 150 Linden St, Oakland, CA 94607
UK: 10A Spring Place, London NW5 3BH
France: 1 rue du Dahomey, 75011 Paris

Or email us at: talk2us@lonelyplanet.com.au

For news, views and updates see our Web site: www.lonelyplanet.com

HOW TO USE A LONELY PLANET GUIDEBOOK

The best way to use a Lonely Planet guidebook is any way you choose. At Lonely Planet we believe the most memorable travel experiences are often those that are unexpected, and the finest discoveries are those you make yourself. Guidebooks are not intended to be used as if they provide a detailed set of infallible instructions!

Contents All Lonely Planet guidebooks follow roughly the same format. The Facts about the Destination chapters or sections give background information ranging from history to weather. Facts for the Visitor gives practical information on issues like visas and health. Getting There & Away gives a brief starting point for researching travel to and from the destination. Getting Around gives an overview of the transport options when you arrive.

The peculiar demands of each destination determine how subsequent chapters are broken up, but some things remain constant. We always start with background, then proceed to sights, places to stay, places to eat, entertainment, getting there and away, and getting around information – in that order.

Heading Hierarchy Lonely Planet headings are used in a strict hierarchical structure that can be visualised as a set of Russian dolls. Each heading (and its following text) is encompassed by any preceding heading that is higher on the hierarchical ladder.

Entry Points We do not assume guidebooks will be read from beginning to end, but that people will dip into them. The traditional entry points are the list of contents and the index. In addition, however, some books have a complete list of maps and an index map illustrating map coverage.

There may also be a colour map that shows highlights. These highlights are dealt with in greater detail in the Facts for the Visitor chapter, along with planning questions and suggested itineraries. Each chapter covering a geographical region usually begins with a locator map and another list of highlights. Once you find something of interest in a list of highlights, turn to the index.

Maps Maps play a crucial role in Lonely Planet guidebooks and include a huge amount of information. A legend is printed on the back page. We seek to have complete consistency between maps and text, and to have every important place in the text captured on a map. Map key numbers usually start in the top left corner.

Although inclusion in a guidebook usually implies a recommendation we cannot list every good place. Exclusion does not necessarily imply criticism. In fact there are a number of reasons why we might exclude a place – sometimes it is simply inappropriate to encourage an influx of travellers.

Introduction

Hanoi, capital of the Socialist Republic of Vietnam, is among the most beguiling cities in Asia. It is an enchanting city of lakes, shaded boulevards and verdant public parks where jean-clad young lovers stroll beside their venerable elders practising elegant, slow-motion shadow-boxing. Hanoi's prosperous shop owners exemplify Vietnam's new economic reforms, while deeply rooted traditional ways live on in pockets of the city's ancient Old Quarter.

This city of three million inhabitants boasts countless attractions, from temples, pagodas and monuments to bustling markets, nightlife and outstanding food. The city centre is an architectural museum piece, its blocks of ochre buildings retaining the air of a provincial French town of the 1930s. By day the city streets are a sea of motorscooters zigzagging between cyclo pedicabs loaded with fruit, livestock and human cargo, but by nightfall the clamour and cornucopia of sounds, sights and smells slips back into a calm and peaceful milieu.

Most foreign visitors find the city slow paced and charming. Physically, it's a more attractive city than Saigon – there is less traffic, noise and pollution, and more greenery and open space. Some have called it the Paris of the Orient – Parisians may find that either an insult or a compliment. For some, Hanoi still carries an indelible stigma of a misguided war.

Over centuries of civil strife and foreign domination, Hanoi has borne a variety of names. In the year 1010 the capital was transferred from the mountains of Hoa Lu to present-day Hanoi, and renamed Thang Long (City of the Soaring Dragon). The city was named Ha Noi (City in a Bend of the River) by Emperor Tu Duc in 1831. In its turbulent 1000 year history, Hanoi has never metamorphosed so much as in the short post-reunification period since 1975. After the fall of South Vietnam to communist forces in 1975, Hanoi became virtually isolated from the world, but in 1989 Vietnam flung open the doors to foreign tourists and investors, becoming a popular travel destination. In the early 1990s, Hanoi earned a bad reputation for routine police harassment of western visitors (both backpackers and businesspeople), as well as for resisting economic reform; as a result, most foreign investment flowed into Saigon and the south. But attitudes have changed remarkably fast, and the Hanoi of today is dramatically different from what it was just a few years ago.

Much of the city's age-old façade has been altered in a euphoric rush to modernise. Shop and restaurant owners have been major beneficiaries of the city's economic resurgence. Colour and liveliness have returned to the streets (and unfortunately so has the traffic). New high-rises crowd out the timeworn French colonial houses, the number of cars and motorbikes increases daily, while postcard vendors and cyclo drivers trawl the streets for tourists. Hotels have improved dramatically and once-bare shelves in state-run stores are now overflowing with goods. Even the staid socialist restaurants have been revamped, or replaced by modern cafés where Hanoian yuppies sip cappuccinos and compare mobile phones.

Birthplace to so much of Vietnam's traditional culture, Hanoi, more than any other city in Vietnam, is a unique fusion of old and new, both personifying the spirit of old Vietnam and its ancient heritage, and perfectly reflecting the rapid changes sweeping the country.

Facts about Hanoi

HISTORY
Prehistory

Archaeological evidence indicates that human habitation of northern Vietnam goes back about 500,000 years. Mesolithic and Neolithic cultures existed 10,000 years ago; these groups may have engaged in primitive agriculture as early as 7000 BC.

The site of present-day Hanoi has been populated since the late Neolithic period. Early inhabitants formed a feudally organised society reliant on slash-and-burn agriculture, hunting and fishing, and animal husbandry; these proto-Vietnamese also carried on trade with other peoples in the area.

Under the Hung kings the Bronze Age Dong Son culture emerged in the first millennium BC. At that time the kingdom was known as Van Lang and included parts of southern China and the Red River delta.

Chinese Rule (circa 250 BC to 938 AD)

In 258 BC the two millennium old Hung kingdom was brought to an end by the warlord Thuc Phan. He established the short-lived Kingdom of Au Lac with its capital at Co Loa (15km north of present-day Hanoi).

In 208 BC Au Lac fell to the former Chinese general Trieu Da, who founded the kingdom of Nam Viet. The Chinese conquered the Red River (Song Hong) Delta in 3 BC and during the ensuing centuries, significant numbers of Chinese settlers, officials and scholars moved to the delta, taking over large tracts of land. They attempted to impose a centralised state system on the Vietnamese and to forcibly Sinocise their culture.

There were major rebellions against Chinese feudal rule in the 3rd and 6th centuries. In 544 Chinese forces were defeated in a revolt led by self-proclaimed King Ly Bi. Ly Bi who transferred the capital to the site near West Lake (Ho Tay) and ordered the building of Chua Tran Quoc, Hanoi's oldest existing pagoda. Later, Ly Bi's nephew Ly Phat Tu relocated the capital back to Co Loa, but in 602 was dethroned when China conquered again.

In 679 the Chinese named the country Annam, which means 'the Pacified South', and on the site of present-day Hanoi made Tong Binh their capital.

Independence from China (10th Century)

In the aftermath of the collapse of the Tang Dynasty in China in the early 10th century, the Vietnamese revolted against Chinese rule. In 938 Ngo Quyen vanquished the Chinese armies at a battle on the Bach Dang River to end 1000 years of Chinese rule.

Ngo Quyen established an independent Vietnamese state, but it was not until 968 that Dinh Bo Linh triumphed, ending the civil anarchy that followed Ngo Quyen's death. In return for recognition of their de facto independence, the Vietnamese accepted Chinese sovereignty and agreed to pay triennial tribute.

The dynasty founded by Dinh Bo Linh survived only until 980, when Le Dai Hanh overthrew it, beginning what is known as the Early Le Dynasty (980-1009).

Ly Dynasty (1010-1225)

From the 11th to 13th centuries, the independence of the Vietnamese Kingdom (Dai Viet) was consolidated under the emperors of the Ly Dynasty, founded by Ly Thai To. Emperor Ly moved his capital from the limestone mountains of Hoa Lu to Dai La (Hanoi) in 1010 AD. He renamed the city Thang Long, City of the Soaring Dragon, claiming to have seen there a golden dragon soaring into the sky.

The foundation of the old Dai La fortress was rebuilt into a grand Royal Enclosure, outside whose walls common people formed guilds. The names of many remain today on the streets of the city's Old Quarter.

Under Ly Thai To, leaders reorganised the administrative system, founded the Temple of Literature as the nation's first university, promoted agriculture, and built the first embankments for flood control along the Red River. Confucian scholars fell out of official favour because of their close cultural links to China; at the same time the early Ly monarchs, whose dynasty had come to power with Buddhist support, promoted Buddhism.

The Confucian philosophy of government and society, emphasising educational attainment, ritual performance and government authority, reasserted itself with the graduation of the first class from the Temple of Literature in 1075. Following years of classical education, these scholars went into government service, becoming what the west came to call mandarins. The outlines of the Vietnamese mandarinal system of government – according to which the state was run by a scholar class recruited in civil service examinations – date from this era.

During the Ly Dynasty, the Chinese, Khmers and Chams repeatedly attacked Thang Long, but were repelled, most notably under the renowned strategist and tactician Ly Thuong Kiet (1030-1105), a military mandarin of royal blood who is still revered as a national hero.

Tran Dynasty (1225-1400)
After years of civil strife, the Tran Dynasty overthrew the Ly Dynasty. The Tran increased the land under cultivation to feed the growing population and improved the dikes on the Red River.

After the dreaded Mongol warrior Kublai Khan completed his conquest of China in the mid-13th century, he demanded the right to cross Dai Viet territory on his way to attack the Champa Kingdom. The Vietnamese refused this demand, but the Mongols – 500,000 of them – came anyway. The outnumbered Vietnamese under Tran Hung Dao twice attacked the invaders, forcing them back to China.

When the Tran Dynasty was overthrown in 1400 by Ho Qui Ly, a mandarin, both the Tran loyalists and the Chams (who had sacked Hanoi in 1371) encouraged Chinese intervention. The Chinese readily complied and took control of Vietnam in 1407, imposing a regime characterised by heavy taxation and slave labour. Chinese culture was forced on the population, and many of the city's cultural and religious treasures were destroyed. The Chinese also took the national archives (and some of the country's intellectuals as well) to China, an irreparable loss to Vietnamese civilisation.

Later Le Dynasty (1428-1524)
Hanoi (then called Dong Kinh) served as the capital of the Later Le Dynasty, founded by Le Loi, from its establishment in 1428 until 1788, when it was overthrown by Nguyen Hué, founder of the Tay Son Dynasty.

In 1418, Le Loi began to organise what came to be known as the Lam Son Uprising, by travelling around the countryside to rally the people against the Chinese. Despite several defeats, he persisted, earning the respect of the peasantry by ensuring that even when facing starvation his guerrilla troops

Dynasties of Independent Vietnam	
dynasty	year
Ngo Dynasty	939-965
Dinh Dynasty	968-980
Early Le Dynasty	980-1009
Ly Dynasty	1010-1225
Tran Dynasty	1225-1400
Ho Dynasty	1400-1407
Post-Tran Dynasty	1407-1413
Chinese Rule	1414-1427
Later Le Dynasty	1428-1524 (nominally until 1788)
Mac Dynasty	1527-1592
Trinh Lords of the North	1539-1787
Nguyen Lords of the South	1558-1778
Tay Son Dynasty	1788-1802
Nguyen Dynasty	1802-1945

did not pillage the land. After his victory in 1428, Le Loi declared himself Emperor Le Thai To, thus beginning the Later Le Dynasty. To this day, Le Loi is revered as one of Vietnam's greatest national heroes.

After Le Loi's victory over the Chinese, Nguyen Trai, a scholar and Le Loi's companion in arms, wrote his famous *Great Proclamation* (Binh Ngo Dai Cao), giving a compelling voice to Vietnam's fierce spirit of independence. His edict is known as Vietnam's second Declaration of Independence:

Our people long ago established Vietnam as an independent nation with its own civilisation. We have our own mountains and our own rivers, our own customs and traditions, and these are different from those of the foreign country to the north ... We have sometimes been weak and sometimes powerful, but at no time have we suffered from a lack of heroes.

Trinh & Nguyen Lords
Throughout the 17th and 18th centuries, Vietnam was divided between the Trinh Lords, who ruled in the North under the titular kingship of the Later Le monarchs, and the Nguyen Lords, who controlled the South and also nominally recognised the Later Le Dynasty. The Trinh Lords repeatedly failed in attempts to take over areas under Nguyen control.

Early Contact with the West
According to Chinese records, the first Vietnamese contact with Europeans took place in 166 AD when travellers from the Rome of Marcus Aurelius arrived in the Red River Delta.

The first Portuguese sailors landed in Danang in 1516. Franciscan missionaries from the Philippines settled in central Vietnam in 1580, followed in 1615 by the Jesuits who had just been expelled from Japan. In 1637 the Dutch were authorised to set up trading posts in the North. The first English attempt to break into the Vietnamese market ended with the murder of an agent of the East India Company in Hanoi in 1613.

Trade with Vietnam, however, had not proved particularly profitable, and by the late 17th century most of the European merchants were gone.

Tay Son Rebellion (1771-1802)
In 1765 a rebellion against misgovernment broke out in the town of Tay Son near Qui Nhon. It was led by three brothers from a wealthy merchant family: Nguyen Nhac, Nguyen Hue and Nguyen Lu. By 1773 the Tay Son Rebels (as they came to be known) controlled the whole of central Vietnam and in 1783 they captured Saigon and the rest of the South.

A few years later the Tay Son Rebels had overthrown the Trinh Lords in the North and proclaimed allegiance to the Later Le Dynasty. The weak Le emperor, however, proved unable to retain his control of the country and rather than calling on the Tay Son Rebels for help, he turned to the Chinese. Taking advantage of the unstable situation, China sent 200,000 troops to Vietnam under the pretext of helping the emperor. In 1788, with popular sentiment on his side, one of the Tay Son brothers, Nguyen Hue, proclaimed himself Emperor Quang Trung and set out with his army to expel the Chinese. In 1789, Nguyen Hue's armed forces overwhelmingly defeated the Chinese army at Dong Da (5km south-west of central Hanoi) in one of the most celebrated military achievements in Vietnamese history.

In the South, Nguyen Anh (a rare surviving Nguyen lord) gradually pushed back the Tay Son. In 1802, Nguyen Anh proclaimed himself Emperor Gia Long, thus beginning the Nguyen Dynasty. When he captured Hanoi his victory was complete and, for the first time in two centuries, Vietnam was united, with Hué as its new national capital.

Nguyen Dynasty (1802-1945)
The decision by Emperor Gia Long to rule from Hué relegated Hanoi to the status of a regional capital. Gia Long also began a large scale program of public works to rehabilitate the country, devastated by almost three decades of warfare.

Emperors of the Nguyen Dynasty

emperor	reign
Gia Long	1802-1819
Minh Mang	1820-1840
Thieu Tri	1841-1847
Tu Duc	1848-1883
Duc Duc	1883
Hiep Hoa	1883
Kien Phuc	1883-1884
Ham Nghi	1884-1885
Dong Khanh	1885-1889
Thanh Thai	1889-1907
Duy Tan	1907-1916
Khai Dinh	1916-1925
Bao Dai	1925-1945

Gia Long's son, Emperor Minh Mang, worked to consolidate the state and establish a strong central government. Profoundly hostile to Catholicism, he emphasised the importance of traditional Confucian education.

Minh Mang was succeeded by Emperor Thieu Tri, who expelled most of the foreign missionaries. He was followed by Emperor Tu Duc, who continued to rule according to conservative Confucian precepts and in imitation of Qing practices in China. Both responded to rural unrest with repression. Under Tu Duc, Hanoi, previously named Dong Kinh, took on its current name (meaning City in a Bend of the River).

In 1858 a joint military force from France and the Spanish colony of the Philippines stormed Danang after the killing of several missionaries. Early the next year they seized Saigon. From 1902 to 1953 Hanoi served as the capital of French Indochina.

French Rule (1859-1954)

In 1862, Emperor Tu Duc signed a treaty that gave the French the three eastern provinces of Cochinchina (the present-day Mekong Delta). Following the French offensive of 1867, Cochinchina became a French colony and the peasantry assumed a position of nonviolent resignation. At the same time, voices among the more educated classes of Vietnamese began to advocate cooperation with, and subordination to, the French in the interests of continuing technical and economic development.

The next major French action came between 1872 to 1874, when merchant Jean Dupuis seized the Hanoi Citadel. Captain Francis Garnier, ostensibly dispatched to reign-in Dupuis, instead took over where Dupuis left off. After capturing Hanoi, Garnier's gunboats proceeded to sail around the Red River Delta demanding tribute from provincial fortresses. Garnier was killed by the Black Flags (Co Den), a semi-autonomous army of Chinese, Vietnamese and hill tribe troops.

These events threw the North into chaos: the Black Flags continued their piratic activities; local bands were organised to take vengeance on the Vietnamese – especially Catholics – who had helped the French; Chinese militias in the pay of both the French and the Nguyen emperors sprang up; Le Dynasty pretenders began asserting their claims; and the hill tribes revolted. As central government authority collapsed and all established order broke down, Tu Duc went so far as to petition for help from the Chinese and to ask for support from the British and even the Americans.

In 1882 a French force under Captain Henri Rivière seized Hanoi. The following year Black Flags units ambushed Rivière at Cau Giay, killing him and 32 other Frenchmen.

Only a few weeks after the death of Tu Duc in 1883, the French attacked Hué and imposed a Treaty of Protectorate on the imperial court. There then began a tragicomic struggle for royal succession notable for its palace coups, mysteriously dead emperors and heavy-handed French diplomacy.

Vietnamese Anti-Colonialism

Throughout the colonial period, the vast majority of Vietnamese retained a strong desire to have their national independence restored. Seething nationalist aspirations often broke out into open defiance of the French.

Some Vietnamese nationalists (such as the scholar and patriot Phan Boi Chau, who rejected French rule but not western ideas and technology) looked to Japan and China for support and political inspiration, especially after Japan's victory in the Russo-Japanese war of 1905 showed all of Asia that western powers could be defeated. Sun Yatsen's 1911 revolution in China was also closely followed in Vietnamese nationalist circles.

Viet Nam Quoc Dan Dang (VNQDD), a predominantly middle class, nationalist party modelled after the Chinese Kuomintang (Nationalist Party), was founded in 1927 by nationalist leaders.

Ultimately, the most successful of the anti-colonialists were the communists, who were uniquely able to relate to the frustrations and aspirations of the population – especially the peasants – and to effectively channel and organise their demands for more equitable land distribution.

The institutional history of Vietnamese communism – which in many ways is the political biography of Ho Chi Minh (1890-1969; see the boxed text 'Ho Chi Minh' in this section) – is rather complicated. In brief, the first Marxist grouping in Indochina was the Viet Nam Cach Menh Thanh Nien Dong Chi Hoi (Vietnam Revolutionary Youth League), founded by Ho Chi Minh in Canton, China, in 1925. The Revolutionary Youth League was succeeded in February 1930 by the Dang Cong San Viet Nam (Vietnamese Communist Party), a union of three groups effected by Ho which was renamed the Dang Cong San Dong Duong (Indochinese Communist Party) in October 1930. In 1941 Ho formed the League for the Independence of Vietnam, better known as the Viet Minh, which resisted the Japanese and carried out extensive political activities during WWII. Despite its broad nationalist program and claims to the contrary, the Viet Minh was, from its inception, dominated by Ho's communists.

WWII

When France fell to Nazi Germany in 1940, the Indochinese government of Vichy-appointed Admiral Jean Decoux concluded an agreement to accept the presence of Japanese troops in Vietnam. For their own convenience the Japanese left the French administration in charge of the day-to-day running of the country. The only group that did anything significant to resist the Japanese occupation was the communist-dominated Viet Minh, which from 1944 received funding and arms from the US Office of Strategic Services (OSS), the predecessor of the CIA. This affiliation offered the Viet Minh the hope of eventual US recognition of their demands for independence; it also proved useful to Ho in that it implied that he had the support of the Americans.

In March 1945, as a Viet Minh offensive was getting under way and Decoux's government was plotting to resist the Japanese, the Japanese overthrew Decoux, imprisoning both his troops and his administrators. Decoux's administration was replaced with a puppet regime (nominally independent within Japan's Greater East-Asian Co-Prosperity Sphere) led by Emperor Bao Dai, who abrogated the 1883 treaty that made Annam and Tonkin French protectorates. During this period, Japanese rice requisitions and the Japanese policy of forcing farmers to plant industrial crops, in combination with floods and breaches in the dikes, caused a horrific famine in which two million of North Vietnam's 10 million people starved to death.

By the spring of 1945 the Viet Minh controlled large parts of the country, particularly in the North. In mid-August – after the atomic bombing of Hiroshima and Nagasaki – Ho Chi Minh formed the National Liberation Committee and called for a general uprising, later known as the August Revolution, to take advantage of the power vacuum. Almost immediately the Viet Minh assumed complete control of the North. On 2 September 1945 Ho – with American OSS agents at his side and borrowing liberally

Ho Chi Minh

Ho Chi Minh is the best known of some 50 aliases assumed over the course of his long career by Nguyen Tat Thanh (1890-1969), founder of the Vietnamese Communist Party and president of the Democratic Republic of Vietnam from 1946 until his death. Born the son of a fiercely nationalistic scholar-official of humble means, he was educated in the Quoc Hoc Secondary School in Hué, before working briefly as a teacher in Phan Thiet. In 1911, he signed on as a cook's apprentice on a French ship, sailing to North America, Africa and Europe. He remained in Europe, where, while working as a gardener, snow sweeper, waiter, photo retoucher and stoker, his political consciousness began to develop.

After living briefly in London, Ho Chi Minh moved to Paris, where he adopted the name Nguyen Ai Quoc (Nguyen the Patriot). During this period, he mastered a number of languages (including English, French, German and Mandarin Chinese) and began to write about and debate the issue of Indochinese independence. During the 1919 Versailles Peace Conference, he tried to present an independence plan for Vietnam to US president Woodrow Wilson. Ho was a founding member of the French Communist Party, which was established in 1920. In 1923, he was summoned to Moscow for training by the Communist International, which later sent him to Guangzhou (Canton), China, where he founded the Revolutionary Youth League of Vietnam, a precursor to the Indochinese Communist Party and the Vietnamese Communist Party.

After spending time in a Hong Kong jail in the early 1930s and more time in the USSR and China, Ho Chi Minh returned to Vietnam in 1941 for the first time in 30 years. That same year – at the age of 51 – he helped found the Viet Minh Front, the goal of which was the independence of Vietnam from French colonial rule and Japanese occupation. In 1942, he was arrested and held for a year by the Nationalist Chinese. As Japan prepared to surrender in August 1945, Ho Chi Minh led the August Revolution, which took control of much of the country; and it was he who composed Vietnam's Declaration of Independence (modelled in part on the American Declaration of Independence) and read it publicly in Ba Dinh Square, very near the site of his mausoleum.

The return of the French shortly thereafter forced Ho Chi Minh and the Viet Minh to flee Hanoi and take up armed resistance. Ho spent eight years conducting a guerrilla war until the Viet Minh's victory against the French at Dien Bien Phu in 1954. He led North Vietnam until his death in September 1969 – he never lived to see the North's victory over the South. Ho Chi Minh is affectionately referred to as 'Uncle Ho' (Bac Ho) by his admirers.

Uncle Ho may have been the father of his country, but he wasn't the father of any children, at least none that are known. Like his erstwhile nemesis, South Vietnamese president Ngo Dinh Diem, Ho Chi Minh never married.

from the stirring prose of the American Declaration of Independence – declared the Democratic Republic of Vietnam independent at a rally in Ba Dinh Square.

Franco-Viet Minh War (1946-54)

In the face of Vietnamese determination that their country regain its independence, the French proved unable to reassert their control. In 1950 the People's Republic of China established diplomatic relations with Hanoi's Democratic Republic of Vietnam; later the Soviet Union did the same. Despite massive American aid and the existence of significant indigenous anti-communist elements, it was an unwinnable war.

After eight years of fighting the Viet Minh controlled much of Vietnam and neighbouring Laos. On 7 May 1954, after a 57 day siege, over 10,000 starving French troops surrendered to the Viet Minh at Dien Bien Phu. The next day the Geneva Conference opened to negotiate an end to the conflict; 2½ months later the Geneva Accords were signed. This provided for an exchange of prisoners, the temporary division of Vietnam into two zones at the Ben Hai River, the free passage of people across the 17th parallel for a period of 300 days and the holding of nationwide elections on 20 July 1956. In the course of the Franco-Viet Minh War more than 35,000 French fighters were killed and 48,000 were wounded – Vietnamese casualties were even greater.

The North-South War

The Geneva Accords allowed the leadership of the Democratic Republic of Vietnam to return to Hanoi and to assert control of all territory north of the 17th parallel. The new government immediately set out to eliminate those elements of the population that threatened its power. Hasty 'trials' resulted in 10,000 to 15,000 executions and the imprisonment of 50,000 to 100,000 people. In 1956 the Party, faced with serious rural unrest caused by the program, recognised that the People's Land Reform Tribunals had gotten out of hand and began a 'Campaign for the Rectification of Errors'.

On 12 December 1955 – shortly after Ngo Dinh Diem had declared the South a republic – the USA closed its consulate in Hanoi.

Although there were communist-led guerrilla attacks on Diem's government during the mid-1950s, the real campaign to 'liberate' the South began in 1959 when Hanoi, responding to the demands of Southern cadres that they be allowed to resist the Diem regime, changed from a strategy of 'political struggle' to one of 'armed struggle'.

In April 1960 universal military conscription was implemented in the North. Eight months later, Hanoi announced the formation of the National Liberation Front (NLF), whose political platform called for a neutralisation of Vietnam, the withdrawal of all foreign troops and gradual reunification of the North and South. In the South the NLF came to be known derogatorily as the 'Viet Cong' or just the 'VC'; both are abbreviations for Viet Nam Cong San, which means 'Vietnamese Communist' (today these terms are no longer considered pejorative). American soldiers nicknamed the VC 'Charlie'.

As the military position of the South Vietnamese government continued to deteriorate, the US Kennedy administration (1961-63) sent more and more military advisers to Vietnam. By the end of 1963 there were 16,300 US military personnel in the country.

When the NLF campaign got under way, the military situation of the Diem government rapidly deteriorated. In 1964 Hanoi began infiltrating regular North Vietnamese Army (NVA) units into the South. By early 1965 the Saigon government was in desperate straits and it was at this point that the USA committed its first combat troops (soon to be joined by soldiers from South Korea, Australia, Thailand and New Zealand).

Ironically, it was 'peace candidate' Lyndon Baines Johnson who rapidly escalated the USA's involvement in the war. On Johnson's orders, carrier-based jets flew 64 sorties against the North – the first of thousands of such missions that would hit every single road and rail bridge in the country, as well as 4000 of North Vietnam's 5788 villages.

VAN MIEU
THE TEMPLE OF LITERATURE

MASON FLORENCE

BETHUNE CARMICHAEL

MASON FLORENCE

Top: Inscriptions in Chinese characters on either side of the Great Portico proclaim the greatness of Confucian teaching. The inscription on the far left proclaims 'All those with mandarinal titles have followed this path'.

Middle: The Constellation of Literature Pavilion (Khue Van Cac), built in 1804, has four suns outlined in wood radiating in four directions.

Bottom: The Great House of Ceremonies leads to the Sanctuary.

Title Page: The statue of Confucius has pride of place in the Sanctuary (photograph by Peter Ptschelinzew).

Inset photograph by Mason Florence

VAN MIEU

Van Mieu was founded in 1070 by Emperor Ly Thanh Tong, who dedicated it to Confucius (in Vietnamese, Khong Tu) in order to honour scholars and men of literary accomplishment. Initially the temple served as a grand study hall for the crown prince. Vietnam's first university was established here in 1076 to educate the sons of mandarins. In 1484 Emperor Le Thanh Tong ordered that stelae be erected in the temple precincts recording the names, places of birth and achievements of men who received doctorates in each triennial examination, commencing in 1442. Between 1442 and 1778, 116 examinations were held, after which the practice was discontinued In 1802 Emperor Gia Long transferred the National University to his new capital, Hué. Major renovations were carried out here in 1920 and 1956.

A walk through Van Mieu serves as an interesting introduction to Confucianism. Its five courtyards represent the essential elements of nature. A central path, symbolising the Confucian Middle Path, symmetrically divides the complex. On their side pillars, all the gates have inscriptions in Chinese characters which contrast and complement each other in meaning and structure.

The central pathways and gates were reserved for the king. The walkways on one side were solely for the use of administrative mandarins, while those on the other side were for military mandarins.

The **main entrance** is preceded by a gate on which an inscription requests that visitors dismount their horses before entering. Upon entering through the **Great Portico** you will find yourself in the courtyard known as **Entrance to the Way**. On either side of the central path are lotus ponds and sacred trees. The path leads to **Dai Trung Mon** (Great Middle Gate) which is flanked by gates whose names symbolise the virtues required to pass from the first to second courtyard: **Thanh**

1 Main entrance
2 Great Portico
3 Entrance to the Way
4 Dai Trung Mon
5 Thanh Duc
6 Dat Tai
7 Great Middle Courtyard
8 Khue Van Cac
9 Thien Quang Tinh
10 Garden of the Stelae
11 Dai Thanh Mon
12 Courtyard of the Sages
13 Great House of Ceremonies
14 Dai Thanh Sanctuary
15 Quoc Tu Giam

VAN MIEU

Duc (Accomplished Virtue) on your right and **Dat Tai** (Attained Talent) on the left.

The **Great Middle Courtyard** leads to the **Khue Van Cac** (Constellation of Literature Pavilion). To pass through this gate the student must have achieved excellence in literary expression. The pavilion was constructed in 1802 and is a fine example of Vietnamese architecture and considered a symbol of the city.

The beautiful square pond known as **Thien Quang Tinh** (Well of Heavenly Clarity) dominates the next courtyard which is called **Garden of the Stelae**. On either side of the pond inscriptions of the names of laureates are borne on the backs of 82 turtles – these are the stelae, the most precious artefacts in the temple.

The fourth courtyard, **Courtyard of the Sages**, is entered through **Dai Thanh Mon** (Gate of the Great Synthesis) which symbolises how the elements of Confucian teaching are brought together to complete a scholar's knowledge. At the open centre of the **Great House of Ceremonies** is an altar to Confucius. Behind the Great House of Ceremonies is **Dai Thanh** (Great Success) Sanctuary featuring a statue of Confucius flanked by smaller statues of his four closest disciples.

The fifth courtyard, **Quoc Tu Giam** (School for the Sons of the Nation), was the site of the classrooms and dormitories of Van Mieu until the college was moved in 1802. At that time it was transformed into Khai Thanh, a shrine to the parents of Confucius. The buildings were destroyed by French shelling in 1947 and little remains of the original courtyard.

MASON FLORENCE

Left: One of 82 giant stone turtles bearing on its back a stele. The stelae are stone slabs on which are engraved the names and native villages of those who achieved the rank of doctor laureate in the national examinations held between 1442 and 1779. Up to thirty stelae have been lost over the years. The remaining ones were restored in 1994.

The Tet Offensive of early 1968 marked a crucial turning point in the war. As the country celebrated Tet, the most impotant date in the Vietnamese calendar, the VC launched a deadly offensive.

The war waged on, and in the spring of 1972 the North Vietnamese launched an offensive across the 17th parallel; the USA responded with increased bombing of the North and mined seven North Vietnamese harbours. The 'Christmas Bombing' of Haiphong and Hanoi at the end of 1972 was meant to wrest concessions from North Vietnam at the negotiating table.

Finally, Henry Kissinger and Le Duc Tho reached agreement. The Paris Agreements, signed by the USA, North Vietnam, South Vietnam and the VC on 27 January 1973, provided for a cease-fire, the establishment of the National Council of Reconciliation and Concord, the total withdrawal of US combat forces and the release by Hanoi of 590 American POWs.

In total, 3.14 million Americans (including 7200 women) served in the US armed forces in Vietnam during the war. Officially, 58,183 Americans (including eight women) were killed in action or are listed as missing in action (MIA).

By the end of 1973, 223,748 South Vietnamese soldiers had been killed in action. North Vietnamese and VC fatalities have been estimated at one million. Approximately four million civilians were killed or injured during the war, many in the North as a result of American bombing. Over 2200 Americans and 300,000 Vietnamese are still listed as MIA.

North Vietnam launched a massive conventional ground attack across the 17th Parallel in January 1975 – a blatant violation of the Paris Agreements. The South Vietnamese military leadership decided to make a 'tactical withdrawal' to more defensible positions. The withdrawal deteriorated into a chaotic rout as soldiers deserted in order to try to save their families. Saigon surrendered to the North Vietnamese Army on 30 April 1975.

Since Reunification

Peace may have arrived, but in many ways the war was far from over. The sudden success of the 1975 North Vietnamese offensive surprised the North almost as much as it did the South. As a result, Hanoi had not prepared specific plans to deal with the integration of the two parts of the country whose social and economic systems could hardly have been more different.

The North was faced with the legacy of a cruel and protracted war that had literally fractured the country and left a mind-boggling array of problems. War damage extended from the unmarked minefields to war-focused, dysfunctional economies, from vast acreages of chemically poisoned countryside to millions of people who had been affected physically or mentally. The country was diplomatically isolated and its old allies were no longer willing or able to provide significant aid.

After months of debate, those in Hanoi who wanted to implement a rapid transition to socialism (including the collectivisation of agriculture) in the South gained the upper hand. Relations with China to the north and its Khmer Rouge allies to the west were rapidly deteriorating and war-weary Vietnam seemed beset by enemies. A campaign of repression against Vietnam's ethnic-Chinese community – plus Vietnam's invasion of Cambodia at the end of 1978 – prompted the Chinese to attack Vietnam in February 1979. The Vietnamese repelled the Chinese invasion forces in a brutal and bloody war that lasted only 17 days.

Opening the Door

The recent liberalisation of foreign investment laws and the relaxation of visa regulations for tourists seem to be part of a general Vietnamese opening-up to the world. The transition was in part spurred on by a brutal famine which by the mid-1980s had ravaged the north and left Hanoi facing severe rice shortages and strict rations.

The Soviet Union began its first cautious opening to the west in 1984 with the appointment of Mikhail Gorbachev as Secretary

Disorderly Departure

One tragic legacy of the American War was the plight of thousands of Amerasians. Marriages and other unions between American soldiers and Vietnamese women – as well as prostitution – were common during the war. But when the Americans were rotated home, all too often they abandoned their 'wives' and mistresses, leaving them to raise children who were half white or half black in a society not particularly tolerant of such racial integration.

After reunification, the Amerasians – living reminders of the American presence – were often mistreated by Vietnamese and even abandoned by their mothers and other relatives, forcing them to live on the streets. They were also denied educational and vocational opportunities and were sadly referred to as 'children of the dust'.

At the end of the 1980s, the Orderly Departure Programme (ODP), carried out under the auspices of the United Nations High Commission for Refugees (UNHCR), was designed to allow for the orderly resettlement in the west (mostly in the USA) of Amerasians and political refugees who otherwise might have tried to flee the country by land or sea. Thousands of Vietnamese and their families were flown via Bangkok to the Philippines, where they underwent six months of English instruction before proceeding to the USA.

Unfortunately, many Amerasian children were adopted by people eager to emigrate, but were then dumped and left to fend for themselves after the family's arrival in the USA. Asian American Lead (☎ 202-518 6737, 1352 Q St NW, Washington, DC 20009, USA) has been doing good work to train and mentor these young Amerasian kids and their parents.

The ODP mainly concerned the South Vietnamese and failed to stem the flow of refugees from the North. After the Vietnam-China border opened in 1990, many simply took the train to China, from where they only had to take a short boat ride across the Pearl River to Hong Kong to be declared 'boat people'. As the refugee camps in Hong Kong swelled to bursting point, the public's patience ran out. 'Refugee fatigue' became the buzzword in Hong Kong and the public demanded that something be done.

Since all but a handful of the arrivals were declared to be economic migrants rather than political refugees, the Hong Kong government experimented with forcible repatriation in 1990. This prompted a vehement protest from the USA and the UNHCR. The Hong Kong government backed off temporarily and finally agreed with Vietnam on a program of combined voluntary and forced repatriation. Those willing to return would not be penalised, would get back their citizenship (the previous policy was to strip all refugees of their citizenship, thus rendering them stateless) and would receive a resettlement allowance of US$30 per month, for several months, from the UNHCR.

The voluntary repatriation didn't go quite as planned; some of the volunteers were back in Hong Kong a few months later seeking another resettlement allowance. In such cases, forcible repatriation swiftly followed. The program produced results – by the end of 1992 practically no new Vietnamese refugees arrived in Hong Kong.

Among the thousands of Vietnamese seeking legitimate refuge in Hong Kong was a small hardcore faction of misfits with a criminal past who the Vietnamese government didn't want back. Hong Kong didn't want them either, nor would any western countries roll out the welcome mat. And so these refugees were stuck in the camps behind razor wire, preying on each other and staging the occasional violent protest over their grim situation. Finally, major riots broke out in the camps in 1995 and 1996, and some of the refugees escaped and could still be hiding in Hong Kong, possibly surviving by theft, smuggling, prostitution and drug dealing.

General of the Communist Party. Vietnam followed suit in 1986 by choosing reform-minded Nguyen Van Linh to be General Secretary of the Vietnamese Communist Party. However, dramatic changes in Eastern Europe and the USSR were not viewed with favour in Hanoi. The Vietnamese Communist Party denounced the participation of non-Communists in Eastern Bloc governments, calling the democratic revolutions 'a counterattack from imperialist circles' against socialism.

General Secretary Linh declared at the end of 1989 that 'we resolutely reject pluralism, a multiparty system and opposition parties'. But in February 1990, the government called for more openness and criticism. The response came swiftly, with an outpouring of news articles, editorials and letters from the public condemning corruption, inept leadership and the high living standards of senior officials while most people lived in extreme poverty. Taken aback by the harsh criticism, official control over literature, the arts and the media were tightened once again in a campaign against 'deviant ideological viewpoints'. An effort was made to blame public dissatisfaction on foreign imperialists.

At age 75, ailing Nguyen Van Linh was replaced as Secretary General in June 1991 by Prime Minister Do Muoi. Regarded as a conservative, Muoi nevertheless vowed to continue the economic reforms started by Linh. At the same time, a major shake-up of the ruling Politburo and Central Committee of the Communist Party saw many members forcibly retired and replaced by younger, more liberal-minded leaders. The sudden collapse of the USSR just two months later caused the government to reiterate its stand that political pluralism would not be tolerated, but at the same time economic reforms were speeded up.

Muoi and Prime Minister Vo Van Kiet visited Beijing in November 1991 to heal Vietnam's 12 year rift with China. The visit was reciprocated in December 1992 when Chinese prime minister Li Peng visited Hanoi. Although it was all smiles and warm handshakes in front of the cameras, relations between Vietnam and China remain tense.

Vietnam has also seen considerable easing of tensions with its old nemesis, the USA. In early 1994 the USA lifted its economic embargo, which had been in place against the old North Vietnam since the 1960s.

Sweden, the first western country to establish diplomatic relations with Hanoi, did so in 1969; since that time most western nations have followed suit, including the USA who have established an embassy in Hanoi. Vietnam now has an embassy in Washington, DC.

GEOGRAPHY

Hanoi lies in the fertile Red River Delta (15,000 sq km) at 106° east longitude and 21° north latitude. The site, enclosed by a rampart connecting the dikes of the Red River (to the east), To Lich River (to the north) and Kim Nguu River (to the south), was chosen nearly a millennium ago. The three rivers formed a strategic moat surrounding Hanoi, and today still play a crucial role in the daily lives of the people.

Hanoi's terrain is relatively flat, though surrounding areas consist of mountains and hills up to over 450m high. Most of the city lies at an average of 5m above sea level, though parts of the north-east Gia Lam District are more than 10m below sea level, protected only by artificial embankments.

Silt carried by the Red River and its tributaries (confined to their paths by 3000km of dikes) has raised the level of the river beds above that of the surrounding plains. Breaches in the levees periodically result in disastrous flooding.

Hanoi is the second largest metropolis in Vietnam – behind Ho Chi Minh City (Saigon) – with a land area of over 900 sq km.

GEOLOGY

The Red River has produced one of the world's great deltas, composed of fine silt which has washed downstream for millions of years. The silt supports lush tropical vegetation and the Hanoi region is an important centre of agriculture.

The northern part of Vietnam has a spectacular assemblage of karst formations, notably around Halong Bay and Tam Coc (see the Excursions chapter). Karst consists of irregular limestone in which erosion has produced fissures, sinkholes, caves and underground rivers. At Halong Bay an enormous limestone plateau has gradually sunk into the ocean – the old mountain tops stick out of the sea like vertical fingers pointing towards the sky. At Tam Coc, the karst formations are similar except they are all still above sea level.

CLIMATE

Northern Vietnam, including Hanoi, has a remarkably diverse climate. Hanoi has four relatively distinct seasons, though temperatures vary considerably from year to year. Weather patterns are highly changeable and warm morning sunshine can turn to cloudy cold by the afternoon, with skies clearing again by nightfall.

Winter is quite cool and dry and usually lasts from November through early February. November typically sees the first monsoon rains, before the dry and chilly winds sweep in from China. In Hanoi an overcoat can be necessary from December through February, with temperatures from 10 to 15°C (48 to 59°F).

Spring lasts from February to April, and is marked by a persistent wet drizzling rain that the Vietnamese call 'rain dust' *(mua bui or mua phun)*. The air is moist, and average temperatures are between 15 and 20°C (59 to 68°F).

The hot summers run from May to September, with humidity rising to 90% in July. Hanoi is subject to occasional devastating typhoons, especially as the weather cools during the late summer months. Summer temperatures reach 30 to 36°C (86 to 97°F).

Autumn (fall) is considered the best season for weather in Hanoi, with October and November becoming cool, sunny and pleasant with temperatures in the 25 to 30°C (75 to 85°F) range.

Hanoi's average annual humidity is around 80%. Annual rainfall averages 170cm. The coldest temperature ever recorded in Hanoi is 2.7°C (in January 1955); the hottest was 42.8°C (in May 1926).

ECOLOGY & ENVIRONMENT

Hanoi was once surrounded by dense woodland, but since the early 20th century, human beings have progressively denuded the forest cover. Each hectare of land stripped of vegetation contributes to the flooding of areas downstream of water catchment areas, irreversible soil erosion (upland soils are especially fragile), the silting up of rivers, streams, lakes and reservoirs, the loss of wildlife habitat and unpredictable climatic changes.

Today, Hanoi's environment is not in the worst shape, though the dramatic increase in noisy, smoke-spewing motorbikes in recent years should be taken as a sign of environmental abominations to come.

Until recently Hanoi suffered little industrial pollution, largely because there was little industry. However, with the city's rapid economic and population growth has come a marked increase in local manufacturing works. Reports in the popular press express a growing concern for air pollution being created by nearby factories producing tobacco, batteries, chemical fertilisers and so on.

FLORA

Hanoi is estimated to contain over 200,000 trees, lining the city streets and filling its parks and gardens and surrounding the city's 27 lakes, countless pools and ponds. The

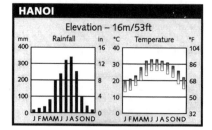

most common tree is the white iron tree *(xa cu)*. Other common varieties include sandalwood *(bach dan)*, willow *(lieu)*, banyan *(da)*, sycamore *(si)* and tamarind *(me)* trees.

Common flowers include chrysanthemums, peach blossoms, roses, violets, carnations, lilies and lotuses.

FAUNA

Vietnam is home to 273 species of mammals, over 800 species of birds, 180 species of reptiles, 80 species of amphibians, hundreds of species of fish and thousands of kinds of invertebrates. Unfortunately, however, most of Hanoi's animal population has been severely degraded, largely because the human population eats both reptiles and amphibians.

Most of Hanoi's birds have also been heavily persecuted, though during migration periods in spring and autumn a fair variety of bird life can be seen in Hanoi's parks and around city lakes. On parts of the Red River live a number of Indochinese endemic species, though the city's birds are scant and ordinary (magpie robins, common tailorbirds, tree sparrows etc). A surprising novelty for some birdwatchers are barn owls, which can occasionally be spotted swooping between city rooftops. These birds are typically found in agricultural areas of rural Europe, but with the local rodent population to feed on they are now one of Hanoi's resident bird species.

Within easy reach of Hanoi are several areas popular with birdwatchers, including the Tam Dao Hill Station and Cuc Phuong National Park. Xuan Thuy is a good wetlands spot near the mouth of the Red River (though access is difficult). In Halong Bay, white-bellied sea eagles are common, but overall there is nothing remarkable there for birdwatchers.

NATIONAL PARKS

There are several national parks and an expanding array of nature reserves within a half-day's journey from Hanoi. Some areas are demonstrating promising potential for ecotourism, and are well worth exploring. The parks are a great escape from the city,

and have the added appeal of being 'protected' in the sense that tourists are rarely, if ever, hassled to buy anything.

Cat Ba National Park is on a beautiful island and attracts a steady stream of travellers willing to make the boat journey. Cuc Phuong National Park is less visited, but is easily reached from Hanoi by rented jeep or motorbike, and offers great hiking.

GOVERNMENT & POLITICS

The Socialist Republic of Vietnam (SRV) came into existence in July 1976 as a unitary state comprising the Democratic Republic of Vietnam (North Vietnam) and the territory of the defeated Republic of Vietnam (South Vietnam). Despite the rapid pace of economic reforms in the 1990s, the government shows no sign of moving towards democracy, and political control remains firmly in the hands of the Communist Party.

Whatever else Ho Chi Minh may have done, he created in Hanoi and much of the north a very effective police state, characterised by ruthless crack-downs on anyone seen as a potential threat to the government. The combination of human rights violations and economic turmoil produced a steady haemorrhage of refugees, even into China, despite that country's less than impressive human rights record.

Officially, the government espouses a Marxist-Leninist political philosophy. Its political institutions have borrowed a great deal from the Soviet and Chinese models, in particular the ability to create mountains of red tape.

Vietnam's political system is dominated by the two million member Communist Party (Dang Cong San Viet Nam), founded by Ho Chi Minh in 1930. Its influence is felt at every level of social and political life. The Party's decentralised structure has allowed local leaders considerable leeway for initiative. Unfortunately, this has also allowed the development of localised corruption, which Hanoi has had difficulty controlling.

The most powerful institution in the Party is the Political Bureau (Politburo), which has about a dozen members. It oversees the

Party's day-to-day functioning and has the power to issue directives to the government. The Politburo is formally elected by the Central Committee, which meets only once or twice a year.

The last few Party Congresses, at which major policy changes are ratified after lengthy behind-the-scenes discussions and consultations, have reflected intense intra-Party disagreements over the path Vietnamese communism should take, with changing coalitions of conservatives and dogmatists squaring off against more pragmatic elements. The position of Party Chairman has been left vacant since Ho Chi Minh's death in 1969. The highest party position is General Secretary, Le Kha Phieu.

Vietnam's unicameral National Assembly (Quoc Hoi) is the highest legislative authority in the country. Its 500 or so deputies each represent around 100,000 voters. The National Assembly's function is basically to rubber-stamp Politburo decisions and Party-initiated legislation during its biannual week-long sessions.

The National Assembly elects the Council of State, which functions as the country's collective presidency. It carries out the duties of the National Assembly when the latter is not in session. The Council of Ministers, similar in style to a western-style cabinet, is also elected by the National Assembly.

During the 1980s and early 1990s thousands of Party members were expelled, in part to reduce corruption (seen by a fed-up public as endemic) and in part to make room for more young people and workers. As in China, Vietnam has been ruled by a gerontocracy of aging officials.

Serving under the command of the men above are 25 official government ministries. Women are under-represented in the Party, especially at the highest levels (there have been no female members of the Politburo since 1945).

Candidates to the National Assembly and local People's Committees are elected to office. Voting is compulsory, though proxy voting is allowed and permits the government to boast of 100% voter partici-pation, thus conferring legitimacy on the process. Only Party-approved candidates are permitted to run and opposition parties are prohibited.

The military does not seem to have any direct political role, even though virtually all of Vietnam's high-ranking politicians and officials came from the military.

Vietnam became a member of the Association of Southeast Asian Nations (ASEAN) in July 1995, and in November of the same year the American President, Bill Clinton, officially announced US-Vietnamese relations 'normalised'.

In 1997 Hanoi hosted the 7th Francophone Summit, an international congregation of French-speaking nations. City residents mostly remember the mass traffic congestion caused by the event, though blue metal signs in French, Vietnamese and English placed at a number of 'cultural vestiges' around the city remain today.

ECONOMY

Vietnam is one of the poorest countries in Asia with an estimated per capita income of less than US$300 per year and US$1.4 billion in hard currency debts (owed mainly to Russia, the IMF and Japan). Unable to repay these loans, Vietnam has been unofficially bankrupt since the 1980s.

Despite its hard-working, educated workforce, the country's economy is beset by low wages, poor infrastructure, a trade deficit, unemployment, under-employment and, until recently, erratic runaway inflation (700% in 1986, 30% in 1989, 50% in 1991, 3% in 1996 and 8% in 1998).

The economy was hurt by wartime infrastructure damage (not a single bridge in the North survived American air raids), but by the government's own admission the present economic fiasco is the result of the ideologically driven policies followed after reunification, plus corruption and the burden of heavy military spending.

Just how the average Vietnamese manages to survive is a mystery; salaries in Hanoi are in the range of only US$40 to US$100 per month.

Economic Reforms

Vietnam might well have collapsed had it not been for Soviet aid and recent capitalist-style reforms. Efforts to restructure the economy really got under way with the Sixth Party Congress held in December 1986. At that time, Nguyen Van Linh (a proponent of reform) was appointed General Secretary of the Communist Party.

Immediately upon the legalisation of limited private enterprise, family businesses began popping up all over the country. But it's the South, with its experience with capitalism, that has the entrepreneurial skills and managerial dynamism needed to effect the reforms. With 'new thinking' in Hanoi now modelling the economic life of the whole country in the mould of the pre-reunification South, some people have remarked that, in the end, the South won the war.

As a direct result of these economic reforms, Vietnam moved from being a rice importer in the mid-1980s to become the world's second largest rice exporter in 1997 (after Thailand).

Vietnam's economy started growing in the late 1980s, reversing the trend of the previous decade when it experienced precipitous negative economic growth. But official growth figures don't record the significant 'black economy' that exists.

But the urban economy is improving much faster than the rural, widening the already significant gap in Vietnamese standards of living. The Vietnamese government fears what China is already experiencing – a mass exodus of countryside residents into the already overcrowded cities.

The transition from an isolated socialist barter economy to a free-market, hard-currency trading economy is not complete and has not been easy. Though the situation is gradually improving, many of Vietnam's manufactured goods (bicycles, shoes, even toothpaste) are of such poor quality that they are practically unsaleable, especially in the face of competition from foreign goods.

One of the first effects of free (or freeish) trade with capitalist countries was the wiping out of many state-run enterprises, leading to job lay-offs and an increase in unemployment.

The Vietnamese government responded with a number of 'temporary import bans' (protectionism). Such bans theoretically give a boost to struggling domestic industries, but also lead to increased smuggling. Slowly but surely, the country is regaining its ability to compete in foreign markets; low wages and the strong Vietnamese work ethic (when offered incentives) bode well for Vietnam's export industries.

Economic Backlash

The reforms have already gained enough momentum to make it hard to imagine reversing them. However, there has been a conservative backlash against them. Rather than shrinking, the state sector has been expanding. Various government regulations make it difficult or impossible for private businesses to function except in a joint venture with a state-owned company. Such joint ventures often come to grief and many foreign investors are becoming disillusioned with Vietnam.

One of the most visible signs of the anti-market backlash was the 'social evils' campaign launched with much fanfare in late 1995. Socially evil foreign video tapes, music tapes, magazines and other paraphernalia were burned in public bonfires, while Vietnam's official *Moi* newspaper reported that, 'thanks to education and propaganda, people voluntarily gave up 27,302 video tapes'.

Privatisation of large state industries, such as Vietnam Airlines, the banking industry and telecommunications, has not yet begun but is being considered. Whether or not the generation of socialist leaders can bring themselves to put the state's prime assets on the auction block remains to be seen.

At the present time, Vietnam has no stock market – establishing one would be a prerequisite to any privatisation moves. In 1995, the government promised to open a capital market by year's end, but it seems to have been postponed indefinitely.

On a more positive note, Vietnam has seen economic growth rates of around 8 to

9% annually in the past few years. Vietnam's joining ASEAN in 1995 should greatly benefit its economy and further spur on reforms.

Hanoi is intent on limiting Vietnam's restructuring *(doi moi)* to the economic sphere, keeping ideas such as pluralism and democracy from undermining the present power structure. Whether it is possible to have economic liberalisation without a concurrent liberalisation in the political sphere remains to be seen.

Vietnam's role model at the moment seems to be China, where economic liberalisation coupled with harsh political controls seems to be at least partially successful in reviving the economy. The role model of the former Soviet Union – where political liberalisation preceded economic restructuring – is pointed to as an example of the wrong way to reform.

The recent economic crisis which has gripped Asia has had a substantial effect on Vietnam. Unemployment has risen and import and export trading have shown a steady decrease since 1996.

POPULATION & PEOPLE

Metropolitan Hanoi's population (including outlying areas) is approximately 3 million, second only to Ho Chi Minh City. The city is made up primarily of ethnic-Vietnamese *(kinh)*, with a light smattering of ethnic minorities – there are 53 in Vietnam – many who migrated to Hanoi from rural areas to find work or pursue a university degree.

The people of Hanoi are known for being more reserved – and at the same time more traditionally hospitable – than their southern compatriots. Hanoians are said to maintain stricter traditional family values than those in the south, this being largely tied to Confucian ideals relating to societal behaviour, discipline, relationships and responsibility.

The communist campaign against the 'bourgeois elements' (considered a euphemism for the ethnic-Chinese) influenced China's decision to attack Vietnam in 1979, causing most of Hanoi's ethnic-Chinese to flee racial persecution to China and the west. Those who remain are almost indis-

tinguishable from the Vietnamese, having completely assimilated into society.

The Vietnamese government takes a carrot and stick approach to family planning. For couples who limit their family size to two children or fewer, there are promises of social benefits in education, housing, health care and employment. The stick comes for those who exceed the two child limit. If the parents have a government job, they may be fined, or even fired. In general, these inducements have succeeded in urban areas – a two child family is now the norm in Hanoi.

Vietnamese who have emigrated abroad are known as Overseas Vietnamese (Viet Kieu). In the late 1980s, returning Viet Kieu were often suspected and followed by the police and the people they spoke to questioned and harassed by the authorities. This has all changed. Indeed, official policy is to welcome the Viet Kieu and encourage them to resettle in Vietnam. Still, many Overseas Vietnamese avoid Hanoi, tending to prefer the atmosphere of the south.

There are around 3000 expats living in Hanoi (about half as many as in 1995). Large numbers have fled in recent years, due to a eroding economic environment or failed business ventures.

EDUCATION

Compared with other developing countries, Vietnam's population is very well educated. Although university education is out of reach for most Vietnamese, the country's literacy rate is estimated at 88.6%, although official figures put it even higher (95%). Before the colonial period, the majority of the population possessed some degree of literacy, but by 1939 only 15% of school-age children were receiving any kind of instruction and 80% of the population was illiterate.

During the late 19th century, one of the few things that French colonial officials and Vietnamese nationalists agreed on was that the traditional Confucian educational system, on which the mandarinal civil service was based, was in desperate need of reform. Mandarinal examinations were held in Tonkin until WWI and in Annam until the war's end.

Unlike in many other poor countries, women in Vietnam generally receive the same access to education as men.

Hanoi has churned out most of Vietnam's intellectual elite. Many of Indochina's independence leaders were educated in exclusive French-language secondary schools such as Hanoi's Lycée Albert Sarraut.

Although the children of foreign residents can theoretically attend Vietnamese schools, the majority go to expensive private academies (see the Facts for the Visitor chapter for details on schools).

ARTS
Dance

Vietnamese traditional dance is relatively simple in comparison to other South-East Asian countries. Not surprisingly, ethnic minorities have their own dancing traditions, which differ sharply from the Vietnamese majority. While in most hill tribes the majority of the dancers are women, a few hill tribe groups allow only the men to dance. A great deal of anthropological research has been carried out in recent years in order to preserve and revive minority traditions, much of this on display at Hanoi's excellent Ethnology Museum (see the Things to See & Do chapter).

Music

The traditional system of writing down music and the five note (pentatonic) scale are of Chinese origin. Vietnamese music, though heavily influenced by the Chinese and (in the South) the Khmer and Indianised Cham musical traditions, has a high degree of originality in style and instrumentation. Vietnamese choral music is unique in that the melody must correspond to the tones of the words; it cannot be rising during a word that has a falling tone. See the Language chapter for an explanation of tone.

There are three broad categories of Vietnamese music:

Folk includes children's songs, love songs, work songs, festival songs, lullabies, lamentations and funeral songs. It is usually sung without instrumental accompaniment.

Classical (or 'learned music') is rather rigid and formal. It was performed at the imperial court and for the entertainment of the mandarin elite. A traditional orchestra consists of 40 musicians. There are two main types of classical chamber music: *hat a dao* (from the North) and *ca Hue* (from central Vietnam).

Theatre includes singing, dancing and instrumentation. There are music conservatories teaching both traditional Vietnamese and western classical music in Hanoi.

Literature

Vietnamese literature can be divided into three types:

Traditional oral literature *(truyen khau)* was begun long before recorded history and includes legends, folk songs and proverbs.

Sino-Vietnamese literature *(Han Viet)* was written in Chinese characters *(chu nho)*. It dates from 939 AD, when the first independent Vietnamese kingdom was established. Sino-Vietnamese literature became dominated by Confucian and Buddhist texts and was governed by strict rules of metre and verse.

Modern Vietnamese literature *(quoc am)* includes anything recorded in *nom* characters or the Romanised *quoc ngu* script (see the Language chapter for a discussion of script). The earliest extant text written in nom is the late 13th century *Van Te Ca Sau* (Ode to an Alligator). Literature written in quoc ngu has played an important role in Vietnamese nationalism.

One of Vietnam's literary masterpieces, *The Tale of Kieu* (Kim Van Kieu) was written during the first half of the 19th century – a period marked by a great deal of literary activity – by Nguyen Du (1765-1820), who was a poet, scholar, mandarin and diplomat.

Sculpture

Vietnamese sculpture has traditionally centred on religious themes and functioned as an adjunct to architecture, especially within pagodas, temples and tombs. Examples of inscribed stelae (carved stone slabs or columns), erected hundreds of years ago to commemorate the founding of a pagoda or important national events, can still be seen at the Temple of Literature in Hanoi.

Architecture

The Vietnamese have not been prolific builders like their neighbours the Khmers, who erected the monuments of Angkor in Cambodia, and the Chams, whose graceful brick towers, constructed using sophisticated masonry technology, adorn many parts of the southern half of the country.

Most of what the Vietnamese have built has been made of wood and other materials that proved highly vulnerable in the tropical climate. This, coupled with the fact that almost all of the stone structures erected by the Vietnamese have been destroyed in countless feudal wars and invasions, means that very little pre-modern Vietnamese architecture remains. Hanoi, however, contains an astounding number of French colonial-style buildings, and some fine examples of traditional Chinese architecture.

Plenty of pagodas and temples founded hundreds of years ago are still functioning, but they have usually been rebuilt many times with little concern for making the upgraded structure an exact copy of the original. As a result, many modern elements have been casually introduced into pagoda architecture – the neon haloes for statues of Buddha is one of the most glaring examples.

Because of the Vietnamese custom of ancestor worship, many graves from previous centuries are extant. These include temples erected in memory of high-ranking mandarins, royal family members and emperors.

The Presidential Palace

Painting

Traditional painting on frame-mounted silk dates from the 13th century. Silk painting was at one time the preserve of scholar-calligraphers, who also painted scenes from nature. Before the advent of photography, realistic portraits for use in ancestor worship were produced. Some of these – usually of former head monks – can still be seen in Buddhist pagodas.

During this century Vietnamese painting has been influenced by western trends. Much recent work has had political rather than aesthetic or artistic motives. According to an official account, the fighting of the French and American forces provided painters with 'rich human material: People's Army combatants facing the jets, peasant and factory women in the militia who handled guns as well as they did their production work, young volunteers who repaired roads in record time ... old mothers offering tea to anti-aircraft gunners ...' – there's lots of this stuff at the Fine Arts Museum.

The recent economic liberalisation has convinced many young artists to abandon the revolutionary themes and concentrate on producing commercial paintings. Some have gone back to the traditional-style silk paintings, while others are experimenting with new subjects.

Pottery

The production of ceramics (gom) has a long history in Vietnam. In ancient times, ceramic objects were made by coating a wicker mould with clay and baking it. Later, ceramic production became very refined, and each dynastic period is known for its particular techniques and motifs. Vietnam's largest ceramics centre is outside Hanoi in the village of Bat Trang.

Lacquerware

The art of making lacquerware was brought to Vietnam from China in the mid-15th century. Before that time, the Vietnamese used lacquer solely for practical purposes (ie making things watertight). During the 1930s the Fine Arts School in Hanoi employed several Japanese teachers who introduced new styles and production methods. Their influence is still evident in some Vietnamese lacquerware.

Lacquer is a resin extracted from the *son* tree *(cay son)*. It is creamy white in raw form but is made black *(son then)* or brown (*canh dan*, 'cockroach wing') by mixing it with resin in an iron container for 40 hours. After an object (traditionally made of teak) has been treated with a fixative, a requisite 10 coats of lacquer are applied. Each coat must be dried for a week and then thoroughly sanded with pumice and cuttlebone before the next layer can be applied. A specially refined lacquer is used for the 11th and final coat, which is sanded with a fine coal powder and lime wash before the object is decorated. Designs may be added by engraving in low relief, by painting or by inlaying mother-of-pearl, eggshell, silver or even gold.

Cinema

One of Vietnam's first cinematographic efforts was a newsreel of Ho Chi Minh's 1945 Proclamation of Independence. Following

this, parts of the battle of Dien Bien Phu were restaged for the benefit of movie cameras.

Until recently, most North Vietnamese film-making efforts have been dedicated to 'the mobilisation of the masses for economic reconstruction, the building of socialism and the struggle for national reunification'. Predictable themes include 'workers devoted to socialist industrialisation', 'old mothers who continuously risk their lives to help the People's Army' and 'children who are ready to face any danger'.

The relaxation of ideological censorship of the arts has proceeded in fits and starts, but in the last few years the gradual increase in artistic freedoms has affected film-making, as well as many other genres. But paranoia concerning the radical changes in Eastern Europe caused a return to greater government control of the arts.

Films Almost all American-made movies about Vietnam are in fact about the war, but most were filmed in the Philippines or Thailand. Some popular ones include *Rambo*, *Full Metal Jacket*, *Platoon*, *The Deer*

Woodcut of young women playing the flute, lute, fan and spoons.

Hunter, Good Morning Vietnam and Apocalypse Now.

The book When Heaven and Earth Changed Places by Le Ly Hayslip was made into the movie Heaven and Earth by director Oliver Stone. Born on the 4th of July by Ron Kovic is another book which made the transition to a Stone blockbuster motion picture.

Indochine, starring Catherine Deneuve, is a French film about France's colonial experience in South-East Asia.

Two more recent films set in Vietnam are Vietnamese director Tran Anh Hung's The Scent of Green Papaya and Cyclo.

Theatre

These days, the various forms of Vietnamese theatre are performed by dozens of state-funded troupes and companies around the country. Vietnamese theatre integrates music, singing, recitation, declamation, dance and mime into a single artistic whole. There are four basic forms:

Classical theatre is known as *hat tuong* in the north. It is based on Chinese opera and was probably brought to Vietnam by the 13th century Mongol invaders eventually chased out by Tran Hung Dao. Hat tuong is very formalistic, employing gestures and scenery similar to Chinese theatre. The accompanying orchestra, which is dominated by the drum, usually has six musicians. Often, the audience also has a drum so it too can comment on the on-stage action. Hat tuong has a limited cast of typical characters who establish their identities using combinations of make-up and dress that the audience can readily recognise. For instance, red face-paint represents courage, loyalty and faithfulness. Traitors and cruel people have white faces. Lowlanders are given green faces; highlanders have black ones. Horizontal eyebrows represent honesty, erect eyebrows symbolise cruelty and lowered eyebrows belong to characters with a cowardly nature. A male character can express emotions (pensiveness, worry, anger etc) by fingering his beard in various ways.

Popular theatre *(hat cheo)* is a typically northern Vietnamese art form and often engages in social protest through satire. The singing and declamation are in everyday language and include many proverbs and sayings. Many of the melodies are of peasant origin.

Modern theatre *(cai luong)* originated in the south in the early 20th century and shows strong western influences. In recent years this form has gained popularity in the north.

Spoken drama *(kich noi* or *kich)*, with its western roots, appeared in the 1920s. It's popular among students and intellectuals.

Puppetry

Conventional puppetry *(roi can)* and that uniquely Vietnamese art form, water puppetry *(roi nuoc)*, draw their plots from the same legendary and historical sources as other forms of traditional theatre. It is thought that water puppetry developed when determined puppeteers in the Red River Delta managed to carry on with the show despite flooding (see the boxed text 'Puppetry in a Pool' in the Things to See & Do chapter).

SOCIETY & CONDUCT
Traditional Culture

Try to learn about the Vietnamese culture before you arrive and respect cultural differences, rather than try to change them.

Face Having 'big face' is synonymous with prestige, and prestige is important in the Orient. All families, even poor ones, are expected to have big wedding parties and throw their money around like it's water in order to gain face. This is often ruinously expensive, but the fact that the wedding results in bankruptcy for the young couple is far less important than losing face.

Geomancy Geomancy is the art (or science) of manipulating or judging the environment. The Vietnamese call it *phong thuy*, meaning 'wind water', but many westerners know it by its Chinese name, *feng shui*.

If you want to build a house or find a suitable site for a grave then you call in a geomancer. The orientation of houses, communal meeting halls *(dinh)*, tombs and pagodas is determined by geomancers, which is why cemeteries have tombstones turned every which way. The location of an ancestor's grave is an especially serious matter – if the grave is in the wrong spot or facing the wrong way, then there is no telling what trouble the spirits might cause. Ditto for the location of the family altar in every Vietnamese home.

Failing businesses may call in a geomancer. Sometimes the solution is to move a door or a window. If this doesn't do the trick, it might be necessary to move an ancestor's grave. Distraught spirits may have to be placated with payments of cash (donated to a temple), especially if one wishes to erect a building or other structure which blocks the spirits' view. The date on which you begin construction of a new building is also a crucial matter.

The concept of geomancy is believed to have originated with the Chinese. Although the communists (both Chinese and Vietnamese) have disparaged geomancy as superstition, it still has a large influence on people's behaviour.

Dos & Don'ts

Clothing Please respect local dress standards, particularly at religious sites (avoid wearing shorts or sleeveless tops and always remove your shoes before entering a temple). In general Vietnamese dress standards are conservative, but the recent influx of foreigners has influenced Vietnamese tastes.

Greetings The traditional Vietnamese form of greeting is to press your hands together in front of your body and bow slightly. These days, the western custom of shaking hands has taken over, but the traditional greeting is still sometimes used by Buddhist monks and nuns – it is proper to respond in kind.

Name Cards Name cards are very popular in Vietnam and, like elsewhere in East Asia, exchanging business cards is an important part of even the smallest transaction or business contact. If you can't get some printed before you arrive in Vietnam, there are plenty of places in Hanoi to get this done cheaply.

Deadly Chopsticks Leaving a pair of chopsticks sticking vertically in a rice bowl looks very much like the incense sticks which are burned for the dead. This is a powerful death sign and is not appreciated anywhere in the Orient.

Mean Feet Shoes are removed inside most Buddhist temples and often in people's homes, but this is not universal so watch what others do. If you are entering a 'shoes off' home, your host will probably provide a pair of slippers.

It's rude to point the bottoms of your feet towards other people; the only exception may be with close friends. When sitting on the floor, you should ideally fold your legs into the lotus position to avoid pointing your soles at others. Most importantly, never point your feet towards anything sacred such as figures of Buddha or the ancestral shrines found in most homes.

In formal situations, when sitting on a chair do not sit with your legs crossed.

Keep Your Hat in Hand As a form of respect to elderly or other respected people (monks etc), take off your hat and bow your head politely when addressing them. The head is the symbolic highest point in Asia – never pat or touch someone on their head.

Show Some Respect In face-conscious Asia, foreigners should pay double attention to showing respect (it's not a bad idea even at home). One expat in Vietnam had this to say on the matter:

The main reason I write is to plead with you to clearly ... and strongly implore your readers to show a little respect for the locals. Fighting over and gloating about ripping off a cyclo driver for US$0.10 is a small 'victory' and shameful thing to do. These people obviously need the money. If nothing else, travellers should at least be cordial and respectful – smile, it works wonders here. What I've seen recently here where I work has made me realise that imperialism is not yet dead. Because of the power of money, some foreigners act like they're inherently superior. The imperialist of old came with a gun and a uniform, the imperialist today comes with a camera.
Steve McNicholas

Vernon Weitzel of the Australian National University sends these 10 tips for successfully dealing with Vietnamese officials, business people etc:

- Always smile and be pleasant.
- Don't run around complaining about everything.
- If you want to criticise someone, do it in a joking manner to avoid confrontation.
- Expect delays – build them into your schedule.
- Never show anger – ever! Getting visibly upset is not only rude – it will cause you to lose face.
- Don't be competitive. Treating your interaction as a cooperative enterprise works much better.
- Don't act as though you deserve service from anyone. If you do, it's likely that you will be delayed.
- Don't be too inquisitive about personal matters.
- Sitting and sipping tea and the exchange of gifts (sharing cigarettes, for instance) are an important prelude to any business interaction.
- The mentality of officialdom is very Confucian. Expect astounding amounts of red tape.

Treatment of Animals

Vietnam, particularly by western standards, has a very low level of awareness when it comes to treatment of animals. See the Responsible Tourism section in the Facts for the Visitor chapter.

RELIGION

Four great philosophies and religions have shaped the spiritual life of the Vietnamese people: Confucianism, Taoism, Buddhism and Christianity.

Over the centuries, Confucianism, Taoism and Buddhism have fused with popular Chinese beliefs and ancient Vietnamese animism to form what is known collectively as Tam Giao (Triple Religion), sometimes referred to as Vietnamese Buddhism. The religious life of the Vietnamese is also profoundly influenced by ancestor worship, which dates from long before the arrival of Confucianism or Buddhism.

Confucianism, more a system of social and political morality than a religion, took on many religious aspects. Taoism, which began as an esoteric philosophy for scholars, mixed with Buddhism, popular among the peasants, and many Taoist elements became an intrinsic part of popular religion. If asked their religion most Vietnamese are likely to say that they are Buddhist, but when it comes to family or civic duties they are likely to follow Confucianism while turning to Taoist conceptions in understanding the nature of the cosmos.

Buddhism

Mahayana Buddhism (Dai Thua, or Bac Tong, which means 'From the North' – ie China) is the predominant religion in Vietnam. It is also known as the Greater Wheel school, Greater Vehicle school and Northern Buddhism.

Mahayana Buddhism differs from Theravada Buddhism (Tieu Thua, or Nam Tong, which means 'From the South') in several important ways. Theravada Buddhism is also known as Hinayana, the Lesser Wheel school, the Lesser Vehicle school and Southern Buddhism; it came to Vietnam directly from India. It is practised mainly in

MASON FLORENCE

Buddhist painting at Tran Quoc Pagoda.

Incense shop in the Old Quarter

Hat and unglazed pots in Phu Lang Village

Offerings for sale at Quan Thanh Temple.

Stacked incense sticks

The wood-carved water buffalos ride out.

Water puppets for sale for bath time back home.

Greet Lunar New Year with a Tet mask.

Ancestor offerings include 'ghost money' and various kinds of foods.

the Mekong Delta region, mostly by ethnic-Khmers.

Whereas the Theravada Buddhist strives to become a perfected saint *(arhat)* ready for nirvana, the Mahayanist ideal is that of the Bodhisattva, one who strives to perfect themselves in the necessary virtues (generosity, morality, patience, vigour, concentration and wisdom), but even after attaining this perfection chooses to remain in the world in order to save others.

Mahayana Buddhist pagodas in Vietnam usually include a number of elements. In front of the pagoda is a white statue of a standing Quan The Am Bo Tat (Avalokitecvara Bodhisattva in Hindi, Guanyin in Chinese, Goddess of Mercy in English). A variation of the Goddess of Mercy shows her with multiple arms and sometimes multiple eyes and ears, permitting her to touch, see and hear all. This version of the Goddess of Mercy is called Chuan De (Qianshou Guanyin in Chinese).

The function of the Vietnamese Buddhist monk *(bonze)* is to minister to the spiritual and superstitious needs of the peasantry, but it is largely up to them whether they invoke the lore of Taoism or the philosophy of Buddhism. A monk may live reclusively on a remote hilltop or may manage a pagoda on a busy city street. And they may choose to fulfil any number of functions: telling fortunes, making and selling talismans *(fu)*, advising where a house should be constructed, reciting incantations at funerals or even performing acupuncture.

Confucianism

While it is more a religious philosophy than an organised religion, Confucianism (Nho Giao, or Khong Giao) has been an important force in shaping Vietnam's social system and the everyday lives and beliefs of its people.

Confucius (Khong Tu) was born in China around 550 BC. He saw people as social beings formed by society yet capable of shaping their own society. He believed that the individual exists in and for society and drew up a code of ethics to guide the individual in social interaction. This code laid down a person's specific obligations to family, society and the state. Central to Confucianism is an emphasis on duty and hierarchy.

According to Confucian philosophy, brought to Vietnam by the Chinese during their 1000 year rule, the emperor alone, governing under the mandate of heaven, can intercede on behalf of the nation with the powers of heaven and earth. Only virtue, as acquired through education, gave one the right (the mandate of heaven) to wield political power. From this it followed that an absence of virtue would result in the withdrawal of this mandate, sanctioning rebellion against an unjust ruler. Natural disasters or defeat on the battlefield were often interpreted as a sign that the mandate of heaven had been withdrawn.

Confucian philosophy in some senses was democratic: education rather than birth made a person virtuous. Therefore, education had to be widespread. Until the beginning of this century, Confucian philosophy and texts formed the basis of Vietnam's educational system. Generation after generation of young people – in villages as well as cities – were taught their duties to family (including ancestor worship) and community and were told that each person had to know their own place in the social hierarchy and should behave accordingly. This is especially true in the north, and Hanoians are known to retain stronger Confucian values than the Saigonese.

Taoism

Taoism (Lao Giao, or Dao Giao) originated in China and is based on the philosophy of Laotse (Thai Thuong Lao Quan). Laotse (literally, The Old One) lived in the 6th century BC. Little is known about Laotse and there is some question as to whether he really existed. He is believed to have been the custodian of the imperial archives for the Chinese government and Confucius is supposed to have consulted him.

Understanding Taoism is not easy. The philosophy emphasises contemplation and simplicity of life. Its ideal is returning to the

FACTS ABOUT HANOI

Tao (the Way – the essence of which all things are made). Only a small elite in China and Vietnam has ever been able to grasp Taoist philosophy, which is based on various correspondences (eg the human body, the microcosmic replica of the macrocosm) and complementary contradictions (*am* and *duong*, the Vietnamese equivalents of Yin and Yang). As a result, there are very few pure Taoist pagodas in Vietnam, yet much of Taoist ritualism has been absorbed into Chinese and Vietnamese Buddhism. The Taoist influence you are most likely to notice is the dragons and demons which decorate temple rooftops.

According to the Taoist cosmology, Ngoc Hoang, the Emperor of Jade (in Chinese: Yu Huang) whose abode is in heaven, rules over a world of divinities, genies, spirits and demons in which the forces of nature are incarnated as supernatural beings and great historical personages have become gods. It is this aspect of Taoism that has become assimilated into the daily lives of most Vietnamese as a collection of superstitions and mystical and animistic beliefs. Much of the sorcery and magic that are now part of popular Vietnamese religion have their origins in Taoism.

Ancestor Worship

Vietnamese ancestor worship, which is the ritual expression of filial piety *(hieu)*, dates from long before the arrival of Confucianism or Buddhism. Some people consider it to be a religion unto itself.

The cult of the ancestors is based on the belief that the soul lives on after death and becomes the protector of its descendants. Because of the influence the spirits of one's ancestors exert on the living, it is considered not only shameful for them to be upset or restless, but downright dangerous. A soul with no descendants is doomed to eternal wandering because it will not receive homage.

Traditionally, the Vietnamese venerate and honour the spirits of their ancestors regularly, especially on the anniversary of their death, when sacrifices are offered to both the god of the household and the spirit of the ancestors. To request intercession for success in business or on behalf of a sick child, sacrifices and prayers are offered to the ancestral spirits. The ancestors are informed on occasions of family joy or sorrow, such as weddings, success in an examination or death. Important elements in the cult of the ancestor are the family altar, a plot of land whose income is set aside for the support of the ancestors, and the designation of a direct male descendent of the deceased to carry on the cult.

Many pagodas have altars on which memorial tablets and photographs of the deceased are displayed. The young faces in so many of these photographs doesn't reflect an early death but, rather than using a picture of an aged, infirm parent, survivors chose a more flattering (though outdated) picture of the deceased in their prime.

Catholicism

Catholicism was introduced into Vietnam in the 16th century by missionaries from Portugal, Spain and France. Pope Alexander VII assigned the first bishops to Vietnam in 1659 and the first Vietnamese priests were ordained nine years later. The first Catholic mission in Hanoi was founded in 1679, and according to some estimates, there were 800,000 Catholics in Vietnam by 1685.

Over the next three centuries, Catholicism was discouraged and at times outlawed. The first known edict forbidding missionary activity was promulgated in 1533. Foreign missionaries and their followers were severely persecuted during the 17th and 18th centuries.

Today, Vietnam has the highest percentage of Catholics (8 to 10% of the population) in Asia outside the Philippines. Since 1954 in the North and 1975 in the South, Catholics have faced severe restrictions on their religious activities and education. As in the former Soviet Union, all churches were viewed as capitalist institutions and rival centres of power which could subvert the government.

Since around 1990, the government has taken a more liberal line. There is no question that the Catholic religion is making a comeback, though the old churches have become quite dilapidated and there is a shortage of trained clergy. Also, a lack of funds prevents many churches from doing necessary restoration work, but donations from both locals and Overseas Vietnamese are gradually solving this problem.

Protestantism
Protestantism was introduced to Vietnam in 1911. The majority of Vietnam's Protestants, who number about 200,000, are Montagnards living in the central highlands. Protestants in Vietnam have been doubly unfortunate in that they were persecuted first by Diem and later by the communists.

Caodaism
Caodaism is an indigenous Vietnamese sect that seeks to create the ideal religion by fusing the secular and religious philosophies of both east and west. It was founded in the early 1920s based on messages revealed in seances to Ngo Minh Chieu, the group's founder. The sect's colourful headquarters is in Tay Ninh, 96km north-west of Saigon. There are currently about two million followers of Caodaism in Vietnam, though just a minute percentage is in Hanoi.

Islam
Muslims, mostly ethnic-Khmers and Chams, constitute less than 0.1% of the city population. Hanoi's Muslims congregate at the Chua An Do Islamic Mosque (Map 5).

Facts for the Visitor

WHEN TO GO

There is really no bad season to visit Hanoi. The city offers countless attractions that can be visited year-round, and aside from some variable weather patterns, the climate is generally pleasant.

The foreign tourist high season runs from late June through August, tapering off in September, and picking up again from October until Tet – the colourful Lunar New Year celebration which falls in late January or February.

Things quieten down again from late February through late April, when the start of summer and the domestic tourist season kicks into high gear. Be aware that public transport can be very busy with large domestic group bookings.

Visitors should allow for the fact that during Tet, public transportation into, out of and around Vietnam can be booked solid.

Cua O Quan Chuong (Old East Gate)

Tet, however, is a fascinating time to be in Hanoi, with lots of colourful festivals and ceremonies in the city and surrounding villages (see the boxed text 'The Tet Festival' later in this chapter).

ORIENTATION

Hanoi sprawls along the banks of the Red River (Song Hong), which is spanned by three bridges.

The 1682m **Long Bien Bridge** (now used only by nonmotorised vehicles and pedestrians) was opened in 1902. It was once named after the turn-of-the-century French governor general of Indochina, Paul Doumer (1857-1932), who was assassinated a year after becoming President of France. Today it is a fantastic hodgepodge of repairs dating from the American War. US aircraft repeatedly bombed the strategic Long Bien Bridge, yet after each attack the Vietnamese somehow managed to improvise replacement spans and return it to road and rail service. It is said that when US POWs were put to work repairing the bridge, the US military, fearing for their safety, ended the attacks.

A few hundred metres south of the Long Bien Bridge is the newer **Chuong Duong Bridge** which took Vietnamese crews just two years to complete.

North of the city, servicing the new road to Noi Bai Airport and northbound National Highway 1, is the **Thang Long Bridge**. Construction lasted over a decade, beginning with the help of the Chinese in 1974 and completed with the help of the Russians. This two-tiered span is the longest bridge in Indochina, stretching 5503m for the railway overpass, 3115m for the motor vehicle section and 2658m on the pedestrian and bicycle crossing. The Chuong Duong and Thang Long bridges were both completed in 1985.

Note that most of Hanoi's streets begin with *pho*, while larger roads and boulevards are called *duong* (abbreviated as Đ in this book).

MASON FLORENCE

Districts

The city proper is geographically divided into seven central districts (or *quan*). In addition there are several outlying areas *(hyyen)* which, while classified as part of Hanoi, operate under independent administration.

The **Hoan Kiem district** – the attractive heart of Hanoi – centres around Hoan Kiem Lake. Just to the north of the lake is *Pho Co*, the Old Quarter (known to the French as the Cité Indigène). This area is characterised by narrow streets whose names change every one or two blocks. Tourists mostly like to base themselves in this part of town as it is convenient for most of the city's major sites – St Joseph's Cathedral, the Hanoi Opera House and several museums, as well as the headquarters of Vietcombank and the main post office. The Hanoi train station is on the far western edge of this district.

The **Hai Ba Trung district**, due south of the Hoan Kiem Lake district, was named after Vietnam's most beloved national heroines, the Trung sisters. It is home to Hai Ba Trung temple, Lenin Park and the Hanoi circus. It boasts several lakes and has a large student population from the Polytechnic, Economic and Construction Universities.

The **Dong Da district**, west of the Hai Ba Trung district, was named after the Dong Da earth mound and has several universities. The must-see Temple of Literature sits on the northern edge of this district.

The **Thanh Xuan district** in the far southwest of town is where you'll find the Air Force Museum, Hanoi University and the Foreign Languages College.

The **Ba Dinh district**, to the west of Hoan Kiem Lake, is a neighbourhood some refer to as the French Quarter. There are several important sites here including Ho Chi Minh's Mausoleum, the Hanoi Citadel, One Pillar Pagoda and the Botanical Gardens. Many foreign embassies and government offices, housed in classical architectural masterpieces from the French colonial era, are also located in this area. On the outer western fringes of Ba Dinh is the Van Phuc Diplomatic Quarter, home to more foreign embassies and medical facilities. Also in this area is a zoo and some posh joint-venture hotels, including the Horizon Hotel, Hanoi Hotel and mammoth Daewoo Hotel (the city's largest and most expensive).

The **Tay Ho district**, due north of Ho Chi Minh's Mausoleum, is Hanoi's newest official district, established in 1995. It forms

---

Urban Orienteering

Urban orienteering is very easy in Hanoi. Vietnamese is written with a Latin-based alphabet. You can at least read the street signs and maps, even if the pronunciation is incomprehensible! In addition, finding out where you are is easy: street signs are plentiful, and almost every shop and restaurant has the street name and number right on its sign. Street names are sometimes abbreviated on street signs with just the initials ('DBP' for 'Dien Bien Phu' etc).

Most streets numbers are sequential, with odd and even numbers on opposite sides of the street, but there are confusing exceptions. In some places, consecutive buildings are numbered 15A, 15B, 15C and so forth, while elsewhere, consecutive addresses read 15D, 17D, 19D etc.

The Vietnamese post office is comfortable with the English words and abbreviations for street (St), road (Rd) and boulevard (Blvd), but this is not what you'll see on street signs. There are several words for 'street', the main ones used in Hanoi being Pho and Duong (Ð). In Vietnamese, the word 'street' comes before the name, so Hang Bac Street becomes Pho Hang Bac.

Many establishments are named after their street addresses. For instance, 'Nha Hang 51 Tran Hung Dao' (*nha hang* means restaurant) would be at number 51 Duong (abbreviated to Ð) Tran Hung Dao.

the periphery of gigantic West Lake (Ho Tay) – Hanoi's largest – and has several important historic and religious sites such as Tran Quoc Pagoda and Quan Thanh Temple.

The **Cau Giay district** occupies the far western edge of Hanoi, and is home to the excellent Museum of Ethnology and a few smaller college campuses.

MAPS

Basic tourist maps of Hanoi are readily available at bookshops and most post offices for around US$1. If you're heading into the countryside, Lonely Planet's *Vietnam travel atlas* gives an in-depth view of towns, highways and topographic features.

RESPONSIBLE TOURISM

The effects of the recent arrival of mass tourism, both positive and negative, are being felt in Vietnam. While positive contributions may include dollars flowing into the local economy, the creation of jobs and a growing sense of globalisation, it is important for travellers to recognise the potentially damaging impact of their visit.

Negative effects of tourism, both domestic and international, can be markedly reduced by responsible travel and a respect for local culture and customs. By minimising impact, each visitor can make a difference. Be sensitive to local customs and take note of what local people do (for more information see Society & Conduct in the Facts about Hanoi chapter).

In Asia, the prevalence of prostitution is unfortunate but real. As part of the social evils campaign, the government regularly cracks down on the sex industry with heavy penalties, but the problem still remains. Avoid patronising bars etc that offer sex as the main service, such as the 'bar oms', and never buy sexual services.

The sexual exploitation of children is another significant problem in Asia. As a direct response to this, a number of countries, including Australia, New Zealand, Germany, Sweden, Norway, France and the USA, now prosecute citizens for paedophilia offences committed abroad.

Vietnam has a low level of environmental awareness and responsibility and many people remain unaware of the implications of littering. Try and raise awareness subtly by example and dispose of rubbish as responsibly as possible.

Vietnam's faunal populations are under considerable threat from domestic consumption and the illegal international trade in animal products. Though it may be 'exotic' to try wild meat such as muntjac, bats, frogs, deer, sea horses, shark fins and snake (wine) etc – or to buy products made from endangered plants and animals – it will indicate your support and acceptance of such practices and add to the demand for them.

Similarly, forest products such as rattan, orchids, medicinal herbs etc are under threat. While some of these products can be grown domestically, earning local people additional income and protecting natural areas from exploitation and degradation, the majority are still collected directly from Vietnam's dwindling forests.

Finally, do not remove or buy 'souvenirs' that have been taken from historical sites and natural areas.

The World Conservation Union (IUCN, Map 5; Vietnam Capacity Building for Sustainable Tourism Project, 13 Pho Tran Hung Dao, ☎ 826-5172, fax 825-8794, tourism .iucnvn@netnam.org.vn) is among the groups working towards reducing the impact of tourism on Vietnam's landscape and cultural heritage. Its free pamphlet entitled *Treading Softly: A Guide to Eco-Friendly Travel in Vietnam* can be picked up at its office in central Hanoi (and hopefully soon at city hotels, tour agencies, etc).

Also consider contacting the Vietnam National Administration of Tourism (Director, Institute for Tourism Development Research), 30A Ly Thuong Kiet.

TOURIST OFFICES

Vietnam's tourist offices are not really in the business of promoting Vietnam as a tourist destination. Rather, they are state-run enterprises which masquerade as tourist offices, and their primary interests are booking tours and earning a profit. In fact, these 'tourist offices' are little more than travel agencies, but they are among the most profitable hard-currency cash cows the Vietnamese government has. There has been talk of creating not-for-profit tourist information offices, as well as a tourist police force such as in Thailand, but these are yet to be realised. Meanwhile, the overall state of tourism continues to suffer.

Perhaps the best sources of independent travel information in Hanoi are the budget tour agencies. Staff are usually willing to part with useful travel information, especially if you approach them in a friendly manner. They will of course also be happy to sell you their tours as well. Most of these places have message boards where travellers post the latest travel tips, praise, gripes, warnings, etc.

For a listing of tour operators, see Organised Tours in the Getting Around chapter.

Tourist Offices Abroad

State-run Vietnamese 'tourist offices' abroad include:

France
    Vietnam Tourism
    (☎ 01-42 86 86 37, fax 42 60 43 32)
    4 Rue Cherubini, Paris 75002
    Saigon Tourist
    (☎ 01-40 51 03 02, fax 43 25 05 70)
    24 Rue des Bernadins, Paris 75005
Germany
    Saigon Tourist
    (☎ 030-786 5056, fax 786 5596)
    24 Dudenstrasse 78 W, 1000 Berlin 61
Japan
    Saigon Tourist
    (☎ 03-3258 5931, fax 3253 6819)
    IDI 6th floor, Crystal Building, 1-2, Kanda Awaji-cho, Chiyoda-ku, Tokyo 101
Singapore
    Vietnam Tourism
    (☎ 02-532 3130, fax 532 2952)
    101 Upper Cross St, No 02-44 People's Park Centre, Singapore 0105
    Saigon Tourist
    (☎ 02-735 1433, fax 735 1508)
    131 Tanglin Rd, Tudor Court, Singapore 1024

DOCUMENTS
Visas

While Vietnamese bureaucracy is legendary, completing the paperwork to obtain a visa is not all that daunting. But it tends to be quite expensive and unnecessarily time-consuming. Furthermore, Vietnamese visas come with numerous restrictions.

One significant restriction is that your visa must specify exactly where you will enter the country and where you will exit. Vietnam might just be the only country in the world to slap on this restriction. This limits your flexibility, but it is possible to change the exit point after you've arrived in Vietnam. This must be arranged through the immigration police, though in many cases people are refused, and instead referred back to local travel agents. You may be best off asking a reliable tour operator to make the arrangements. The cost for this rubber stamp is around US$25. Making this simple change can take from one to three days – if you want it fast then it may cost more.

In most cases getting your visa from a travel agent rather than directly through the Vietnamese embassy can save time and headaches. The travel agency doing your visa usually needs a photocopy of your passport and two or three photos.

Passing through Vietnamese immigration at Hanoi's Noi Bai Airport is far easier and smoother than in past years. However, many entering via overland still face hassles. Immigration authorities at the Chinese border checks at Lao Cai and Dong Dang, as well as the crossings into Laos, are notorious for extorting extra fees (typically around US$40) from travellers who have gone to the expense and trouble of getting all the paperwork in order.

If you plan to enter Vietnam overland, be *absolutely* sure that the border point you're using is in fact what is stamped in your passport. Even still, border guards have complete authority to decide whether or not you can enter, and how long you can stay. While most people get through OK, immigration staff may arbitrarily give you a shorter stay than what your visa calls for. Immediately after your visa has been stamped by the immigration officer, check to see how many days they've given you. If it's not enough, sometimes you can get it changed right at the border checkpoint – otherwise you will be forced to go through the immigration police and apply for an extension.

Always have some photos with you because immigration police have been known to inexplicably give travellers more forms to fill out, requiring photos. Of course, there is a photographer right there to serve you – for a substantial fee.

Regarding visa processing in Vietnam, and changes or extensions to visas, the less you personally get involved with immigration officials, the better off you are. Although travellers can theoretically secure a visa without going through a travel agent, Vietnamese bureaucrats usually thwart such individual efforts. Usually things go smoothly if you work through a reliable agent.

See the Internet Resources section later in this chapter for details of Lonely Planet's Web site which has hot links to the most up-to-date visa information.

Tourist Visas Tourist visas are only valid for a single 30 day stay within specified dates. You cannot arrive even one day earlier than your visa specifies. And if you postpone your trip by two weeks, then you'll only have 16 days remaining on your visa instead of 30 days.

Prices for single-entry tourist visas are around US$45 to US$60. In Bangkok they can be issued in about four days, in Hong Kong five days, but in other places (Taiwan, for example) as long as 10 working days. Many travel agencies offer package deals with visa and air ticket included.

Business Visas There are several advantages in having a business visa: they are usually valid for three or six months, can be issued for multiple-entry journeys and will

look more impressive when you have to deal with bureaucratic authorities. Also, they permit you to work.

Business visas can be prearranged through a local sponsor in Vietnam (usually a company). If approved, you must receive confirmation from the sponsor, and then pick up the visa from a Vietnamese embassy abroad. This usually costs around US$90.

It is also possible to arrive on a tourist visa and make arrangements locally for a business visa. In this case you'll either have to go abroad (most people go to Vientiene, Laos or Phnom Penh, Cambodia) to get the actual visa put into your passport; or you pay dearly to have it issued in Vietnam (they appear to figure into the cost a round-trip air ticket abroad!).

Student Visas A student visa is something you usually arrange after arrival. It's acceptable to enter Vietnam on a tourist visa, enrol in a Vietnamese language course and then apply through the immigration police for a change in status. A minimum of 10 hours of study per week is needed to qualify for student status.

Resident Visas Only a few foreigners can qualify for a resident visa. Probably the easiest way to do this is to marry a local, though anyone contemplating doing this had best be prepared for the mountains of paperwork.

Visa Extensions If you've got the dollars, they've got the rubber stamp. In Hanoi, visa extensions cost around US$25. You should probably go to a travel agency to get this taken care of, rather than fronting up at the immigration police yourself. The procedure typically takes three working days. You can apply for your extension several weeks before it's necessary. You are officially permitted one visa extension only, for up to 30 days. In some cases a second extension (10 day maximum) may be granted, but you'll need to cough up another US$25 and show proof (in the form of an air ticket) of your departure date.

Re-Entry Visas It's possible to enter China, Laos or Cambodia from Vietnam and then re-enter on your original single-entry Vietnamese visa. However, you must apply for a re-entry visa *before* you leave Vietnam. If you do not have a re-entry visa, then you will have to go through the whole expensive and time-consuming procedure of applying for a new Vietnamese visa. Re-entry visas are easy enough to arrange in Hanoi, but you will almost certainly have to ask a travel agent to do the paperwork for you. They charge about US$25 for this three day service.

Travel Insurance

A travel insurance policy is a very good idea – it can protect you against cancellation penalties on advance purchase flights, medical costs through illness or injury, theft or loss of possessions and the cost of additional air tickets if you get really sick and have to fly home.

If you do have to undergo medical treatment, be sure to collect all receipts and copies of your medical report – in your native language if possible – for your insurance company.

If you get robbed, you'll need to get a police report if you want to claim from your insurance company.

Many student travel organisations offer insurance policies. Some of these are very cheap, but only offer very minimal coverage. Read the small print *very* carefully to avoid being caught out by exclusions.

Driving Licence

If you plan to drive in Vietnam, get an International Driver's Licence before you leave home. You must carry a valid driver's licence from your home country together with this licence. Make sure your licence states that it is valid for motorbikes if you plan to ride one. Note that self-drive car hire is not an option in Vietnam. See Car & Motorbike in the Getting Around chapter and the Motorbiking in Northern Vietnam appendix following the Excursions chapter for further details.

Student & Youth Cards

Full-time students coming from the USA, Australia and Europe can often get some good discounts on international (not domestic) air tickets with the help of an International Student Identity Card (ISIC). To get this card, inquire at your campus.

International Health Card

Useful (though not essential) is an International Health Certificate to record any vaccinations you've had. These can also be issued in Vietnam.

Other Documents

Losing your passport is very bad news indeed. Getting a new one takes time and money. It's wise to have a driver's licence, student card, ID card or something else with your photo on it – some embassies want to see this picture ID before issuing a replacement passport. Keeping the original of an old expired passport is also very useful.

If you're travelling with your spouse, a photocopy of your marriage certificate might come in handy should you become involved with the law, hospitals or other bureaucratic authorities.

If you're planning on working or studying in Vietnam, it could be helpful to bring copies of transcripts, diplomas, letters of reference and other relevant professional qualifications.

Photocopies

It certainly helps to keep a separate record of the number and issue date of your passport as well as a photocopy of it, or your birth certificate. While you're compiling that info, add the serial numbers of your travellers cheques, credit card numbers, travel insurance details, and about US$50 or so in emergency cash (better hotels have a safe for these valuables).

If police stop you on the street and ask for your passport, give them a photocopy and explain your hotel has the original. Trusting anyone with your documents always makes you very vulnerable.

Photocopy shops – signposted in English – are never far away.

EMBASSIES & CONSULATES

It's important to realise what your own embassy can and can't do to help you if you get into trouble.

Generally speaking, it won't be much help in emergencies if the trouble you're in is remotely your own fault. You are bound by Vietnamese laws; your embassy will not be sympathetic if you end up in jail after committing a crime locally, even if such actions are legal in your own country.

In genuine emergencies you might get some assistance, but only if other channels have been exhausted.

Vietnamese Embassies & Consulates

The following addresses are for Vietnamese embassies and consulates abroad.

Australia
(☎ 02-6286 6059, fax 6286 4534)
6 Timbarra Crescent, O'Malley, Canberra, ACT 2603
Consulate: (☎ 02-9327 2539, fax 9328 1653)
489 New South Head Rd, Double Bay, NSW 2028
Cambodia
(☎ 05-1881 1804, fax 236 2314)
436 Blvd Preach, Monivong, Phnom Penh
Canada
(☎ 613-236 0772, fax 236 2704)
226 Maclaren St, Ottawa, Ontario K2P 0L9
China
(☎ 010-532 1125, fax 532 5720)
32 Guanghua Lu, Jianguomen Wai, Beijing
Consulate: (☎ 020-652 7908, fax 652 7808)
Jin Yanf Hotel, 92 Huanshi Western Rd, Guangzhou
Consulate: (☎ 22-591 4510, fax 591 4524)
15th floor, Great Smart Tower Bldg, 230 Wanchai Rd, Hong Kong
France
(☎ 01-44 14 64 00, fax 45 24 39 48)
62-66 Rue Boileau, Paris 75016
Germany
(☎ 228-357021, fax 351866)
Konstantinstrasse 37, 5300 Bonn 2
Italy
(☎ 06-854 3223, fax 854 8501)
34 Via Clituno, 00198 Rome
Japan
(☎ 03-3446 3311, fax 3466 3312)
50-11 Moto Yoyogi-Cho, Shibuya-ku, Tokyo 151

Consulate: (☎ 06-263 1600, fax 263 1770)
10th floor, Estate Bakurocho Bldg, 4-10 Bakurocho, 1-chome, Chuo-ku, Osaka
Laos
(☎ 214-13409)
1 Thap Luang Rd, Vientiane
Consulate: (☎ 412-12239, fax 12182)
418 Sisavang Vong, Savannakhet
Philippines
(☎ 2-500 364/508 101)
54 Victor Cruz, Malate, Metro Manila
Thailand
(☎ 2-251 7201/251 5836)
83/1 Wireless Rd, Bangkok
UK
(☎ 0171-937 1912, fax 937 6108; or after April 2000 ☎ 020-7937 1912, fax 7937 6108)
12-14 Victoria Rd, London W8 5RD
USA
(☎ 202-861 0737, fax 861 0917)
1233 20th St NW, Washington, DC 20036

Embassies in Hanoi

If you're staying a long time in Vietnam you should register your passport at your embassy (which makes it much easier to issue a new one if yours is lost or stolen). Consider registering with your embassy if you intend on travelling to more remote areas. They can help you obtain a ballot for absentee voting or provide forms for filing income tax returns. Embassies can also advise businesspeople and will sometimes intervene in trade disputes.

The following list contains the addresses of some foreign embassies:

Australia
(☎ 831 7755, fax 831 7711)
Map 2; Van Phuc Diplomatic Quarter (next to Daewoo Hotel)
Cambodia
(☎ 825 3788, fax 826 5225)
Map 5; 71 Pho Tran Hung Dao
Canada
(☎ 823 5500, fax 823 5333)
Map 3; 31 Đ Hung Vuong
China
(☎ 845 3736, fax 823 2826)
Map 3; 46 Pho Hoang Dieu
European Union (EU)
(☎ 934 1300, fax 934 1361)
56 Ly Thai To
France
(☎ 825 2719, fax 826 4236)
Map 5; 57 Pho Tran Hung Dao

Germany
(☎ 845 3836, fax 845 3838)
Map 3; 29 Đ Tran Phu
Japan
(☎ 846 3000, fax 846 3043)
Map 2; 27 Pho Lieu Giai
Laos
(☎ 825 4576, fax 822 8414)
Map 5; 22 Pho Tran Binh Trong; visas processed at Laos Consulate (Map 5), 40 Pho Quang Trung
Netherlands
(☎ 843 0605, fax 843 1013)
Block D1, Van Phuc Diplomatic Quarter
New Zealand
(☎ 824 1481, fax 824 1480)
Map 5; 32 Pho Hang Bai
Philippines
(☎ 825 7948, fax 826 5760)
Map 5; 27B Pho Tran Hung Dao
Thailand
(☎ 823 5092, fax 823 5088)
Map 3; 63-65 Pho Hoang Dieu
UK
(☎ 825 2510, fax 826 5762)
Map 5; 31 Pho Hai Ba Trung
USA
(☎ 843 1500, fax 843 1510)
Map 2; 7 Pho Lang Ha

CUSTOMS

Travellers occasionally report trouble with Vietnamese customs. Some travellers have even had their Lonely Planet books seized or sections of it torn out! Ditto for video tapes. It's best to keep such dangerous items buried deep down in your luggage or else in your coat pocket.

You are not permitted to take antiques or other 'cultural treasures' out of the country. If you purchase fake antiques, be sure that you have a receipt and a customs clearance form from the seller. Suspected antiques will be seized, or else you'll have to pay a 'fine'.

If you enter Vietnam by air, the customs inspection is usually fast and cursory. However, if you enter overland, you may be subjected to a rigorous search.

You are permitted to bring in a duty-free allowance of 200 cigarettes, 50 cigars or 250g of tobacco; 2L of liquor; gifts worth up to US$50; and a reasonable quantity of luggage and personal effects.

FACTS FOR THE VISITOR

Social Evils

... we were advised by other tourists that the Vietnamese Department of Cultural Exports had to approve any tourist photographs prior to departure from the country or have the films confiscated at the airport. This rumour was confirmed after contacting the Australian embassy.

After getting five weeks of films developed, we sought out the relevant office on the far side of Hanoi. The films were taken off us and we were told to return immediately with any souvenirs that we had purchased so they could also be assessed. After doing this we were told we should return the next day, as we were flying out that day.

The next day – running out of time – we were interrogated for over an hour about photographs they deemed to reflect Vietnamese culture in a poor light.

The relevant photographs and negatives were confiscated. We were charged for the assessment of the photographs, negatives and souvenirs, and threatened with a hefty fine.

We were advised that a sculpture we had would take three days to assess, and should therefore be left in the country if we wished to leave that day. Finally talking our way out of the office, we proceeded to the airport (with sculpture) only to find that the airport customs officials didn't bother to check our bags, camera or even the documentation we'd been given by the Department of Cultural Exports.

We felt sorry for the guy behind us in Hanoi who had 52 films and a year of souvenirs for these same officials to paw over. This whole scam could have been avoided by going directly to the airport to begin with.

Nigel & Michelle Gough

Items which you cannot bring into Vietnam include opium, weapons, explosives and 'cultural materials unsuitable to Vietnamese society'.

Tourists can bring an unlimited amount of foreign currency into Vietnam, but they are required to declare it on their customs form upon arrival. Theoretically, when you leave the country you should have exchange receipts for all the foreign currency you have spent, but in practice the authorities really don't care.

When entering Vietnam, visitors must also declare all precious metals, jewellery, cameras and electronic devices in their possession. This should mean that when you leave, you will have no hassles taking these items out with you. It also means that you could be asked to show these items so that customs officials know you didn't sell them on the black market, though in practice you will seldom be troubled unless you bring in an unreasonable amount of goods or something of great value.

The import and export of Vietnamese currency and live animals is forbidden.

MONEY
Currency

The currency of Vietnam is the dong (abbreviated to 'd'). The banknotes come in denominations of 200d, 500d, 1000d, 2000d, 5000d, 10,000d, 20,000d and 50,000d.

Now that Ho Chi Minh has been canonised (against his wishes), you'll find his picture on *every* banknote. There are no coins currently in use in Vietnam, though the dong used to be subdivided into 10 hao and 100 xu. All dong-denominated prices in this book are from a time when US$1 was worth 13,800d.

The US dollar virtually acts as a second local currency, and hotels, airlines and travel agencies all normally quote their prices in dollars. This is in part because

Money for Nothing

The dong has certainly had a rocky history. In the days of French Indochina, the local currency was known as the *piastre*. The partitioning of Vietnam in 1954 created separate versions of the dong for North and South Vietnam. In 1975, US$1 was equal to 450d in South Vietnam. In 1976, the Communist Provisional Revolutionary Government (PRG) cancelled the South Vietnamese dong and issued its own PRG dong. The swap rate between the two dong was not set at 1:1, but rather at 500:1 in favour of the PRG dong. Furthermore, southerners were only permitted to exchange a maximum of 200d per family. This sudden demonetarisation of South Vietnam instantly turned much of the affluent population into paupers and caused the swift collapse of the economy. Those with the foresight to have kept their wealth hidden in gold or jewellery escaped some of the hardships.

In 1977, both the North Vietnamese dong and the PRG dong were done away with and swapped for a reunification dong. In the North the swap was 1:1, but in the South the ratio was 1:1.2. This time the southerners got a slightly better deal, though it was small compensation for the 500:1 loss of the previous year.

The last great attempt at currency swapping was in 1985. Realising that inflation was rapidly eroding the value of the dong, the government decided to solve the problem by reissuing a new dong at a swap ratio of 10:1 in favour of the new dong. This time each family was allowed only 2000d of the new banknotes, though on special application more was allotted. Rather than controlling price increases as the government had hoped, the currency reissue ignited yet another round of hyper-inflation. These days, the old 20d notes are literally not worth the paper they're printed on.

Vietnamese prices are so unwieldy, since US$100 is well over one million dong! For this reason, we also quote prices in US dollars. However, you can, and should, pay dong. Indeed, Vietnamese law requires that all transactions be in dong, though in practice many people will accept dollars.

A small pocket calculator is useful for converting currency.

Exchange Rates

Country	Unit		Dong
Australia	A$1	=	9094d
Canada	C$1	=	9415d
China	Y1	=	1679d
euro	€1	=	14,727d
France	1FF	=	2262d
Germany	DM1	=	7588d
Hong Kong	HK$1	=	1794d
Japan	¥100	=	11,615d
Malaysia	RM1	=	3659d
New Zealand	NZ$1	=	7670d
Singapore	S$1	=	8177d
Thailand	B1	=	371d
UK	UK£1	=	22,509d
USA	US$1	=	13,906d

Exchanging Money

Although you can at least theoretically exchange most major currencies, the reality is that US dollars are still much preferred.

Once in Vietnam beware of counterfeit cash, especially the 20,000d and 50,000d notes. There shouldn't be any problem if you've changed money in a bank, but out on the free market it's a different story.

You can reconvert 'reasonable' amounts of dong back into dollars on departure without an official receipt. Most visitors have had no problem, but having an official receipt should settle any arguments that may arise. You cannot legally take the dong out with you.

For cashing travellers cheques or taking a credit card cash advance, you are required to show your passport as ID.

Banks Vietcombank is another name for the state-owned Bank for Foreign Trade of Vietnam (Ngan Hang Ngoai Thuong Viet Nam).

Banking hours are normally from 8 am to 3 pm Monday to Friday, 8 am to noon on Saturday; most banks also close for 1½ hours during lunch and all day Sunday and public holidays.

The mammoth main branch of Vietcombank is at 47-49 Pho Ly Thai To (Map 5). There are numerous smaller branches around town. Two central locations are 12 Pho Hang Trong (Map 5; ☎ 828 5143) and 198 Pho Tran Quang Khai (Map 5; ☎ 826 7622).

Foreign or joint-venture banks with fully functioning branches can be found, though some are forced to impose higher fees than Vietcombank. They include (all on Map 5):

ANZ Bank
(☎ 825 8190, fax 825 8188)
14 Pho Le Thai To
(western shore of Hoan Kiem Lake)
Bangkok Bank
(☎ 826 0886, fax 826 7397)
41B Pho Ly Thai To
Bank of America
(☎ 825 0003, fax 824 9322)
27 Pho Ly Thuong Kiet
Chinfon Commercial Bank
(☎ 825 0555, fax 825 0566)
55 Pho Quang Trung
Citibank
(☎ 825 1950, fax 824 3960)
17 Pho Ngo Quyen
Credit Lyonnais
(☎ 825 8102, fax 826 0080)
10 Pho Trang Thi
Hong Kong Bank
(☎ 934 1887, fax 825 0199)
31 Pho Hai Ba Trung
ING Bank
(☎ 824 6888/826 9216)
International Centre Building,
17 Pho Ngo Quyen
Standard Chartered Bank
(☎ 825 8970, fax 825 8880)
27 Pho Ly Thai To

Foreign exchange banks observe all major public holidays. During the Lunar New Year, banks may close for three or four days in a row.

Cash Large-denomination bills (US$100) are preferred when changing into dong, but a small supply (say US$20 worth) of ones and fives may prove useful. Be very careful with your money – travellers cheques and large-denomination cash belong in a money belt or a hotel safe.

Travellers Cheques Travellers cheques can be exchanged, for dong or for US dollars cash, only at authorised foreign exchange banks. These banks usually charge a 2% commission to change US dollar travellers cheques into US dollars cash (other banks may charge more). Vietcombank charges no commission if you exchange travellers cheques for dong.

If your travellers cheques are in other currencies besides US dollars, you may find them difficult to exchange. If you insist, the banks may exchange non-US dollar cheques for dong, but they will charge a hefty commission to protect themselves against any possible exchange rate fluctuations.

ATMs ANZ Bank has a 24 hour automatic teller machine (ATM) which dispenses US dollars if you have an internationally accepted Visa, MasterCard or Cirrus card. There is no longer a service fee, though there is a daily maximum of US$500.

Credit Cards Visa, MasterCard, American Express and JCB cards are now acceptable at many places in Hanoi – typically mid-range and upmarket hotels, restaurants, and shops. But you may be charged up to 4% commission each time you use a credit card.

Getting a cash advance is possible at Vietcombank, but you'll be charged between 2% and 4% commission.

Black Market The black market is Vietnam's unofficial banking system, and is almost everywhere. Perhaps the term 'black market' is really too strong since it implies some cloak and dagger operation. It's in fact very open. Private individuals and some shops (jewellery stores, travel agencies) will exchange US dollars for dong and vice versa. While the practice is supposedly illegal, enforcement is virtually nonexistent. But it's important to realise that black

market exchange rates can be *worse* than the official exchange rates.

If people approach you on the street with offers to change money at rates better than the official bank rate, then you can rest assured that you are being set up for a rip-off. Don't even think about trying it. Remember, if an offer seems too good to be true, that's because it is. The most common place to be approached is around Hoan Kiem Lake.

Costs
Foreigners are frequently overcharged, particularly when buying souvenirs, and occasionally in restaurants. But don't assume that everyone is trying to rip you off – despite being poor, many Vietnamese will only ask the local price for most goods and services.

The cost of staying in Hanoi depends on your tastes and susceptibility to luxuries. Ascetics can get by on US$10 a day while most backpackers can live very well on US$20 to US$25.

Bare-bones private hotel rooms come as cheap as US$6, but for around US$10 to US$15 you can get something decent with an attached bath and air-con. Once you pass the US$20 limit, expect to be spoiled with satellite TV, IDD phones, etc.

While it is theoretically possible to eat in Hanoi on about US$2 to US$4 per day, most budget travellers would require something closer to US$10 for three square meals. Sampling some of the city's finer fare could push this over US$20 in no time.

Transportation expenses can be kept down by walking (which Hanoi is well suited to). Travelling by rented bicycle (about US$1 per day) can also save you a considerable sum.

Tipping & Bargaining
Tipping is not expected but it's enormously appreciated. For a person who earns US$50 per month, a US$1 tip is about half a day's wages.

In general, if you stay a couple of days in the same hotel it's not a bad idea to tip the staff who clean your room – US$0.50 to US$1 should be enough. You should also tip drivers and guides, especially on trips out of the city.

It is considered proper to make a small donation at the end of a visit to a pagoda, especially if the monk has shown you around; most pagodas have contribution boxes for this purpose.

Many foreigners just assume that every Vietnamese is out to rip them off. That just isn't true. Bargaining is common, even with the police if you are fined! In touristy areas, postcard vendors have a reputation for charging about five times the going rate. Many cyclo and motorbike drivers also try to grossly overcharge foreigners – try to find out the correct rate in advance and then bargain accordingly. Remember, bargaining should be good-natured; always be polite and smiling when bargaining – screaming and arguing will get you nowhere. And don't take bargaining too seriously.

Security

Though Hanoi's street crime pales in comparison to Ho Chi Minh City, it does have its share of pickpockets. To avoid losing your precious cash, travellers cheques or passport, keep any valuables far from sticky fingers – devices include pockets sewn on the inside of your trousers, Velcro tabs to seal pocket openings, a moneybelt under your clothes or a pouch under your shirt. A vest (waistcoat) worn under your outer jacket is another option.

Taxes

After years on the drawing board, Vietnam introduced a controversial value added tax (VAT) on 1 January 1999. The new tax technically applies to all consumer goods, and is set at four levels (0%, 5%, 10% or 20%) depending on the sector of the economy. So far it has created nothing but confusion. The government has aired a special TV program aimed at clarifying the issue, but, currently, the public still remains largely perplexed.

On many goods you pay for, the marked or stated price includes any relevant taxes. Only in some hotels, restaurants and shops is the VAT added separately.

If you're working in Vietnam, the issue of paying income taxes is totally flaky. Normal income taxes are 40% to 50% depending on how much you earn. In reality, few Vietnamese report all their income. As a foreign resident, you can theoretically be taxed on your 'worldwide income', which includes money not earned in Vietnam! Needless to say, most expats 'forget' to report their foreign-earned income.

The Vietnamese government is said to be looking at ways to crack down on tax evasion. If the tax collectors really get their act together, it will be a disaster for the economy.

POST & COMMUNICATIONS

The main post office (Buu Dien Trung Vong, Map 5; ☎ 825 7036, fax 825 3525), which occupies a full city block facing Hoan Kiem Lake, is at 75 Pho Dinh Tien Hoang (between Pho Dinh Le and Pho Le Thach). The entrance in the middle of the block leads to the postal services windows, which are open daily from 6.30 am to 8 pm.

The same entrance leads to the telex, telegram and domestic telephone office (☎ 825 5918), to the left as you enter. These services are available from 6.30 am to 8 pm, except for telegrams, which can be sent 24 hours a day.

International telephone calls can be made and faxes sent from the office (☎ 825 2030) on the corner of Pho Dinh Tien Hoang and Pho Dinh Le, open daily from 7.30 am to 9.30 pm.

Postal Rates

Domestic postal rates are sinfully cheap; just US$0.04 to mail a letter.

International postal rates are similar to those in European countries, ie postcards to Europe or the USA cost about US$0.50. While these rates might not seem expensive to you, the tariffs are so out of line with most salaries that locals literally cannot afford to send letters to friends and relatives abroad. If you would like to correspond with Vietnamese whom you meet during your visit, try leaving them enough stamps to cover postage for several letters, explaining that the stamps were extras you didn't use. Or buy a bunch of Vietnamese stamps to take home and when you write to Vietnamese friends include a few stamps for their replies.

Sending Mail

Air mail sent from Hanoi takes approximately 10 days to most western countries. Express mail service (EMS) can take as little as four days; the EMS office is on the north side of the main post office. There is also a reasonably priced domestic EMS between Hanoi and Saigon promising next-day delivery.

Foreigners wishing to send parcels out of Vietnam sometimes have to deal with time-consuming inspections of the contents, but this happens less frequently now. The most important thing is to keep the parcel small. If it's documents only you should be OK.

Private Couriers For a price, private couriers can deliver both international and domestic small parcels or documents. Companies include:

Airborne Express
    (☎ 824 1689, fax 824 1514)
    Map 5; 1 Pho Le Thach
DHL Worldwide Express
    (☎ 833 3999, fax 823 5698)
    Map 5; 75 Pho Dinh Tien Hoang
Federal Express
    (☎ 824 9054, fax 825 2479)
    Map 5; 6C Pho Dinh Le
TNT Express Worldwide
    (☎ 843 4535, fax 843 4550)
    Map 5; 15 Pho Ly Nam De
United Parcel Service
    (☎ 824 6483, fax 824 6464)
    Map 5; 4C Pho Dinh Le

Freight Forwarders Planning on shipping home Vietnamese furniture or moving an entire household? For this you need the services of an international mover.

Much of this business goes to Saigon Van (☎ 943 0610, fax 824 0944) at 21 Pho Ngo Van So. This company is associated with the international company Atlas Van Lines.

Receiving Mail

Every district and sub-district in Hanoi has some sort of post office; all are signposted with the words 'Buu Dien'.

Mail delivery is mostly reliable and fast. But this reliability becomes questionable if your envelope or package contains something worth stealing. Normal letters and postcards should be fine.

The poste restante service at Hanoi post offices works well. It is possible to receive mail at any post office, but the sender will need to specify when addressing the envelope or package. Generally speaking, the GPO is the best bet. Foreigners have to pay a US$0.04 service charge for each letter they pick up from poste restante.

Receiving even a small package from abroad can cause a headache and large ones will produce a migraine. If you're lucky, customs will clear the package and the clerks at the post office will simply let you take it away. If you're unlucky, customs will demand an inspection, at which lengthy process you must be present, and pay some small fees.

Telephone

Useful Phone Numbers The following free phone services are available, but don't be surprised if the person answering only speaks Vietnamese:

Ambulance	☎ 115
Fire Brigade	☎ 114
General Information	☎ 118
International Operator	☎ 110
International Prefix	☎ 00
Local Directory Assistance	☎ 116
Police	☎ 113
Time Information	☎ 117

Kudos to Vietnam's ☎ 108 information service, from which you can request an amazing array of facts, figures and trivia. For a mere US$0.03 per minute, you can ask everything from phone numbers to

MASON FLORENCE

SARA-JANE CLELAND

BERNARD NAPTHINE

MASON FLORENCE

MASON FLORENCE

The young and old of Hanoi and its surrounding villages will impress you with their industry and smiling good humour – and they might even try and sell you stuff.

You can move just about anything on two wheels, but you need the sturdy three wheels of a cyclo (top right) for really precious cargo.

train and plane timetables, to exchange rates and the latest football scores. We have used ☎ 108 to confirm historical dates, economic statistics, and receive a morning wake-up call. You can even order up a bedtime story for your child (told in a sweet voice)! Most of the time it is possible to be connected to an operator who speaks English or French.

International Calls International telecommunications charges from Vietnam are among the highest in the world, so unless you have some matter of earthshaking importance, you might rely on email or conventional post (or ring home and leave a number where you can be called back).

International and domestic long distance calls from hotels are expensive. A cheaper alternative is to call from the post office. Operator assisted calls will incur a three minute minimum charge – even if you only talk for one minute – at an inflated rate. The cheapest way to make a long distance call is to dial direct.

The cheapest and simplest way to make an International Direct Dial (IDD) call is with a telephone card, known as a 'UniphoneKad', available from post offices and bookstores. UniphoneKads can only be used in special telephones found on street corners. The cards are issued in four denominations; 30,000d (US$2.30), 60,000d (US$4.60), 150,000d (US$11.50) and 300,000d (US$23). The 150,000d and 300,000d cards can be used to make both domestic and international calls, while the 30,000d and 60,000d cards work for domestic calls only.

Foreigners are not permitted to make international reverse-charge (collect) calls. So if your credit cards or travellers cheques are stolen, you cannot make a collect call to report the loss to the issuing company!

There is a 15% discount for calls placed between 11 pm and 7 am and on Sunday and public holidays.

Domestic Calls Except for some special numbers (eg fire brigade and directory assistance), all phone numbers in Hanoi have seven digits (in addition to the 04 area code if you are calling from outside the city).

Local calls can usually be made from any hotel or restaurant phone and are often free – perhaps with the exception of calling a mobile phone (mobile telephone numbers begin with 090 and are followed by six more digits).

Domestic long distance calls are reasonably priced and are cheaper if you dial direct. Calls between Hanoi and Saigon at the full daytime rate will cost US$0.45 per minute. An operator-assisted call is US$0.82 per minute and there is a three minute minimum charge. You can save up to 20% by calling between 10 pm and 5 am.

Cellular Phones Vietnam is pouring a lot of money into the cellular network and more and more Hanoians are depending on the portability and convenience of mobile phones. Foreigners too can buy or rent them.

Companies offering sales, rental and service in Hanoi are Vina-Phone (Map 3; ☎ 843 9889), 51-53 Pho Nguyen Thai Hoc, and VMS Mobi-Fone (Map 2; ☎ 864 9660), 8/11A Đ Giai Phong.

Fax, Email & Internet Access
Most of Hanoi's post offices and tourist hotels offer domestic and international fax, as well as telegraph and telex services. Hotels generally charge more than the post office.

Access to online services is available through cybercafés and a growing number of hotels. Most long term visitors sign up with one of Hanoi's three Internet service providers.

If you have an established email account with a non-Vietnamese service provider, access from Vietnam will require you to download your mail through a Web-based service such as Hotmail. Unfortunately, other popular international email service providers such as CompuServe, America Online and Asia Online do *not* have local nodes in Vietnam.

There are a rapidly expanding number of Internet cafés in Hanoi, the best equipped of which is the Emotion Cybernet Café (Map 5;

☎ 934-1066, emotion@fpt.vn) at 52 Pho Ly Thuong Kiet (rear entrance at 60 Pho Tho Nhuom). The 'cyber' part of the café is on the second floor, and is open daily from 7.30 am to 11 pm.

There are also several backpacker café/travel agents (mainly in the Old Quarter) offering Internet service. These include the A to Z Queen Café (Map 5; ☎ 826 0860, queenaz@fpt.vn), 65 Pho Hang Bac; TF Handspan (Map 5; ☎ 828 1996, tfhandspn @hn.vnn.vn), 116 Pho Hang Bac; and the Love Planet Café (Map 5; ☎ 828 4864, loveplanet@hn.vnn.vn), 25 Pho Hang Bac.

Two more popular places for emailing include Old Street Tony's Café (Map 5; 118 Pho Hang Bac) – also a great place to drink *real* Vietnamese coffee – and Kim Café – no relation to the one in Saigon – (Map 5; ☎ 826 6901, 135 Pho Hang Bac).

Most places charge about US$0.05 per minute for Internet access, but you can pay as much as US$0.25. Printing usually costs between US$0.08 and US$0.16 per page.

INTERNET RESOURCES

The World Wide Web is a rich resource for travellers. You can research your trip, hunt down bargain air fares, book hotels, check on weather conditions or chat with locals and other travellers about the best places to visit (or avoid!).

There's no better place to start your Web explorations than the comprehensive Lonely Planet site www.lonelyplanet.com /dest/sea/vietnam.htm.

One of the best all-round sites on contemporary Vietnam is Destination Vietnam (www.destinationvietnam.com), a one-stop Vietnam information zone covering travel, art, history and culture.

Vietnam Adventures Online (www .vietnamadventures.com) is full of practical travel information and special travel deals.

Vietnam Online (www.vietnamonline .com) is loaded with useful travel lore and coverage of employment and business opportunities in Vietnam.

Images of Hanoi (travel.to/hanoi) has plenty of historical and cultural information, plus interesting links.

BOOKS

An increasing variety of English and French books are now available in Hanoi. For a listing of bookshops, see the Bookshops section of the Shopping chapter.

Lonely Planet

Our *Vietnamese Phrasebook* is not only educational and practical, but will also give you something to do on a rainy day. If you're going further afield, Lonely Planet's *Vietnam* covers the entire country inside out, while *South-East Asia on a shoestring* has a chapter on Vietnam. You may also want to score a copy of the *Vietnam travel atlas*. And if you'd like the latest details on Saigon, there is the *Ho Chi Minh City guide*.

Guidebooks

There are a handful of locally published books on Hanoi worth a look. For a detailed treatment of Hanoi's long history and cultural attractions, Nguyen Vinh Phuc's *Hanoi: Past & Present* is an excellent reference.

Published in hard cover coffee-table book format, *Sketches for a Portrait of Hanoi* by Huu Ngoc paints a vivid picture of the city through text and colour photographs.

Hanoi: Practical Guide Book by Pham Hoang Hai gives a basic overview of tourist facilities in the city, but was published in 1996 and some of the information is out of date.

Travel

A Dragon Apparent is about author Norman Lewis' fascinating journeys through Vietnam, Laos and Cambodia in 1950. This classic travelogue is now available as a reprint from Eland in London and Hippocrene in New York.

Sparring with Charlie: Motorbiking down the Ho Chi Minh Trail by Christopher Hunt is a light-hearted travelogue about modern Vietnam.

The impressive *Ten Years After* by Tim Page boasts '12 months worth of photos taken 10 years after the war'. Page also returned to Vietnam to write *Derailed in Uncle Ho's Victory Garden.*

Karin Muller's *Hitchhiking in Vietnam* (1998) is a travelogue detailing this intrepid young woman's tumultuous seven month journey through Vietnam. Also see her website at www.pbs.org/hitchhikingvietnam.

History & Politics

Vietnam: Politics, Economics and Society by Melanie Beresford (1988) gives a good overview of post-reunification Vietnam. *The Vietnamese Gulag* by Doan Van Toai tells of one man's experiences in the post-reunification re-education camps. *The Birth of Vietnam* by Keith Weller Taylor tackles the country's early history.

For a very readable account of Vietnamese history from prehistoric times until the fall of Saigon, try Stanley Karnow's *Vietnam: A History*, published as a companion volume to the American Public Broadcasting System series *Vietnam: A Television History.*

A number of biographies of Ho Chi Minh have been written, including *Ho Chi Minh: A Political Biography* by Jean Lacouture and *Ho* by David Halberstam.

An excellent reference work is *Vietnam's Famous Ancient Pagodas (Viet Nam Danh Lam Co Tu)*, written in Vietnamese, English, French and Chinese. The publisher is the Social Sciences Publishing House and you should be able to find copies in Hanoi.

Franco-Viet Minh War

Worthwhile books covering this topic include Peter M Dunn's *The First Vietnam War* and two works by Bernard B Fall: *Street Without Joy: Indochina at War 1946-54* (1961) and *Hell in a Very Small Place: The Siege of Dien Bien Phu* (1967).

Graham Greene's 1954 novel *The Quiet American*, set during the last days of French rule, is probably the most famous western work of fiction on Vietnam.

American War

The earliest days of US involvement in Indochina – when the US Office of Strategic Services (OSS; predecessor of the CIA) was providing funding and weapons to Ho Chi Minh at the end of WWII – are recounted in *Why Vietnam?*, a riveting work by Archimedes L Patti. Patti was the head of the OSS team in Vietnam and was at Ho Chi Minh's side when he declared Vietnam independent in 1945.

Three of the finest essays on the war are collected in *The Real War* by Jonathan Schell. An overview of the conflict is provided by George C Herring's *America's Longest War.*

An excellent autobiographical account of the war by a Vietnamese woman is Le Ly Hayslip's *When Heaven and Earth Changed Places.*

A highly acclaimed biographical account of the US war effort is *A Bright Shining Lie* by Neil Sheehan. It won both the Pulitzer Prize and the National Book Award, and was also made into a major motion picture under the same name.

Another fine biography is Tim Bowden's *One Crowded Hour* which details the life of Australian film journalist Neil Davis.

Some of the horror of what American POWs endured comes through in *Chained Eagle* by Everett Alvarez Jr, a US pilot who was imprisoned in North Vietnam for 8½ years.

Viet Cong Memoir by Truong Nhu Tang is the autobiography of a Viet Cong cadre who later became disenchanted with post-1975 Vietnam.

One of the finest books about the war written by a Vietnamese is *The Sorrow of War* by Bao Ninh. English-language photocopies are available from bookstalls and street vendors in Hanoi.

CD-ROMS

The classic choice here is 'Passage to Vietnam', a collection of beautiful photos and narrative. This CD was produced by Rick Smolan, who created the famed *Day in the Life* series.

NEWSPAPERS & MAGAZINES

The *Vietnam News* is an English-language newspaper published daily, if you're desperate for some news of the outside world.

One of Vietnam's best magazines is the monthly *Vietnam Economic Times* (VET). Its free insert, *The Guide*, is an excellent source of leisure information. The supplement can be picked up in most hotels, and some bars and restaurants.

The weekly *Vietnam Investment Review* is a broadsheet economic newspaper. VIR's free supplement, *Time Out*, is also useful for finding what's going on in town.

Imported newspapers and magazines are available in most large bookshops and hotels.

RADIO & TV

The Voice of Vietnam broadcasts on short wave, AM and FM for about 18 hours a day. The broadcasts consist mostly of music, but there are also news bulletins in Vietnamese, English, French and Russian.

Visitors wishing to keep up on events in the rest of the world – and in Vietnam itself – may want to bring along a small short-wave receiver.

Vietnamese TV

Vietnamese TV began broadcasting in 1970 and it's fair to say that the content has improved little since then. There are currently three channels in Hanoi and Saigon, and two channels elsewhere. Broadcast hours from Monday to Saturday are 9 to 11.30 am and 7 to 11 pm. On Sunday there is an extra broadcast from 3 to 4 pm. English-language news follows the last broadcast sometime after 10 pm. Sometimes soccer or other sports come on at strange hours like 1.30 am.

Satellite TV

Satellite TV, now widely available, is a boon for foreign visitors. You're most likely to find it in the better hotels and some pubs. Hong Kong's Star TV is the most popular station, along with CNN, the Sports Channel, Asia Business News (ABN) and Channel V (an MTV station).

VIDEO SYSTEMS

It's hard to know what Vietnam's official video standard is. That's because most new TVs and video players sold in Vietnam are multistandard: PAL, NTSC and SECAM.

PHOTOGRAPHY & VIDEO
Film & Equipment

Colour print film is widely available, but look for shops which get traffic, and always check the expiration date printed on the box. Avoid buying film from outdoor souvenir stalls – the film may have been cooking in the sun for the past three months. Negative film prices are perfectly reasonable and you won't save much by bringing film from abroad.

Colour slide film and black and white film is mostly found in speciality shops. If you really need the stuff then you'd best bring a supply from abroad.

Photo processing shops have become ubiquitous in places where tourists congregate. Most of these shops are equipped with the latest one hour, colour printing equipment. Printing costs are about US$5 per roll depending on print size. The quality tends to be quite good. One such place is Super Photo Noritsu (Map 4; ☎ 822 6147) at 154 Pho Ba Trieu. Be sure to specify if you want glossy or matte finish prints.

Colour slide film can be developed quickly (three hours) and costs about US$5 per roll, but most shops do not mount the slides unless you request (and pay for) it.

Plastic laminating is cheap. Just look for signs saying 'Ep Plastic'.

Cameras are fairly expensive in Vietnam and the selection is limited – bring one from abroad. Happily, lithium batteries (needed by many of today's point-and-shoot cameras) are widely available.

Restrictions

The Vietnamese police usually don't care what you photograph, but on occasion they get pernickety. Obviously, don't photograph something militarily sensitive (airports, military bases, border checkpoints etc).

Don't even think of trying to get a snapshot of Ho Chi Minh in his glass sarcophagus!

Some touristy sites charge a camera fee of about US$0.50, or a video fee of US$2 to US$5.

Photographing People

Photographing people demands the utmost respect for local customs. The beauty and colour of the Vietnamese people and their surrounding scenery provides ample opportunity, but it is important to remember you are a guest in Vietnam and that your actions might be interpreted as rude or offensive.

Airport Security

The dreaded old x-ray machines at the airports are no longer a problem – they have been replaced with modern, film-safe equipment. But don't attempt to film the airport security procedures (the film will most likely be ripped out of your camera).

The authorities seem to be more sensitive about video tape material than film. Video tapes are deemed to be 'cultural materials' which may be screened in advance by 'experts' from the Department of Culture.

TIME

Hanoi, like the rest of the country, is seven hours ahead of Greenwich Mean Time/Universal Time Coordinated (GMT/UTC). Because it is so close to the equator, Vietnam does not observe daylight saving time. Thus, without allowing variations for daylight saving, when it's noon in Hanoi or Saigon it is 9 pm the previous day in Los Angeles, midnight in New York, 5 am in London and 3 pm in Sydney.

ELECTRICITY
Voltages & Cycles

Electric current in Hanoi is mostly 220V at 50Hz (cycles), but often you'll still find 110V (also at 50Hz).

Plugs & Sockets

In Hanoi, most outlets are the Russian-inspired round pins and also usually carry 220V. If the voltage is not marked on the socket try finding a light bulb or appliance with the voltage written on it. Sockets are two-prong only – you won't find a third wire for ground (earth).

WEIGHTS & MEASURES

The Vietnamese use the international metric system (see the back of this book for a metric conversion table). In addition, two weight measurements have been borrowed from the Chinese: the tael and the catty. A catty equals 0.6kg (1.32lb). There are 16 taels to the catty, so one tael equals 37.5g (1.32oz). Gold is always sold by the tael.

LAUNDRY

It is usually easy to find a hotel attendant who can get your laundry spotlessly clean for the equivalent of one or two US dollars. There have, however, been a number of reports of gross overcharging at some hotels, so check on the price beforehand. Larger hotels might display a price list.

Budget hotels do not have clothes dryers – they rely on the sunshine – so allow at least a day and a half for washing and drying, especially during the wet season.

BEAUTY SALONS

The Aussie-run QT Salon (Map 4; ☎ 826 3823) at 48 Pho Mai Hac De captures a large share of the expat hair and beauty market. Local beauticians are expertly trained and the salon maintains a high international standard. QT offers over 50 different beauty treatments (all legitimate), from haircutting, facials and massage to aromatherapy.

There are also respectable beauty salons in the Daewoo and Sofitel hotels.

TOILETS

Better hotels will have the more familiar western-style sit-down toilets, but squat toilets still exist in cheaper hotels and public places like restaurants, bus stations etc.

The scarcity of public toilets seems to be a greater problem for women than for men. Vietnamese males (and children) are often seen urinating in public, but this appears to be socially unacceptable for women.

Toilet paper is seldom provided in the toilets at bus and train stations or in other public buildings, though hotels usually supply it. You'd be wise to keep a stash of your own with you at all times.

LEFT LUGGAGE

You may find baggage storage at some train and bus stations, but in general these are not reliable. Hotels or budget cafés are a better bet, though it never hurts to padlock your bag.

HEALTH
Immunisations

There are no compulsory vaccinations for travel to Hanoi, unless you will be coming from an area infected with yellow fever (most of subSaharan Africa and parts of South America). However it's a good idea to ensure routine vaccinations against diphtheria, tetanus and polio are up to date. Discuss your requirements with your doctor but other vaccinations you might consider before coming to Hanoi are hepatitis A, which is a common food and water- borne disease, typhoid, rabies and hepatitis B, which is transmitted through sexual activity and blood products. Vaccinations for a longer term stay could include tuberculosis and Japanese B encephalitis. While there is no risk of malaria in Hanoi, if you plan to travel outside the city make sure you are protected. Discuss your requirements with your doctor at least six weeks before travel.

Further Information

If you are looking for more detailed information, *Staying Healthy in Asia, Africa & Latin America* by Dirk Schroeder, Moon Publications, or *Travellers' Health* by Dr Richard Dawood, Oxford University Press, are both good all-round guides. There are also a number of excellent travel health sites on the Internet. From the Lonely Planet site at www.lonelyplanet.com /weblinks/wlprep.htm#heal there are useful links to health organisations.

Medical Kit Check List

Consider travelling with a basic medical kit including:

- ☐ **Aspirin** or **paracetamol** (acetaminophen in the USA) – for pain or fever.
- ☐ **Antihistamine** (such as Benadryl) – a decongestant for colds and allergies, eases the itch from insect bites or stings and helps prevent motion sickness. They may cause sedation and interact with alcohol, so care should be taken when using them; take one you know and have used before, if possible.
- ☐ **Antibiotics** – useful if you're travelling well off the beaten track, but they must be prescribed; carry the prescription with you.
- ☐ **Lomotil** or **Imodium** – to treat diarrhoea; prochlorperazine (eg Stemetil) or metaclopramide (eg Maxalon) is good for nausea and vomiting.
- ☐ **Rehydration mixture** – to treat severe diarrhoea; particularly important when travelling with children.
- ☐ **Antiseptic**, such as povidone-iodine (eg Betadine) – for minor cuts and grazes.
- ☐ **Multivitamins** – especially useful for long trips when dietary vitamin intake may be inadequate.
- ☐ **Calamine lotion** or **aluminium sulphate spray** (eg Stingose) – to ease irritation from bites or stings.
- ☐ **Bandages** and **Band-aids**.
- ☐ **Scissors, tweezers** and a **thermometer** – (note that mercury thermometers are prohibited by airlines).
- ☐ **Cold and flu tablets** and **throat lozenges** – Pseudoephedrine hydrochloride (Sudafed) may be useful if you're flying with a cold to avoid ear damage.
- ☐ **Insect repellent, sunscreen, Chapstick** and **water purification tablets**.
- ☐ **A couple of syringes** – in case you need injections in a country with medical hygiene problems. Ask your doctor for a note explaining why they have been prescribed.

Other Preparations

Make sure you're healthy before you start travelling and a trip to the dentist to make sure your teeth are OK is not a bad idea. If you wear glasses take a spare pair and your prescription.

If you require a particular medication take an adequate supply, as it may not be available locally. Take part of the packaging showing the generic name rather than the brand, which will make getting replacements easier. It's a good idea to have a legible prescription or letter from your doctor to show that you legally use the medication, to avoid any problems.

Basic Rules

Many health problems can be avoided by taking care of yourself. Wash your hands frequently – it's quite easy to contaminate your own food. Clean your teeth with purified water rather than straight from the tap. Avoid climatic extremes: keep out of the sun when it's hot, dress warmly when it's cold. Avoid potential diseases by dressing sensibly – you can get worm infections through walking barefoot. Avoid insect bites by covering bare skin when insects are around, by screening windows or beds or by using insect repellents. Seek local advice on specific health risks; and in situations where there is no information, it's better to be safe than sorry.

Food & Drink

Vegetables and fruit should be washed with purified water or peeled where possible. Beware of ice cream which is sold in the street or anywhere it might have been melted and refrozen; if there's any doubt (eg a power cut in the last day or two), steer well clear. Shellfish such as mussels, oysters and clams should be avoided as well as undercooked meat, particularly in the form of mince. Steaming does not make shellfish safe for eating.

If a place looks clean and well run and the vendor also looks clean and healthy, then the food is probably safe. In general, places that are packed with travellers or locals will be fine, while empty restaurants are questionable. The food in busy restaurants is cooked and eaten quite quickly with little standing around or reheating. You may want to consider carrying your own set of chopsticks (very cheap to buy in Hanoi) with you; at least this way you know exactly how clean they are.

The number one rule is *be careful of the water* and especially ice. Although tap water in Hanoi is chlorinated, it is still recommended you only drink boiled or bottled water. Reputable brands of bottled water or soft drinks are generally fine. Only use water from containers with a serrated seal – not tops or corks. Take care with fruit juice, particularly if water may have been added. Milk should be treated with suspicion as it is often unpasteurised, though boiled milk is fine if it is kept hygienically. Tea or coffee should also be OK, since the water should have been boiled.

Environmental Hazards

Cuts & Scratches Wash well and treat any cut with an antiseptic such as povidone-iodine. Where possible avoid bandages and Band-Aids, which can keep wounds wet.

Heat Exhaustion Dehydration and salt deficiency can cause heat exhaustion. If you arrive in Hanoi during the summer (May until October) take time to acclimatise to high temperatures, drink sufficient liquids and do not do anything too physically demanding.

Salt deficiency is characterised by fatigue, lethargy, headaches, giddiness and muscle cramps; salt tablets may help, but adding extra salt to your food is better.

Prickly Heat Prickly heat is an itchy rash caused by excessive perspiration trapped under the skin. It usually strikes people who have just arrived in a hot climate. Keeping cool, bathing often, drying the skin and using a mild talcum or prickly heat powder, or resorting to air-conditioning may help.

Warm, moist conditions also encourage fungal skin infections. To prevent them wear loose clothes, avoid artificial fibres, wash frequently and dry yourself carefully. If you do get an infection, an antifungal cream or powder may help. Try to expose the infected area to air or sunlight as much as possible.

Sunburn You can get sunburnt surprisingly quickly, even through cloud. Use a sunscreen, a hat, and a barrier cream for your nose and lips. Calamine lotion or a commercial after-sun preparation are good for mild sunburn. Protect your eyes with good quality sunglasses.

Medical Problems & Treatment

Diarrhoea Simple things like a change of water, food or climate can all cause a mild bout of diarrhoea, but a few rushed toilet trips with no other symptoms is not indicative of a major problem.

Dehydration is the main danger with any diarrhoea, particularly in children or the elderly, and can occur quite quickly. Under all circumstances *fluid replacement* (at least equal to the volume being lost) is the most important thing to remember. Weak black tea with a little sugar, soda water, or soft drinks allowed to go flat and diluted 50% with clean water are all good. With severe diarrhoea a rehydrating solution is preferable to replace minerals and salts lost. Commercially available oral rehydration salts (ORS) are very useful; add them to boiled or bottled water. In an emergency you can make up a solution of six teaspoons of sugar and a half-teaspoon of salt to a litre of boiled or bottled water. You need to drink at least the same volume of fluid that you are losing in bowel movements and vomiting. Urine is the best guide to the adequacy of replacement – if you have small amounts of concentrated urine, you need to drink more. Keep drinking small amounts often. Stick to a bland diet as you recover.

Gut-paralysing drugs such as loperamide or diphenoxylate can be used to bring relief from symptoms, although they do not actually cure the problem. Only use them if you do not have access to toilets, eg if you *must* travel. Note that these drugs are not recommended for children under 12 years.

In certain situations antibiotics may be required: diarrhoea with blood or mucus (dysentery), any diarrhoea with fever, profuse watery diarrhoea, persistent diarrhoea not improving after 48 hours and severe diarrhoea. These suggest a more serious cause of diarrhoea and in these situations gut-paralysing drugs should be avoided. In these situations, a stool test may be necessary to diagnose what bug is causing your diarrhoea, so you should seek medical help urgently.

Hepatitis Hepatitis is a general term for inflammation of the liver. It is a common disease worldwide. There are several different viruses that cause hepatitis, and they differ in the way that they are transmitted. The symptoms are similar in all forms of the illness, and include fever, chills, headache, fatigue, feelings of weakness and aches and pains, followed by loss of appetite, nausea, vomiting, abdominal pain, dark urine, light-coloured faeces, jaundiced (yellow) skin and yellowing of the whites of the eyes. People who have had hepatitis should avoid alcohol for some time after the illness, as the liver needs time to recover.

Hepatitis A is transmitted by contaminated food and drinking water. You should seek medical advice, but there is not much you can do apart from resting, drinking lots of fluids, eating lightly and avoiding fatty foods. Hepatitis E is transmitted in the same way as hepatitis A; it can be particularly serious in pregnant women.

There are almost 300 million chronic carriers of **hepatitis B** in the world. It is spread through contact with infected blood, blood products or body fluids; for example, through sexual contact, unsterilised needles and blood transfusions, or contact with blood via small breaks in the skin. Other risk situations include having a shave, tattoo or body piercing with contaminated equipment. The symptoms of hepatitis B may be more severe than type A and the disease can lead to long term problems such as chronic liver damage, liver cancer or a long term carrier state. Hepatitis C and D are spread in the same way as hepatitis B and can also lead to long term complications.

There are vaccines against hepatitis A and B, but there are currently no vaccines against the other types of hepatitis. Following the basic rules about food and water (hepatitis A and E) and avoiding risk situations (hepatitis B, C and D) are important preventative measures.

HIV/AIDS & Sexually-Transmitted Diseases Infection with the human immunodeficiency virus (HIV) may lead to acquired immune deficiency syndrome (AIDS), which is a fatal disease. Any exposure to blood, blood products or body fluids may put the individual at risk. The disease is often transmitted through sexual contact or dirty needles – vaccinations, acupuncture, tattooing and body piercing can be potentially as dangerous as intravenous drug use. HIV/AIDS can also be spread through infected blood transfusions; some developing countries cannot afford to screen blood used for transfusions. Hepatitis B is transmitted the same way as HIV/AIDS; for more details, see the previous paragraph.

If you do need an injection, ask to see the syringe unwrapped in front of you, or take a needle and syringe pack with you.

While abstinence from sexual contact is the only 100% effective prevention, using condoms is also effective against contracting sexually transmitted diseases including gonorrhoea, herpes and syphilis. Condoms are widely available in Hanoi.

Dengue Fever This viral disease is transmitted by mosquitoes and is fast becoming one of the top public health problems in the tropical world, including Vietnam. Unlike the malaria mosquito, the *Aedes aegypti* mosquito, which transmits the dengue virus, is most active during the day, and is found mainly in urban areas, in and around human dwellings.

Signs and symptoms of dengue fever include a sudden onset of high fever, headache, joint and muscle pains (hence its old name 'breakbone fever') and nausea and vomiting. A rash of small red spots sometimes appears three to four days after the onset of fever. In the early phase of illness, dengue may be mistaken for other infectious diseases, including malaria and influenza. Minor bleeding such as nose bleeds may occur in the course of the illness, but this does not necessarily mean that you have progressed to the potentially fatal dengue haemorrhagic fever (DHF). This is a severe illness, characterised by heavy bleeding, thought to be a result of second infection due to a different strain (there are four major strains) and usually affects residents of the country rather than travellers. Aspirin should be avoided, as it increases the risk of haemorrhaging. Recovery even from simple dengue fever may be prolonged, with tiredness lasting for several weeks.

You should seek medical attention as son as possible if you think you may be infected. A blood test can exclude malaria and indicate the possibility of dengue fever. There is no specific treatment for, or vaccine against, dengue fever. The best prevention is to avoid mosquito bites at all times by covering up, using insect repellents containing the compound DEET and mosquito nets.

Other Diseases

Although these don't pose a big risk for most travellers, be aware that cholera and typhoid (both spread via contaminated food and water) occur in Vietnam. Other food risks include liver and intestinal flukes that you can pick up from eating raw or undercooked fish or from swimming in the Mekong Delta, and various worms, including roundworm and hookworm. These worms generally don't cause any symptoms, but consider having a test when you get home if you think you may be at risk or if you have spent a long time away.

Japanese encephalitis, a viral infection of the brain, is transmitted via mosquitoes and may be a health risk if you are travelling in rural areas; cover up and use insect repellent.

Other risks include bed bugs, lice, leeches and snake bites.

Women's Health

Gynaecological Problems Antibiotic use, synthetic underwear, sweating and contraceptive pills can lead to fungal vaginal infections, especially when travelling in hot climates. Fungal infections are characterised by a rash, itch and discharge and can be treated with a vinegar or lemon-juice douche, or with yoghurt. Nystatin, miconazole or clotrimazole pessaries or vaginal cream are the usual treatment. Maintaining good personal hygiene and wearing loose-fitting clothes and cotton underwear may help prevent these infections.

Sexually transmitted diseases are a major cause of vaginal problems. Symptoms include a smelly discharge, painful intercourse and sometimes a burning sensation when urinating. Medical attention should be sought and male sexual partners must also be treated. Besides abstinence, the best thing is to practise safe sex using condoms.

Pregnancy Most miscarriages occur during the first three months of pregnancy. Miscarriage is not uncommon and can occasionally lead to severe bleeding. The last three months should also be spent within reasonable distance of good medical care. A baby born as early as 24 weeks stands a chance of survival, but only in a good modern hospital. Pregnant women should avoid all unnecessary medication, although vaccinations and malarial prophylactics should still be taken where needed. Additional care should be taken to prevent illness and particular attention should be paid to diet and nutrition. Alcohol and nicotine, for example, should be avoided.

Medical Services

The Hanoi Family Medical Practice (Map 2; ☎ 843 0748, fax 846 1750, mobile ☎ 090-401919, A1, Van Phuc Diplomatic Quarter, 109-112 Pho Kim Ma) is headed by Hanoi's most respected foreign private physician, Dr Rafi Kot. This clinic comes highly recommended by travellers and expats alike, and provides 24 hour emergency service and evacuations.

Affiliated with the above, in Building A2 of the same complex, is The Dental Clinic (Map 2; ☎ 846 2864, ☎/fax 823 0281, mobile ☎ 090-401919), also recommended and staffed by foreign dentists.

Asia Emergency Assistance (AEA International, ☎ 934 0555, fax 934 0556) has a clinic at 31 Pho Hai Ba Trung. Resident foreigners can contact AEA for information about a long term medical and emergency evacuation plan. A similar plan is offered by International SOS Assistance (☎ 824 2866).

The Vietnam International Hospital (Map 4; ☎ 574 0740) is staffed by international, multilingual doctors and offers 24 hour emergency service (☎ 547 1111). This hospital also has dentists on staff.

Traditional Medicine

Hanoi has a long history of traditional medicine and doctors who can treat patients with a variety of natural remedies.

Dr Le Anh Tuan, a young doctor fluent in English and French, has combined knowledge of traditional and modern medicine and specialises in acupuncture and acupressure. He can treat functional diseases including body pain, and psychological disorders caused by stress and overwork. Some have even called on him for anti-ageing treatment and smoking cessation assistance. Dr Tuan provides home services only, and can come to your hotel. Sessions last from 45 minutes to one hour, and cost between US$15 and US$20 (inclusive of disposable needles). He is best reached on ☎ 090-443529, or tuanlehanoi@hotmail.com.

Other places to consider include:

National Institute of Traditional Medicine
(Vien Y Hoc Co Truyen Viet Nam, ☎ 826 4462) Map 4; 29 Pho Nguyen Binh Khiem. Specialises in massage, exercise, acupuncture and herbal remedies.

Hanoi Traditional Medicine Hospital
(Benh Vien Y Hoc Co Truyen Ha Noi, ☎ 828 3253) Map 3; 34 Pho Hoe Nhai. An inexpensive option (acupuncture costs just US$0.25 a session), though very few foreigners take advantage of this.

Institute of Acupuncture
  (Vien Cham Cuu, ☎ 853 4253) Map 3; Vinh Ho
  Condominium. Focuses on acupuncture and
  acupressure treatment.

WOMEN TRAVELLERS

Like Thailand and other predominantly Buddhist countries, Vietnam is in general relatively free of serious hassles for female western travellers.

It's a different story for some Asian women, particularly one who is young and accompanied by a western male – she may automatically be labelled a 'Vietnamese whore'. The fact that the couple could be married (or just friends) doesn't seem to occur to anyone, nor does it seem to register that the woman might not be Vietnamese at all. If she's Asian then she's Vietnamese, and if she's with a western male then she must be a prostitute. It may be difficult to convince many Vietnamese otherwise.

The problem is basically that Vietnamese men believe western men are out to steal their women. Asian women travelling in Vietnam with a western male companion have reported frequent verbal abuse.

For racially mixed couples in Vietnam, no easy solution exists. There's no need to be overly paranoid, but a few precautions and words of advice are helpful: if you do face a confrontation, don't lose your top; maintain your cool and walk away. Dressing 'like a foreigner' make help – sewing patches on your clothing with Japanese or Chinese characters can work wonders. One traveller got good results by sewing a Korean flag onto her backpack.

Attitudes Towards Women

As in most parts of Asia, Vietnamese women are given plenty of hard work to do, but have little authority at the decision-making level. Vietnamese women proved to be highly successful as guerrillas and brought plenty of grief to US soldiers. After the war, their contribution received plenty of lip service, but all the important government posts were given to men. In the countryside, you'll see women doing such jobs as farm labour, crushing rocks at construction sites and carrying baskets weighing 60kg. It's doubtful that most western men are capable of such strenuous activity.

Vietnam's two children per family policy appears to be benefiting women, and more women are delaying marriage to get an education. About 50% of students are female, but their skills don't seem to be put to much use after graduation.

Organisations

Consider contacting the International Relations Department of the Vietnam Women's Union (☎ 971 7225), 39 Pho Hang Chuoi.

GAY & LESBIAN TRAVELLERS

On the whole Vietnam is a relatively hassle-free place for homosexuals. There are no official laws on same-sex relationships in Vietnam, nor much in the way of official harassment.

Common local attitudes suggest a general social prohibition, though the lack of any laws makes things fairly safe (even if the authorities do break up a party on occasion). Major headlines were made in 1997 with Vietnam's first gay male marriage, and again in 1998 at the country's first lesbian wedding, in the Mekong Delta.

With the vast number of same-sex travel partners, gay or not, it is fair to say there is little scrutiny over how travelling foreigners are related. However it would be prudent not to flaunt your sexuality. Likewise with heterosexual couples, passionate public displays of affection are considered a basic no-no.

Perhaps the best way to tap into what's what is on the Net. Check out Utopia at www.utopia-asia.com. The site is chock-full of information and contacts, including detailed sections on the legality of homosexuality in Vietnam and some local gay terminology.

Douglas Thompson's *The Men of Vietnam* is a comprehensive gay travel guide to Vietnam. The book can be ordered at the abovementioned Internet site.

DISABLED TRAVELLERS

Hanoi is not a particularly good city for disabled travellers, despite the fact that many Vietnamese are disabled with war injuries. Tactical problems include the crazy traffic, a lack of pedestrian footpaths, a lack of lifts (elevators) in buildings and the ubiquitous squat toilets.

SENIOR TRAVELLERS

There is a deep and definite sense of respect for the elderly in Vietnam, though seniors are likely to encounter problems similar to those that affect disabled people. And, as in other Asian countries, it is not uncommon to be elbowed out of line at a post office by a 1m-tall, 97-year-old woman.

There are no discounts as such for pensioners, nor international cards which are officially recognised, but it may be worth flashing your card and seeing what you can get.

HANOI FOR CHILDREN

Hanoi is an excellent city for kids, and there are a good number of attractions to keep them busy. Water puppet performances, the circus and city zoo are Hanoi's top three drawcards for people travelling with kids. Other popular places include city parks, and the Air Force Museum. Of course, a cyclo ride alone should keep most kids enthralled for a while, not to mention some of the best ice cream shops in South-East Asia!

Nature lovers with children may choose to hike in one of the national parks or nature reserves near Hanoi. Cuc Phuong National Park (see the Excursions chapter), in particular, has the interesting Endangered Primate Rescue Centre.

Schools

Popular choices for expats considering schools in Hanoi include:

Amsterdam School
 (☎ 832 7379, fax 832 7535)
 Map 2; Pho Giang Vo
Hanoi International School
 (☎ 832 9828) Map 2; 301 Pho Lieu Giai

Rainbow Montessori School
 (☎ 826 6194)
 Map 5; 18B Pho Ngo Van So
United Nations School
 (☎ 823 4910, fax 846 3635)
 Map 2; 2C Pho Van Phuc

TRAVEL WITH CHILDREN

In general, foreign children have a good time in Vietnam mainly because of the overwhelming amount of attention they attract and the fact that almost everybody wants to play with them!

Babies and unborn children can present their own peculiar problems when travelling. Lonely Planet's *Travel with Children* by Maureen Wheeler gives a rundown on health precautions to be taken with kids and advice on travel during pregnancy.

USEFUL ORGANISATIONS
Multilateral Organisations

The following is a list of foreign-aid and United Nations (UN) organisations with offices in Hanoi:

Asian Development Bank
 (☎ 733 0923, fax 733 0925)
 15 Pho Dang Dung
Food & Agricultural Organisation
 (☎ 825 7239, fax 825 9257)
 3 Pho Nguyen Gia Thieu
International Monetary Fund
 (☎ 825 1927, fax 825 1885)
 Room 308-9, 12 Pho Trang Thi
UNAIDS
 (☎ 846 0739, fax 846 0740)
 138 Pho Giang Vo
UN Drug Control Programme
 (☎ 825 7495, fax 825 9267)
 25-29 Pho Phan Boi Chau
UN Development Programme
 (☎ 825 7495, fax 825 9267)
 25-29 Pho Phan Boi Chau
UN High Commissioner for Refugees
 (☎ 845 7871, fax 823 2055)
 60 Pho Nguyen Thai Hoc
UNICEF (Children's Emergency Fund)
 (☎ 826 1170, fax 826 2641)
 72 Pho Ly Thuong Kiet
UN Industrial Development Organization
 (☎ 825 7495, fax 825 9267)
 25-29 Pho Phan Boi Chau

UN Population Fund
(☎ 845 4763, fax 823 2822)
B3 Giang Vo Quarter
World Bank Resident Mission
(☎ 843 2461, fax 843 2471)
53 Pho Tran Phu
World Conservation Union
(☎ 826 5172, fax 825 8794)
13 Pho Tran Hung Dao, IPO Box 60
World Food Programme
(☎ 846 3896, fax 823 2072)
2B Van Phuc Quarter, IPO Box 25
World Health Organization
(☎ 825 7901, fax 823 3301)
2A Van Phuc Quarter, IPO Box 52

LIBRARIES
Hanoi's three largest libraries are:

Hanoi Library
(☎ 825 4817) Map 5; 47 Pho Ba Trieu
National Library and Archives
(☎ 825 3357) Map 5; 31 Pho Trang Thi
Science Library
(☎ 825 2345) Map 5; 26 Pho Ly Thuong Kiet

UNIVERSITIES
Hanoi is the country's centre of education and home to large student population. There are currently more than 30 universities and colleges in the city, the largest being:

Foreign Languages College
(☎ 854 4338) Map 2; Km 9, Pho Nguyen Trai
Hanoi National University
(☎ 824 5365) 19 Pho Le Thanh Tong
Polytechnic University
(☎ 869 2743) Map 4; Pho Dai Co Viet

CULTURAL CENTRES
France's Alliance Française de Hanoi (Map 5; ☎ 826 6970, fax 826 6977) is located near the Hanoi train station at 42 Pho Yet Kieu. It is open from 8 am to noon, and 1 to 5 pm.

Germany's Goethe Institute (☎ 923 0035, fax 923 0038) is in the Old Quarter at 64/66 Pho Hang Duong. Opening hours are from 8 am to noon, and 1.30 to 5 pm.

DANGERS & ANNOYANCES
Culture Shock
The dangerous thing in Vietnam is your own psyche and its ability to cope with the shock of the sights, sounds and smells of this country, for which you can never be fully prepared. Of course, things can go wrong, and there are some things you should definitely be concerned about. But worrying about all the 'problems' you may encounter can do more to ruin your trip than the problems themselves. Just take necessary precautions to guard yourself against the ever-present minority of schemers and thieves so you can get back to connecting with the other 99.9% of the population who are genuinely honest and delightful.

Theft
To avoid theft, probably the best advice is to not bring anything valuable that you don't need. Expensive watches, jewellery and electronic gadgets invite theft – do you really need these things while travelling?

We have also had reports of people being drugged and robbed on long distance public buses. It usually starts with a friendly fellow passenger offering you a free Coke, which in reality turns out to be a chloral hydrate cocktail. You wake up hours later to find your valuables and new 'friend' gone.

Still, you should not be overly paranoid. Although crime certainly exists, don't assume that everyone's a thief – most Vietnamese are poor but reasonably honest.

Violence
Unlike in some western cities, recreational homicide is not a popular sport in Hanoi and the city is virtually free of terrorists with political agendas. Violence against foreigners is extremely rare.

Scams
Beware of a motorcycle rental scam which some travellers have encountered. What happens is that you rent a bike and the owner supplies you with an excellent lock. What he doesn't tell you is that he, too, has a key and that somebody will follow you and 'steal' the bike at the first opportunity. You then have to pay for a new bike or forfeit your passport, visa, deposit or whatever

security you left with him. And the person who rented the bike to you still has it!

More common is when your motorcycle won't start after you parked it in a 'safe' area with a guard. But yes, the guard knows somebody who can repair your bike. The mechanic shows up and goes about reinstalling the parts they removed earlier and now the bike works fine. That will be US$10 please.

Despite an array of scams, it is important to keep in mind the Vietnamese are not always out to get you. Con artists and thieves are, however, always seeking new tricks to separate naive tourists from their money and are becoming more savvy in their ways. We can't warn you about every trick you might encounter, so perhaps the best advice we can give is to maintain a healthy suspicion and be prepared to argue when unnecessary demands are made for your money.

Beggar Fatigue

Though far worse in Saigon and other parts of the country, Hanoi does have its fair share of beggars. If you feel like giving something, it's probably better to give food than money – little children are often forced to beg for money, sometimes with the cash going towards their parents' drinking and gambling habits rather than food or schooling for the children. Of course, that's if the kids have parents, which many of them don't.

So what can you do to help these street people, many of whom are malnourished and illiterate with no future? Good question – we wish we knew (see Useful Organisations earlier in this chapter for reputable aid organisations that accept donations). As for what to do when you are approached by beggars, give or refuse as you wish, but spare a moment to think of just how lucky you are.

I will always remember the beam of delight that came over the face of a hard-bitten child beggar when I offered him a cake similar to the one I was eating.

Gordon Balderston

Noise

One thing that can be insidiously draining on your energy during a trip to Vietnam is noise.

Fortunately, most noise subsides around 10 or 11 pm. Unfortunately, though, the Vietnamese are very early risers; most are up and about from around 5 am onwards and traffic noise starts early. It's worth trying to get a room at the back of a hotel, or wherever else the street noise looks likely to be diminished. Other than that, consider bringing a set of earplugs.

LEGAL MATTERS
Civil Law

The French gave the Vietnamese the Napoleonic Code, much of which has still to be repealed, although these laws may conflict with later statutes. Since reunification, Soviet-style laws have been applied to the whole country with devastating consequences for private property owners. The recent economic reforms have seen a flood of new property legislation, much of it the result of advice from the United Nations, International Monetary Fund and other international organisations. The rapid speed at which legislation is being enacted is a challenge for those who must interpret and enforce the law.

Today most legal disputes are settled out of court. In general, you can accomplish more with a carton of cigarettes and a bottle of good cognac than you can with a lawyer.

Drugs

You may well be approached with offers to buy marijuana and occasionally opium. Giving in to this temptation is risky at best. There are many plain-clothes police in Vietnam – just because you don't see them doesn't mean they aren't there. If arrested, you could be subjected to a long prison term and/or a large fine.

The illegal drug export market has also been doing well and Vietnam's reputation is such that customs officials at your next destination might be inclined to vigorously search your luggage. In short, drug use in Vietnam is still a very perilous activity and taking some samples home with you is even riskier.

Police

The problem of police corruption has been acknowledged in official newspapers. The same problems that plague many Third World police forces – very low pay and low levels of training – certainly exist in Hanoi. The government has attempted to crack down on abuses and has warned that any police caught shaking down foreign tourists will be fired.

The crackdown has dented the enthusiasm of the police to confront foreigners directly with demands for bribes. However, it has not eliminated the problem altogether.

BUSINESS HOURS

Vietnamese rise early (and consider sleeping in to be a sure indication of illness). Offices, museums and many shops open from 7 or 8 am and close at 4 or 5 pm. Lunch is taken very seriously and virtually everything shuts down between noon and 1.30 pm.

Most government offices are open on Saturday until noon, and closed all day on Sunday. Most museums are closed on

---

Lunar Calendar

The Vietnamese lunar calendar closely resembles the Chinese one. Year 1 of the Vietnamese lunar calendar corresponds to 2637 BC and each lunar month has 29 or 30 days, resulting in years with 355 days. Approximately every third year is a leap year; an extra month is added between the third and fourth months to keep the lunar year in sync with the solar year. If this weren't done, you'd end up having the seasons gradually rotate around the lunar year, playing havoc with all elements of life linked to the agricultural seasons. To find out the Gregorian (solar) date corresponding to a lunar date, check any Vietnamese or Chinese calendar.

Instead of dividing time into centuries, the Vietnamese calendar uses units of 60 years called *hoi*. Each hoi consists of six 10-year cycles *(can)* and five 12-year cycles *(ky)* which run simultaneously. The name of each year in the cycle consists of the can name followed by the ky name, a system which never produces the same combination twice.

The 10 heavenly stems of the can cycle		The 12 zodiacal stems of the ky cycle	
giap	water in nature	*tý*	rat
at	water in the home	*suu*	cow
binh	lighted fire	*dan*	tiger
dinh	latent fire	*mau*	rabbit
mau	wood	*thin*	dragon
ky	wood prepared to burn	*ty*	snake
canh	metal	*ngo*	horse
tan	wrought metal	*mui*	goat
nham	virgin land	*than*	monkey
quy	cultivated land	*dau*	rooster
		tuat	dog
		hoi	pig

Thus in 1999 the Vietnamese year is Ky Mau (rabbit), in 2000 it's Canh Thin (dragon) and in 2001 it's Tan Ty (snake).

Monday. Temples on the tourist circuit are usually open all day every day.

Many small privately owned shops, restaurants and street stalls stay open seven days a week, often until late at night.

PUBLIC HOLIDAYS & SPECIAL EVENTS

Politics affects everything, including public holidays. As an indication of Vietnam's new openness, Christmas, New Year's Day, Tet (Lunar New Year) and Buddha's Birthday were re-established as holidays after a 15 year lapse. The following are Vietnam's public holidays:

New Year's Day (Tet Duong Lich)
1 January
Anniversary of the Founding of the Vietnamese Communist Party (Thanh Lap Dang CSVN)
3 February – the Party was founded on this date in 1930.
Liberation Day (Saigon Giai Phong)
30 April – the date on which Saigon surrendered is commemorated nationwide on this day. Many cities and provinces also commemorate the anniversary of the date in March or April of 1975 on which they were 'liberated' by the North Vietnamese Army.
International Workers' Day (Quoc Te Lao Dong)
1 May – also known as May Day, this falls back-to-back with Liberation Day, giving everyone a two day holiday.
Ho Chi Minh's Birthday (Sinh Nhat Bac Ho)
19 May
Buddha's Birthday (Dan Sinh)
Eighth day of the fourth moon (usually June)
National Day (Quoc Khanh)
2 September – commemorates the proclamation of the Declaration of Independence of the Democratic Republic of Vietnam by Ho Chi Minh in 1945. It is celebrated at Ba Dinh Square (the expanse of grass in front of Ho Chi Minh's Mausoleum) with a rally and fireworks; boat races are held on Hoan Kiem Lake.
Christmas (Giang Sinh)
25 December

Special prayers are held at Vietnamese and Chinese pagodas when the moon is full or just the thinnest sliver. Many Buddhists eat only vegetarian food on these days, which, according to the Chinese lunar calendar, fall on the 14th and 15th days of the month and from the last (29th or 30th) day of the month to the first day of the next month.

The following major religious festivals include the lunar date (check against any Vietnamese calendar for the Gregorian dates):

Tet (Tet Nguyen Dan)
First to seventh days of the first moon – the Vietnamese Lunar New Year is the most important festival of the year and falls in late January or early February (see the boxed text 'The Tet Festival'). This public holiday is officially three days, but many people take an entire week off work and few businesses are open.
Holiday of the Dead (Thanh Minh)
Fifth day of the third moon – people pay solemn visits to graves of deceased relatives, specially tidied up a few days before, and make offerings of food, flowers, joss sticks and votive papers.
Buddha's Birth, Enlightenment and Death
Eighth day of the fourth moon – this day is celebrated at pagodas and temples which, like many private homes, are festooned with lanterns. Processions are held in the evening. This festival has been redesignated a public holiday.
Summer Solstice Day (Doan Ngu)
Fifth day of the fifth moon – offerings are made to spirits, ghosts and the God of Death to ward off epidemics. Human effigies are burned to satisfy the requirements of the God of Death for souls to staff his army.
Wandering Souls Day (Trung Nguyen)
Fifteenth day of the seventh moon – this is the second largest Vietnamese festival of the year. Offerings of food and gifts are made in homes and pagodas for the wandering souls of the forgotten dead.
Mid-Autumn Festival (Trung Thu)
Fifteenth day of the eighth moon – this festival is celebrated with moon cakes of sticky rice filled with lotus seeds, watermelon seeds, peanuts, the yolks of duck eggs, raisins, sugar and other such things. This festival is like Christmas day for children, who carry colourful lanterns in the form of boats, unicorns, dragons, lobsters, carp, hares, toads etc in an evening procession accompanied by the banging of drums and cymbals.
Confucius' Birthday
Twenty-eighth day of the ninth moon

The Tet Festival

Tet Nguyen Dan (Festival of the First Day) announces Lunar New Year and is the most important date in the Vietnamese festival calendar. Commonly known as Tet, it is much more than your average Gregorian (western) New Year's celebration; it's a time when families reunite in the hope of good fortune for the coming year, ancestral spirits are welcomed back into the family home and all loose ends are tied up. And Tet is everybody's birthday; on this day everyone becomes one year older.

The festival falls some time between 19 January and 20 February on the western/solar calendar. The exact dates vary from year to year due to differences between the lunar and solar calendars. The first three days after New Year's day are the official holidays but many people take the whole week off.

Tet rites begin seven days before New Year's Day. This is when the Tao Quan – the three Spirits of the Hearth found in the kitchen of every home – ascend to the heavens to report on the past year's events to the Jade Emperor. The Tao Quan ride fish on their journey to heaven, so on this day people all over Vietnam release live carp into rivers and lakes. Altars, laden with offerings of food, fresh water, flowers, betel and more live carp for celestial transport, are assembled in preparation for the gods' departure, all in the hope of receiving a favourable report and ensuring good luck for the family in the coming year.

Other rituals performed during pre-Tet week include visiting cemeteries and inviting the spirits of dead relatives home for the celebrations. Absent family members start to make their way home so the whole family can celebrate Tet under the same roof. All loose ends are tied up so that the new year can be started with a clean slate; debts are paid and absolutely everything is cleaned, including ancestors' graves.

Much like the tradition of Christmas trees in the west, Vietnamese homes are decorated with trees at this time. A New Year's tree *(cay neu)* is constructed to ward off evil spirits. Kumquat trees are popular throughout the country, while branches of pink *dao* peach blossoms grace houses in the north, and yellow *mai* apricot blossoms can be found in southern and central Vietnamese homes. For a spectacular sight, the area around Pho Hang Dau and Pho Hang Ma is transformed into a massive peach blossom and kumquat tree market. Or be dazzled by the blocked-off streets near the Dong Xuan market, ablaze with red and gold decorations for sale.

A few days before the New Year is heralded in, the excitement at these markets is almost palpable as people rush to buy their food and decorations, and motorbikes laden with blossoms and two or three kumquat trees jam the streets.

This is an expensive time of year for most families. The kumquat trees alone cost up to US$50 – in many cases a family's entire year's savings. In addition, children are given red envelopes containing substantial amounts of *li xi*, or lucky money. The Vietnamese see all this expense as being necessary to gain favour with the gods for the coming year.

MASON FLORENCE

The Tet Festival

Like special events anywhere, a large part of the celebrations revolve around food. A Tet staple is *banh chung*. These intriguing square parcels are made of fatty pork and bean paste sandwiched between two layers of glutinous *nep* rice. They're wrapped in green *dong* (banana) leaves and tied with bamboo twine, giving them the appearance of a present. You'll see mountains of them everywhere and will no doubt be invited to taste one.

Banh chung is often accompanied by *mang*, a dish made with boiled bamboo shoots and fried pork marinated in *nuoc mam*. Many visitors don't appreciate these dishes but they have a symbolic significance for Vietnamese people, their simple ingredients being reminders of past hard times. For sweets, *mut* – candied fruit such as sugared apples, plums and even tomatoes – is popular. Fresh fruit is another essential element of Tet: in the north, grapefruit, green bananas and kumquats are big favourites.

On New Year's Eve, the Tao Quan return to earth. At the stroke of midnight, all problems from the previous year are left behind and jubilant celebrations ensue. The goal seems to be to make as much noise as possible: drums and percussion are popular and so were firecrackers until their ban in 1995, although you might still hear recordings of exploding firecrackers blaring from cassette players. Any noise will do really, as long as it provides a suitable welcome back for the gods while scaring off any evil spirits which may be loitering.

The events of New Year's Day are very important as they're believed to affect the course of life in the year ahead. People take extra care not to be rude or show anger. Other no-nos include sewing, sweeping, swearing and breaking things, all acts which might attract bad spirits. Similarly, it's crucial that the first visitor of the year to each household is suitable. They're usually male – best of all is a wealthy married man with several children. Foreigners are sometimes welcomed as the first to enter the house, although not always, so it's wise not to visit any Vietnamese house on the first day of Tet unless you are explicitly invited (and make sure you confirm the time they want you to arrive). Those blacklisted as first visitors include single middle-aged women, and anyone who has lost their job, had an accident or lost a family member during the previous year – all signs of bad luck. Such unfortunates and their families can be ostracised from their community and sometimes stay home during the whole Tet period.

In Hanoi a flower market is held during the week preceding Tet, on Pho Hang Luoc. A two week flower exhibition and competition, beginning on the first day of the new year, takes place in Lenin Park. Wrestling matches are held on the 15th day of the first lunar month at Dong Da Mound, site of the uprising against Chinese invaders led by Emperor Quang Trung (Nguyen Hue) in 1788.

A popular activity in Hanoi during the weeks that follow Tet is *co nguoi*, or human chess. All the human chess pieces come from the same village, Lien Xa in the northern province of Ha Tay, and they're chosen because they're attractive, young, unmarried and have had no recent deaths in their families or other signs of bad luck. The form of chess played is Chinese. Although the pieces and moves are different from western chess, the objective remains the same: to capture the opposing leader, in this case the 'general'. The final is held at the Temple of De Thich, who was the right-hand man of the Jade Emperor, and the celestial God of Chess.

On the 13th day of the first lunar month boys and girls in Lim village (Ha Bac Province) engage in *hat doi*, a traditional game in which groups conduct a sung dialogue with each other; other rural activities include rice field water puppetry, human chess and cock fighting.

Tet is not a particularly boisterous celebration, except on New Year's Eve itself. It's closer to a western Christmas day, a quiet family affair. Difficulty in booking transport and accommodation

The Tet Festival

aside, this is an excellent time to visit the country, especially to witness the contrasting frenzied activity before the New Year and the calm (and quiet streets!) afterwards. Wherever you're staying, it's more than likely you'll be invited to join in the celebrations.

New Year's Day is due to fall on the following dates: 5 February 2000, 24 January 2001, 12 February 2002 and 1 February 2003.

If visiting Hanoi at this time, just make sure you learn this phrase: *Chúc mừng nam mới!* (Happy New Year!).

Michelle Bennett

Banh Chung

The fable behind *banh chung* cakes originated with King Huong Vuong the Sixth, who fathered 22 sons, all worthy heirs. In order to select his successor, the king instructed them to search the globe for delicacies unknown to him. Whoever returned with the best dish would rule the kingdom. Twenty-one of them did as they were told, but one young prince, Lang Lieu, remained in the palace with no idea of where to start looking. He was filled with gloom until one night a genie appeared in his dreams. 'Man cannot live without rice', she said, and told him the recipe for banh chung. When the time came for the king to taste the 22 dishes, he was bitterly disappointed with the 21 from the princes who had travelled abroad. Finally he tasted the rice creations of Lang Lieu and was amazed at how delicious they were. When told of the genie's assistance with the recipe, the king was impressed with this divine support and named Lang Lieu his successor.

Tao Quan

One legend behind the Tao Quan is based on the story of a woodcutter and his wife. They lived happily together until the man was driven to drink through the worry of being unable to provide enough food for them both. He became violent towards his wife and eventually she could no longer bear it and left him. After some time she married a local hunter, forgetting the terrors of her previous marriage.

One day, a few days before the Vietnamese New Year, the woman received a beggar at the front door while the hunter was searching for game. She offered the beggar a meal and soon realised that he was her former husband. Panicked by the sound of her current husband returning, she hid the beggar under a pile of hay. The hungry hunter promptly set the hay alight and placed his recently caught game on it to roast, unaware that there was someone there. Fearing that the hunter might kill the woman if he cried out, the beggar remained silently burning to death. The poor woman was torn with grief, realising that her former husband was dying for her sake. With little hesitation, she threw herself onto the fire to die with him. The confused hunter thought that he must have driven her to such desperation, so he too jumped into the fire, unable to contemplate life without her.

All three perished, an act of devotion which so deeply touched the Jade Emperor that he made them gods. In their new role, they were to look out for the wellbeing of the Vietnamese people from the vantage point of the hearth. Often these kitchen gods are described as a single person and may be called Ong Tao, Ong Lo or Ong Vua Bep.

DOING BUSINESS

The recent liberalisation of rules has had a dramatic effect on foreign joint venture operations. Some of the most successful joint ventures to date have involved hotels, though some of these 'investments' are clear cases of real-estate speculation (foreigners cannot buy land directly, but businesses with a Vietnamese partner can). The leading foreign investors are the Koreans, Singaporeans and Taiwanese. There has also been a large amount of Overseas Vietnamese money invested.

Hanoi's foreign investment environment, however, has grown shaky lately. The crippling economic crisis which has gripped Asia in recent years has had a substantial effect on Vietnam. Countless promising joint business ventures, in particular those depending on Asian funding, have collapsed. Stories abound of foreigners being burned in business deals in Vietnam. While multinational companies and huge hotel chains can afford to dump a few million dollars into a risky venture, a lot of smaller start-up companies and individuals have lost their shirts.

While on paper, it all looks good, in practice the rule of law barely exists in Vietnam these days. Local officials interpret the law any way it suits them, often against the wishes of Hanoi. This poses serious problems for joint ventures – foreigners who have gone to court in Vietnam to settle civil disputes have generally fared pretty badly. It's particularly difficult to sue a state-run company, even if that company committed obvious fraud. The government has a reputation for suddenly revoking permits and licences and tearing up written contracts. There is no independent judiciary.

One successful foreign entrepreneur in Hanoi drew this analogy: 'Vietnamese do business like they drive – that is to say, recklessly, and with little thought for the future, and no respect for others'.

Foreigners who stay in Vietnam long term and attempt to do business can expect periodic visits from the police collecting 'taxes' and 'donations'. Often they will direct their requests towards the Vietnamese employees rather than confront a foreign manager directly. It's just one of those things that makes doing business in Vietnam so exciting. Good luck.

The Vietnamese bureaucracy, official incompetence, corruption and the ever-changing rules and regulations continue to irritate foreign investors. On paper, intellectual property rights are protected, but enforcement is lax – patents, copyrights and trademarks are widely and blatantly pirated (including Lonely Planet guidebooks!).

Vietnam's legal system is complex, but fortunately today there are several Vietnamese and foreign law firms available in Hanoi to help.

For foreign language translation services, consider contacting Intraco (☎ 826 5911), 34 Pho Tran Hung Dao, or the Translation Centre (☎ 943 1880), 238 Pho Hue.

Personal and corporate bank accounts can be set up at Vietcombank, or at one of several foreign banks in Hanoi (see the Banks listing earlier in this chapter under Money).

Useful Organisations

Vietcochamber, the Chamber of Commerce & Industry, is supposed to initiate and facilitate contacts between foreign business and Vietnamese companies. Vietcochamber publishes a listing of government companies and their contact details.

The head office of Vietcochamber (☎ 574 2122, fax 574 1759) and the Chamber of Commerce & Industry of Vietnam (☎ 574 2143, fax 574 2030) is at 9 Pho Dao Duy. The Trade Service Company (affiliated with Vietcochamber) has its offices at 33 Pho Ba Trieu.

Business travellers could also talk to the Vietnam Trade Information Centre (☎ 826 3227/826 4038), at 46 Pho Ngo Quyen.

The Ministry of Foreign Affairs (☎ 199 2000) is located at 1 Pho Ton That Dam. The Foreign Affairs Ministry Consular Office (☎ 845 6891, fax 823 6928) is at 6 Pho Chu Van An, near Ho Chi Minh's Mausoleum. The Foreign Press Centre of the Foreign Affairs Ministry (☎ 825 5075) is at 10 Pho Le Phung Hieu.

Contacts for the International Relations Departments of various government ministries are:

Ministry of Construction
(☎ 978 0674)
37 Pho Le Dai Hanh
Ministry of Culture & Information
(☎ 826 2972)
51-53 Pho Ngo Quyen
Ministry of Finance
(☎ 824 0437)
8 Pho Phan Huy Chu
Ministry of Industry
(☎ 826 7988)
54 Ha Ba Trung
Ministry of Planning & Investment
(☎ 823 0628)

WORK

From 1975 to about 1990, Hanoi's foreign workers were basically technical specialists and military advisers from Eastern Europe and the now defunct Soviet Union. The declining fortunes of the former Eastern Bloc have caused most of these advisers to be withdrawn.

Vietnam's opening to capitalist countries has suddenly created more work opportunities for westerners, though less so today in the corporate sector than a few years ago. Today some of the best-paid westerners living in Vietnam are those working for the diplomatic corps, official foreign-aid organisations or private foreign companies setting up joint venture operations.

Foreigners who look like Rambo are occasionally approached by talent scouts recruiting for extras in war movies, but for most travellers, the main work opportunities will be teaching a foreign language. Watch for ads in the *Vietnam News* newspaper.

English is by far the most popular foreign language with Vietnamese students. Some foreign language students in Vietnam also want to learn French and Japanese. There is also a limited demand for teachers of German, Spanish, Chinese and Korean.

Government-run universities in Vietnam hire some foreign teachers. Pay is generally around US$2 per hour, but benefits such as free housing and unlimited visa renewals are usually thrown in. Teaching at a university requires some commitment (eg you may have to sign a one year contract).

There is also a budding free market in private language centres and home tutoring – this is where most newly arrived foreigners seek work. Pay in the private sector is slightly better, but it is likely that these private schools won't be able to offer the same benefits as government-run schools.

Private tutoring pays even better – up to US$15 per hour. In this case, you are in business for yourself. The authorities may or may not turn a blind eye to such activities.

Some western journalists and photographers manage to make a living in Hanoi by selling their stories and pictures to western news organisations and domestic English-language media outlets. Most journalists, however, are forced to work freelance and pay can vary from decent to dismal.

Volunteer Work

There are various nongovernmental organisations (NGOs), including religious, environmental and humanitarian aid groups with offices in Hanoi. If you're looking to volunteer in Vietnam, you may wish to contact the NGO Resource Centre (Map 2; ☎ 832 8570, fax 832 8611, ngocentr@netnam.org.vn), La Thanh Hotel, 218 Pho Doi Can. This organisation has links with most international NGOs in Vietnam and can sell you a copy of their *Vietnam NGO Directory* (US$10) with detailed listings and contacts.

Getting There & Away

AIR

Hanoi's Noi Bai airport is second in air traffic volume only to Ho Chi Minh City's (Saigon) Tan Son Nhat airport. For a capital city, there are surprisingly few flights in and out of Hanoi, but this is gradually changing.

Vietnam Airlines, the nation's state-owned flag carrier, has a near-monopoly on domestic flights. Pacific Airlines flies a handful of both domestic and international routes, charging the same fares as Vietnam Airlines on domestic routes but lower fares on international routes. Vasco (Vietnam Air Services Company), a foreign joint venture, runs charters using small, fixed-wing aircraft and helicopters.

The Vietnam Airlines booking office in Hanoi is one of the busiest in Vietnam. There are many travel agents around which sell air tickets and do not charge any more than the airline.

Departure Tax

Vietnam's departure tax for international flights is US$10, or US$1.60 for domestic flights, payable in Vietnamese dong or US dollars. Children under two are exempt.

Other Parts of Vietnam

There are direct flights between Hanoi and most major cities in Vietnam.

USA & Canada

At the time of writing, no US air carriers were flying into Vietnam. China Airlines and EVA Airways (both Taiwanese) typically offer the cheapest fares on US-Vietnam flights, all of which transit in Taipei.

Other possible US-Vietnam tickets are available from Cathay Pacific (via Hong Kong), Singapore Airlines (via Singapore), Thai Airways (via Bangkok) and Asiana (via Seoul).

There are currently no direct flights between Canada and Vietnam. Most Canadian travellers transit at Hong Kong.

UK

There are no direct flights between the UK and Vietnam, but relatively cheap tickets are available on the London-Hong Kong run. From Hong Kong you will find it easy enough to make onward arrangements to Hanoi.

There are a number of magazines in Britain which have good information about flights and agents. These include the weekly *Time Out* along with free publications such as *TNT*, *LAM*, *New Zealand News UK* and *Trailfinder* which are available from distribution bins around London.

Discount tickets are available almost exclusively in London. Try calling STA Travel (☎ 020-7937 1221), Trailfinders (☎ 020-7938 3366) or Campus Travel (☎ 020-7730 8111).

Warning

The information in this chapter is particularly vulnerable to change: prices for international travel are volatile, routes are introduced and cancelled, schedules change, special deals come and go, and rules and visa requirements are amended. Airlines and governments seem to take a perverse pleasure in making price structures and regulations as complicated as possible. You should check directly with the airline or a travel agent to make sure you understand how a fare (and ticket you may buy) works. In addition, the travel industry is highly competitive and there are many lurks and perks.

The upshot of this is that you should get opinions, quotes and advice from as many airlines and travel agents as possible before you part with your hard-earned cash. The details given in this chapter should be regarded as pointers and are not a substitute for your own careful, up-to-date research.

Continental Europe

Vietnam Airlines operates three weekly flights between Paris and Hanoi via Bangkok. Cheaper Paris-Hanoi flights are operated by Aeroflot (via Moscow), Lauda Air (via Vienna), and Malaysian Airlines (via Kuala Lumpur).

One French travel agent specialising in tickets and tours to Asia is Nouvelles Frontières (☎ 08-03 33 33 33).

Australia

Vietnam Airlines offers weekly direct flights between Hanoi and both Sydney and Melbourne. The weekend travel sections of major newspapers are good sources of discount travel information. Also check out STA Travel's *Escape* magazine.

Thailand

Bangkok, only 90 minutes flying time from Hanoi, has emerged as the main port of embarkation for air travel to Vietnam. Thai Airways, Air France and Vietnam Airlines offer daily Bangkok-Hanoi services. Khao San Rd in Bangkok is the budget travellers' headquarters.

Hong Kong

After Bangkok, Hong Kong is the second most popular point for departures to Vietnam. Cathay Pacific and Vietnam Airlines offer a daily joint service between Hong Kong and Hanoi.

Phoenix Services (☎ 2722 7378, fax 2369 8884), Room B, 6th floor, Milton Mansion, 96 Nathan Rd, Tsimshatsui, Kowloon, specialises in discount tickets and customised tours to Vietnam.

Other Asian Countries

Vietnam Airlines operates joint services with the following airlines.

Cambodia In conjunction with Royal Air Cambodge, there are daily flights between Phnom Penh and Hanoi. There is a US$5 airport tax when flying out of Cambodia. One-month visas for Cambodia are available on arrival at Phnom Penh airport for US$20.

China A joint service with China Southern Airlines flies the Guangzhou-Hanoi route, as well as the Beijing-Hanoi flight which stops at Nanning (Guangxi) en route – you can board or exit there.

Japan In conjunction with Japan Airlines or Cathay Pacific, there is a daily route between Tokyo and Hanoi (via Hong Kong).

Korea A shared service with Korean Air and Asiana flies the Seoul-Saigon route at least three times weekly, with connections on to Hanoi.

Joy Travel Service (☎ 776 9871, fax 756 5342), 10th floor, 24-2 Mukyo-dong, Chung-gu, Seoul, sells discounted tickets.

Laos A daily joint service with Lao Aviation operates between Vientiane and Hanoi.

Malaysia Malaysia Airlines offers a joint service from Kuala Lumpur to Hanoi.

Singapore In conjunction with Singapore Airlines, there is a daily Saigon-Singapore service. Most flights from Singapore continue to Hanoi.

Taiwan Taiwan's China Airlines offers a joint service three times weekly between Hanoi and Taipei. There are no diplomatic relations between Taiwan and Vietnam, so visa processing goes via Bangkok and takes 10 working days.

A good discount travel agent is Jenny Su Travel (☎ 02-2594 7733/2596 2263, fax 2592 0068), 10th floor, 27 Chungshan N Rd, Section 3, Taipei.

Airline Offices

Hanoi booking offices for international airlines are:

Aeroflot
    (☎ 825 6742, fax 824 9411)
    Map 5; 4 Pho Trang Thi
Air France
    (☎ 825 3484, fax 826 6694)
    Map 5; 1 Pho Ba Trieu

Air Travel Glossary

Baggage Allowance This will be written on your ticket and usually includes one 20kg item to go in the hold, plus one item of hand luggage.

Bucket Shops These are unbonded travel agencies specialising in discounted airline tickets.

Bumped Just because you have a confirmed seat doesn't mean you're going to get on the plane (see Overbooking).

Cancellation Penalties If you have to cancel or change a discounted ticket, there are often heavy penalties involved; insurance can sometimes be taken out against these penalties. Some airlines impose penalties on regular tickets as well, particularly against 'no-show' passengers.

Check-In Airlines ask you to check in a certain time ahead of the flight departure (usually one to two hours on international flights). If you fail to check in on time and the flight is overbooked, the airline can cancel your booking and give your seat to somebody else.

Confirmation Having a ticket written out with the flight and date you want doesn't mean you have a seat until the agent has checked with the airline that your status is 'OK' or confirmed. Meanwhile you could just be 'on request'.

Courier Fares Businesses often need to send urgent documents or freight securely and quickly. Courier companies hire people to accompany the package through customs and, in return, offer a discount ticket which is sometimes a phenomenal bargain. In effect, what the companies do is ship their freight as your luggage on regular commercial flights. This is a legitimate operation, but there are two shortcomings - the short turnaround time of the ticket (usually not longer than a month) and the limitation on your luggage allowance. You may have to surrender all your allowance and take only carry-on luggage.

Full Fares Airlines traditionally offer 1st class (coded F), business class (coded J) and economy class (coded Y) tickets. These days there are so many promotional and discounted fares available that few passengers pay full economy fare.

ITX An ITX, or 'independent inclusive tour excursion', is often available on tickets to popular holiday destinations. Officially it's a package deal combined with hotel accommodation, but many agents will sell you one of these for the flight only and give you phoney hotel vouchers in the unlikely event that you're challenged at the airport.

Lost Tickets If you lose your airline ticket an airline will usually treat it like a travellers cheque and, after inquiries, issue you with another one. Legally, however, an airline is entitled to treat it like cash and if you lose it then it's gone forever. Take good care of your tickets.

MCO An MCO, or 'miscellaneous charge order', is a voucher that looks like an airline ticket but carries no destination or date. It can be exchanged through any International Association of Travel Agents (IATA) airline for a ticket on a specific flight. It's a useful alternative to an onward ticket in those countries that demand one, and is more flexible than an ordinary ticket if you're unsure of your route.

No-Shows No-shows are passengers who fail to show up for their flight. Full-fare passengers who fail to turn up are sometimes entitled to travel on a later flight. The rest are penalised (see Cancellation Penalties).

On Request This is an unconfirmed booking for a flight.

Air Travel Glossary

Onward Tickets An entry requirement for many countries is that you have a ticket out of the country. If you're unsure of your next move, the easiest solution is to buy the cheapest onward ticket to a neighbouring country or a ticket from a reliable airline which can later be refunded if you do not use it.

Open Jaw Tickets These are return tickets where you fly out to one place but return from another. If available, this can save you backtracking to your arrival point.

Overbooking Airlines hate to fly empty seats and since every flight has some passengers who fail to show up, airlines often book more passengers than they have seats. Usually excess passengers make up for the no-shows, but occasionally somebody gets bumped. Guess who it is most likely to be? The passengers who check in late.

Point-to-Point Tickets These are discount tickets that can be bought on some routes in return for passengers waiving their rights to a stopover.

Promotional Fares These are officially discounted fares, available from travel agencies or direct from the airline.

Reconfirmation At least 72 hours prior to departure time of an onward or return flight, you must contact the airline and 'reconfirm' that you intend to be on the flight. If you don't do this the airline can delete your name from the passenger list and you could lose your seat.

Restrictions Discounted tickets often have various restrictions on them - such as needing to be paid for in advance and incurring a penalty to be altered. Others are restrictions on the minimum and maximum period you must be away, such as a minimum of 14 days or a maximum of one year.

Round-the-World Tickets RTW tickets give you a limited period (usually a year) in which to circumnavigate the globe. You can go anywhere the carrying airlines go, as long as you don't backtrack. The number of stopovers or total number of separate flights is decided before you set off and they usually cost a bit more than a basic return flight.

Stand-by This is a discounted ticket where you only fly if there is a seat free at the last moment. Stand-by fares are usually available only on domestic routes.

Transferred Tickets Airline tickets cannot be transferred from one person to another. Travellers sometimes try to sell the return half of their ticket, but officials can ask you to prove that you are the person named on the ticket. This is less likely to happen on domestic flights, but on an international flight tickets are compared with passports.

Travel Agencies Travel agencies vary widely and you should choose one that suits your needs. Some simply handle tours, while full-services agencies handle everything from tours and tickets to car rental and hotel bookings. If all you want is a ticket at the lowest possible price, then go to an agency specialising in discounted tickets.

Travel Periods Ticket prices vary with the time of year. There is a low (off-peak) season and a high (peak) season, and often a low-shoulder season and a high-shoulder season as well. Usually the fare depends on your outward flight - if you depart in the high season and return in the low season, you pay the high-season fare.

GETTING THERE & AWAY

Cathay Pacific Airways
(☎ 826 7298, fax 826 7709)
Map 5; 49 Hai Ba Trung
China Airlines (Taiwan)
(☎ 824 2688, fax 824 2588)
Map 5; 18 Pho Tran Hung Dao
China Southern Airlines
(☎ 826 9233/826 9234)
Map 5; Binh Minh Hotel, 27 Pho Ly Thai To
Czech Airlines
(☎ 845 6512, fax 846 4000)
103 A2 Van Phuc Diplomatic Quarter
Japan Airlines
(☎ 826 6693, fax 826 6698)
Map 5; 1 Pho Ba Trieu
Lao Aviation
(☎ 826 6538, fax 822 9951)
Map 5; 41 Pho Quang Trung
Malaysia Airlines
(☎ 826 8820, fax 824 2388)
Map 5; 15 Pho Ngo Quyen
Pacific Airlines
(☎ 851 5356, fax 851 5350)
Map 2; 100 Pho Le Duan
Singapore Airlines
(☎ 826 8888, fax 826 8666)
Map 5; 17 Pho Ngo Quyen
Thai Airways
(☎ 826 6893, fax 826 7934)
Map 5; 44B Pho Ly Thuong Kiet
Vasco
(☎ 827 1707, fax 827 2705)
Gia Lam airport
Vietnam Airlines
(☎ 825 0888, fax 824 8989)
Map 5; 1 Pho Quang Trung

BORDER CROSSINGS

There are currently five places where foreigners may cross overland into Vietnam. In addition to the two crossings into China listed here, there are two legal ways into Laos, and one into Cambodia.

The Vietnamese require travellers to have a special visa for entering overland. These visas cost more and take longer to issue than those for entering by air.

Vietnamese police at the land border crossings are known to be particularly problematic. Upon entry, they may only give you a one week stay rather than the one month indicated on your visa. Most travellers find that it's much easier to exit Vietnam overland than it is to enter that way.

There are no legal moneychanging facilities on the Vietnamese side of any of these crossings, so be sure to have some US dollars cash handy. Try to find a bank or legal moneychanger, to avoid short-changing or outright theft.

Be warned that drugs checks are reportedly common, and that the Vietnamese border guards routinely ask for an 'immigration fee' and/or a 'customs fee', although this is illegal.

China

As well as the two checkpoints described below, there is a third (Mong Cai) open to Vietnamese and Chinese nationals only. The crossings are only open from 7 am to 4 pm Vietnam time, or 8 am to 5 pm China time.

Friendship Pass The busiest border crossing is at the Vietnamese town of Dong Dang, 164km north-east of Hanoi. The closest town on the Chinese side of the border is Pinxiang (about 10km north). The crossing point (Friendship Pass) is known as Huu Nghi Quan in Vietnamese or Youyi Guan in Chinese.

Lao Cai-Hekou Another transit point for Hanoi is at the border town (on the Vietnamese side) of Lao Cai (294km from Hanoi). On the Chinese side, the border town is Hekou (468km from Kunming).

BUS

Figuring out the bus system is anything but easy. Hanoi has several bus stations, and responsibilities are divided according to the location of the destination and the type of service being offered.

Hanoi's Gia Lam bus station (Ben Xe Gia Lam) is where you catch buses to points north-east of Hanoi. This includes Halong Bay, Haiphong and Lang Son (near the China border). The bus station is 2km north-east of the centre, across the Red River (Song Hong). Cyclos won't cross the bridge so take a taxi or motorbike.

Kim Ma bus station (Ben Xe Kim Ma, Map 3) is opposite 166 Pho Nguyen Thai

Hoc (corner Pho Giang Vo). This is where you get buses to the north-west part of Vietnam, including Pho Lu and Dien Bien Phu. Tickets should be purchased the day before departure.

Son La bus station (Ben Xe Son La, Map 2) at Km 8, Pho Nguyen Trai also has buses to the north-west (Hoa Binh, Mai Chau, Son La, Tuan Giao, Dien Bien Phu, Lai Chau).

Giap Bat bus station (Ben Xe Giap Bat, Map 2) serves points south of Hanoi, including Saigon. The station is 7km south of the Hanoi train station on Đ Giai Phong.

Other Parts of Vietnam

Vietnam has an extensive network of dirt-cheap buses and other passenger vehicles which reaches virtually every corner of the country. Riding the public buses will give you ample opportunity to have 'personal contact', literally, with the Vietnamese people. However, few travellers use them, for reasons of safety. Vietnam's network of two-lane highways is becoming more and more dangerous due to the rapid increase in the number of motor vehicles. In addition, Vietnam does not have an emergency rescue system or even a proper ambulance network.

If possible, try to travel during daylight hours. The dangers of driving after dark in rural areas include unlit highways with huge potholes, occasional collapsed bridges and lots of bicycles and pedestrians oblivious to the traffic.

The appellation 'express' *(toc hanh)* is applied rather loosely in Vietnam, but express buses are usually faster than local buses, which stop at each cluster of houses along the highway.

Most long distance buses depart in the early morning. Often, half a dozen vehicles for the same destination will leave at the same time, usually around 5.30 am. If you don't plan to bargain with the bus driver, purchase your ticket at the bus station the day before departure.

Open Date Ticket In backpacker haunts throughout Vietnam you'll see signs advertising the 'Open Date Ticket' or just 'Open

Ticket'. This is a bus service catering to foreign budget travellers. The buses run between Hanoi and Saigon and you may enter and exit the bus at any major city along the route.

There are two tickets available: Hanoi-Hué-Hanoi for as low as US$16 and Hué-Saigon for as little as US$27, though individual legs of the trip can be purchased for less. Buying minibus tickets all along the way costs a bit more, but you achieve maximum flexibility.

Other Countries

Most travellers to and from the Chinese borders prefer to travel by train, though there are frequent buses and minibuses on both the Hanoi-Lang Son and Hanoi-Lao Cai routes.

MINIBUS

Tourist-style minibuses can be booked through most hotels and cafés. There are two categories of minibus:

Public Minibus Public minibuses cater for the domestic market. They depart when full and will pick up as many passengers as possible along the route, becoming ridiculously crowded, uncomfortable and slow. They are really a small scale version of the large public buses. They congregate around the bus stations.

Chartered Minibus A large majority of independent travellers in Vietnam choose this form of transport. Chartered minibuses are just what the name implies.

Air-conditioning is standard and you'll have enough space to sit comfortably. Prices will of course be a lot higher than on public buses, but are still very cheap. Budget hotels and cafés are the best places to inquire about these vehicles.

TRAIN

Hanoi's main train station (Ga Hang Co, Map 5; ☎ 825 3949), at 120 Đ Le Duan, is at the western end of Pho Tran Hung Dao. Trains from here go to destinations south.

The ticket office is open from 7.30 to 11.30 am and 1.30 to 3.30 pm only and there is a special counter for foreigners.

Where you purchase the ticket is not necessarily where the train departs; northbound trains leave from Tran Quy Cap station (or 'B station') on Pho Tran Qui Cap (Map 5; ☎ 825 2628), a two-block walk from the front station entrance.

To complicate matters some northbound (Viet Tri, Yen Bai, Lao Cai, Lang Son) and eastbound (Haiphong) trains depart from both Gia Lam and Long Bien (☎ 826 8280) train stations (both across the bridge on the east side of the Red River). Some of the local southbound trains leave from the Giap

Bat train station (Map 2) about 7km south of Hanoi train station. Be sure to ask just where you need to go to catch your train; you can try phoning for information, but don't expect much.

Other Parts of Vietnam

The 2600km Vietnamese railway system (Duong Sat Viet Nam) runs along the coast between Hanoi and Saigon, and also links Hanoi with other parts of northern Vietnam. One line takes you east to Haiphong. A second heads north-east to Lang Son, crosses the border and continues to Nanning, China. A third goes north-west to Lao Cai and on to Kunming, China.

The Hanoi-Saigon Railway

Construction of the 1726km Hanoi-Saigon railway – the Transindochinois – began in 1899 (under Governor-General Paul Doumer) and was completed in 1936. In the late 1930s, the trip from Hanoi to Saigon took 40 hours and 20 minutes at an average speed of 43km/h. During WWII, the Japanese made extensive use of the rail system, resulting in Viet Minh sabotage on the ground and US bombing from the air. After WWII, efforts were made to repair the Transindochinois, major parts of which were either damaged or had become overgrown.

During the Franco-Viet Minh War, the Viet Minh engaged in massive sabotage against the rail system. Sometimes they would pry up and carry off several kilometres of track in a single night. In 1948 the French responded by introducing two armoured trains which were equipped with turret-mounted cannon, anti-aircraft machine guns, grenade launchers and mortars (similar trains are used in Cambodia today on the Phnom Penh-Battambang line). The Viet Minh used their bounty to create a 300km network of tracks in an area wholly under their control (between Ninh Hoa and Danang) – the French quickly responded with their own sabotage.

In the late 1950s, the South, with US funding, reconstructed the track between Saigon and Hué, a distance of 1041km. But between 1961 and 1964 alone, 795 Viet Cong attacks were launched on the rail system, forcing the abandonment of large sections of track (including the Dalat spur). A major reconstruction effort was carried out between 1967 and 1969, and three sections of track were put back into operation: one in the immediate vicinity of Saigon, another between Nha Trang and Qui Nhon, and a third between Danang and Hué.

By 1960, the North had repaired 1000km of track, mostly between Hanoi and China. During the US air war against the North, the northern rail network was repeatedly bombed. Even now clusters of bomb craters can be seen around virtually every rail bridge and train station in the north.

After reunification, the government immediately set about re-establishing the Hanoi-Ho Chi Minh City rail link as a symbol of Vietnamese unity. By the time the *Reunification* (Thong Nhat) *Express* trains were inaugurated on 31 December 1976, 1334 bridges, 27 tunnels, 158 stations and 1370 shunts (switches) had been repaired.

While sometimes even slower than buses, Vietnam's dilapidated trains offer a more relaxing and roomy way to get around, and are much safer than the country's kamikaze bus fleet. Facilities are regularly being upgraded to accommodate foreign tourists – express trains even have air-conditioned sleeping berths now.

There are five classes of train travel in Vietnam: hard seat (usually packed), soft seat, hard sleeper, soft sleeper (normal) and soft sleeper (air-con). Foreigners are required to pay a substantial surcharge above what Vietnamese pay.

The quickest journey between Hanoi and Saigon (1726km) takes 36 hours at an average speed of 48km/h, on the *Reunification Express*, with the slowest express train taking 44 hours.

It's important to realise that the train schedule is 'bare-bones' during Tet.

It's also *very* important that you hang onto your ticket until you've exited the train station at your final destination, or you could be forced to purchase another ticket at the full price to leave the station. Train personnel may ask to have a look at your passport and visa.

Reservations for all trips should be made at least one day in advance (further in advance for sleepers). You can also get tickets from many travel agencies, hotels and cafés (for a small commission). In any given city,

Reunification Express Fares from Hanoi

Hanoi-Ho Chi Minh City (HCMC); 44/40 hours

station	distance from Hanoi	hard seat	soft seat	bottom berth	middle berth	top berth	soft sleeper
Nam Dinh	87km	US$3/3	US$3/3	US$5/6	US$5/5	US$4/5	US$5/6
Ninh Binh	115km	US$4/4	US$4/4	US$6/7	US$6/6	US$6/6	US$7/8
Thanh Hoa	155km	US$5/6	US$6/6	US$9/10	US$9/9	US$8/9	US$10/11
Vinh	319km	US$9/10	US$9/10	US$17/18	US$15/18	US$14/15	US$17/19
Dong Hoi	522km	US$14/16	US$16/17	US$27/29	US$24/27	US$22/27	US$28/32
Dong Ha	622km	US$17/18	US$18/20	US$32/35	US$27/32	US$26/29	US$33/38
Hué	688km	US$19/20	US$20/22	US$35/38	US$32/35	US$28/32	US$36/32
Danang	791km	US$21/23	US$23/25	US$40/44	US$36/40	US$33/32	US$42/36
Quang Ngai	928km	US$25/27	US$27/29	US$47/51	US$43/49	US$38/43	US$49/56
Dieu Tri	1096km	US$29/32	US$32/35	US$55/61	US$50/55	US$45/55	US$57/50
Tuy Hoa	1195km	US$32/35	US$35/38	US$60/66	US$55/60	US$53/55	US$62/72
Nha Trang	1315km	US$38/41	US$41/45	US$72/79	US$65/72	US$59/65	US$75/86
Thap Cham	1408km	US$41/44	US$44/48	US$77/84	US$70/77	US$62/70	US$80/92
HCMC	1726km	US$46/49	US$49/54	US$87/95	US$78/87	US$70/78	US$90/103

Hanoi-HCMC; 36 hours

station	distance from Hanoi	soft seat	bottom berth	middle berth	top berth	hard sleeper	soft sleeper	AC soft sleeper
Vinh	319km	US$12	US$20	US$18	US$17	US$21	US$21	US$27
Hué	688km	US$25	US$41	US$38	US$35	US$45	US$45	US$57
Danang	791km	US$29	US$48	US$44	US$40	US$51	US$51	US$66
Dieu Tri	1096km	US$40	US$66	US$61	US$55	US$71	US$71	US$91
Nha Trang	1315km	US$52	US$85	US$79	US$72	US$93	US$93	US$119
HCMC	1726km	US$82	US$103	US$95	US$89	US$111	US$111	US$143

reservations can be made only for travel originating in that city.

Petty crime is a problem on Vietnamese trains, especially in budget class. Thieves have become proficient at grabbing packs through the windows as trains pull out of stations. Always keep your luggage near you and lock or tie it to something, especially at night.

There is supposedly a 20kg limit for luggage. Enforcement isn't really strict, but if you have excess you might have to send it in the freight car and pay a small extra charge. Bicycles can also be sent in the freight car. Just make sure that the train you are on *has* a freight car (most have) or your luggage will arrive later than you do.

Privately Run Services Victoria Hotels and Resorts (Map 5; ☎ 933 0318, fax 933 0319, victoria@fpt.vn), 33A Pham Ngu Lao, Hanoi, recently inaugurated an upmarket train service between Hanoi and Sapa. The service is luxurious, but expensive.

China

There is a twice-weekly international train between Beijing and Hanoi via Friendship Pass. You can board or exit the train at numerous stations in China. The entire 2951km run takes approximately 55 hours, including a three hour delay (if you're lucky) at the border checkpoint.

There is also a direct service between Hanoi and Kunming in the Yunnan Province.

Domestic trains also run daily on both sides of the border, from the border towns of Lao Cai and Hekou.

CAR & MOTORBIKE

In general, the major highways are hard surfaced and reasonably well maintained, but seasonal flooding can be a problem. In remote backwaters, such as in north-west Vietnam, roads are not surfaced and become a sea of mud in bad weather – such roads are best tackled with a 4WD vehicle or sturdy motorbike. Mountain roads are particularly dangerous – landslides, falling rocks and runaway vehicles can add unwelcome excitement to your journey.

See the Getting Around chapter for details on renting vehicles and the Motorbiking in Northern Vietnam appendix for more information on motorbiking.

Land distances from Hanoi are as follows:

destination	distance (km)
Ba Be National Park	240
Bac Giang	51
Bac Ninh	29
Bach Thong (Bac Can)	162
Cam Pha	190
Cao Bang	272
Da Bac (Cho Bo)	104
Danang	763
Dien Bien Phu	420
Ha Dong	11
Ha Giang	343
Hai Duong	58
Haiphong	103
Halong City	165
Hoa Binh	74
Ho Chi Minh City	1710
Hué	658
Lai Chau	490
Lang Son	146
Lao Cai	294
Ninh Binh	93
Sapa	324
Son La	308
Tam Dao	85
Thai Binh	109
Thai Nguyen	73
Thanh Hoa	175
Tuyen Quang	165
Viet Tri	73
Vinh	319
Yen Bai	155

BICYCLE

Vietnam is an appealing (if dangerous) place for long distance cycling. Most of the terrain in and around Hanoi is flat or only moderately hilly, and most major roads are of a serviceable standard, but roads in the north-west in particular are mountainous.

Bicycles can be transported around the country on the top of buses or in train baggage compartments.

HITCHING

Hitching is never entirely safe in any country in the world, and we don't recommend it. Travellers who hitch should understand that they are taking a small but potentially serious risk. You'll be safer if you travel in pairs, and let someone know where you are planning to go.

ORGANISED TOURS

While it's easy to make all travel arrangements upon arrival in Hanoi (see Organised Tours in the Getting Around chapter), this does demand time, and some flexibility. If your time is more precious than your money, consider a pre-booked package tour. Nearly all package tours to Vietnam include a stop in Hanoi.

Almost any reputable travel agency worldwide can book you onto a standard mad-dash minibus tour around Vietnam. There are also adventure tours or speciality tours for cyclists, trekkers, birdwatchers, war veterans, 4WD enthusiasts and Vietnamese cuisine buffs.

Consider contacting the following speciality travel outfits:

Australia
Griswalds Vietnamese Vacations (☎ 02-9564 5040, fax 9564 1373, binh@magna.com) PO Box 501, Leichhardt, NSW 2040. Its slogan is 'Your dong is in our hands!'
Orbitours (☎ 02-9954 1399, fax 9954 1655) 3rd floor, 73 Walker St (PO Box 834), North Sydney, NSW 2059
Peregrine (☎ 02-9290 2770) 5/38 York St, Sydney, NSW 2000
(☎ 03-9662 2800, fax 9663 8618) 258 Lonsdale St, Melbourne, Vic 3000

Canada
Club Adventure (☎ 514-699 7764, fax 514-699 8756, info@clubadventure.com) 200 Rene-Levesque, Lery, Quebec J6N 3N6
Global Adventures (☎ 800-781 2269/604-940 2220, fax 940 2233, www.portal.ca/~global). Runs 12-day sea kayaking trips in scenic Halong Bay.

France
Nouveau Monde Voyages (☎ 01-43 29 40 40, fax 46 34 19 67) 8 rue Mabillon, Paris 75006

Germany
Geoplan Touristik (☎ 307-954021, fax 954025) Steglitzer Damm 96B, D-12 169, Berlin

Netherlands
Baobab Reizen (☎ 31-20-6275129, fax 20-6245401, baobob@dds.nl) Haarlemmerstraat 24-26, 1013 ER, Amsterdam
Tradewind Holidays (☎ 20-661 0101, fax 642 0137) PO Box 70449, Amsterdam 1007 KK

New Zealand
Adventure World (☎ 09-524 5118, fax 520 6629) 101 Great South Rd, Auckland
Go Orient Holidays (☎ 09-379 5520, fax 377 0111) 151 Victoria St West, Auckland

UK
Asian Journeys (☎ 1604-234855, fax 234866) 32 Semilong Rd, Northampton NN2 6BT

USA
Wild Card Adventures (☎ 800-590 3776, fax 360-387 9816, www.awildcard.com) 751 Maple Grove Rd, Camano Island, WA 98292 (close to Seattle). Customised Vietnam travel itinereries and unusual destinations.
Asia Transpacific Journeys (☎ 800-642 2742, www.SoutheastAsia.com) PO Box 1279, Boulder, CO 80306. Offers unique trekking tours and cycling trips to suit all budgets.
The Global Spectrum (☎ 800-419 4446, gspectrum @gspectrum.com) Suite 204, 1901 Pennsylvania Ave NW, Washington, DC 20006
Asian Pacific Adventures (☎ 800-825 1680/323-935 3156) 826 South Sierra Bonita Ave, Los Angeles, CA 90036. Arranges cycling trips.
Latitudes-Expeditions East (☎ 800-580 4883/415-398 0458, fax 680 1522, www.weblatitudes .com) 870 Market St, Suite 482, San Francisco, CA 94102. South-East Asian specialist running small group expeditions to Vietnam.
Sea Canoe International Adventures (☎ 800-444 1043, fax 888-824 5621, www.seacanoe.com). Offers kayaking trips on rivers and lakes near the Chinese border, and in Halong Bay.
Vietnam Tours (☎ 206-824 9946, fax 824 9982, www.bmi.net/vntours/index.html)
China Span (☎ 425-882 8686, fax 882 8880, www.chinaspan.com) 18419 NE 27th Way, Redmond, WA 98052. Runs photographic speciality tours to Vietnam.

Vietnam
Vidotour (☎ 08-829 1438, fax 829 1435, vidotour @bdvn.vnmail.vnd.net) 41 Đ Dinh Tien Hoang, District 1, Ho Chi Minh City. Offers a spectrum of upmarket tours throughout Indochina and Vietnam.

GETTING THERE & AWAY

Getting Around

TO/FROM THE AIRPORT

Noi Bai airport is about 35km north of the city, a 45-60 minute drive. The airport freeway is one of the most modern roads in Vietnam, and it's curious to see oxen herded by farmers crossing it.

Minibuses from Hanoi to Noi Bai airport depart every half-hour from opposite the Vietnam Airlines International Booking Office on Pho Quang Trung. It's best – though not essential – to book the day before. Tickets (US$4) are sold inside the booking office. Coming from the airport, the driver will drop you at your hotel rather than the booking office for US$1 extra. The minibus service works OK but beware of the usual scams, involving additional 'payments', especially at the airport.

Airport Taxi (☎ 873 3333) charges just US$3 for a seat on a minibus, or US$10 for a private sedan to or from the airport. They do *not* require that you pay the toll for the bridge which must be crossed en route. Some other taxi drivers require that you pay the toll, so ask first. If you are travelling solo, the minibus is practical. It will drop you at the Vietnam Airlines office in town, from where you can cheaply hire a cyclo to get to most hotels. For two or more people, sharing a taxi is recommended. There is an Airport Taxi booking counter in the terminal building. Out in the airport car park, taxis can usually be negotiated for whatever the market will bear (usually around US$10), though it is generally best to avoid the freelancers.

Cafés, travel agents and hotels can often arrange a (usually dilapidated) private car to the airport for as cheap as US$8.

BUS

There are 13 bus lines in Hanoi. Figuring out exactly where the buses go can be a challenge, and service on some of the lines is infrequent. Still, when it comes to economy, only walking is cheaper. Fares are typically US$0.10 to US$0.20.

No bus route guides or maps are published, as yet, so we list the routes and stops here as a guide.

Bus No 1 Ha Dong – Yen Phu
Nguyen Trai, Nguyen Luong Bang, Kham Thien, Nguyen Thuong Hien, Yet Kieu, Quan Su, Hang Da, Hang Cot, Hang Dau

Bus No 2 Ha Dong – Bac Co
Nguyen Trai, Nguyen Luong Bang, Ton Duc Thang, Nguyen Thai Hoc, Hai Ba Trung, Phan Chu Trinh, Bac Co

Bus No 3 Giap Bat – Gia Lam bus station
Vong, Kim Lien bus station, Hanoi train station, Tran Hung Dao, Phan Chu Trinh, Bac Co, Tran Quang Khai, Long Bien bus station, Gia Lam bus station

Bus No 4 Long Bien bus station – Giap Bat train station
Long Bien bus station, Nguyen Huu Huan, Phan Chu Trinh, Lo Duc, Mai Dong, Nguyen Thi Minh Kahi, Mo Market, Truong Dinh, Duoi Ca (Giap Bat train station)

Bus No 5 Nhon – Phan Chu Trinh
Nhon, Cau Dien, Cau Giay, Kim Ma bus station, Nguyen Thai Hoc, Tran Phu, Cua Nam, Hai Ba Trung, Phan Chu Trinh

Bus No 6 Long Bien bus station – Ngoc Hoi
Long Bien bus station, Nguyen Huu Huan, Ly Thai To, Co Tan, Phan Chu Trinh, Le Van Huu, Nguyen Du, Le Duan, Kim Lien bus station, Giai Phong, Duoi Ca, Van Dien, Ngoc Hoi

Bus No 7 Bo Ho – Cua Nam – Cau Giay
Bo Ho, Hang Gai, Hang Bong, Dien Bien Phu, Le Hong Phong, Doi Can, Buoi, Cau Giay

Bus No 8 Long Bien bus station – Mo Market
Long Bien bus station, Hang Dau, Hang Can, Bo Ho, Dinh Tien Hoang, Ba Trieu, Le Dai Hanh, Bach Mai, Mo Market

Bus No 9 Long Bien bus station – Cau Bieu
Bus No 10 Bac Co – Yen Vien
Bac Co, Tran Quang Khai, Tran Nhat Duat, Long Bien bus station, Gia Lam bus station, Yen Vien

Bus No 11 Kim Lien bus station – Phu Thuy
Bus No 12 Giap Bat – Kim Ma
Kim Lien bus station, Trung Tu, Chua Boc, Thai Ha, Lang Ha, Giang Vo, Kim Ma bus station

Bus No 14 Nghia Do – Bo Ho
Nghia Do, Hoang Hoa Tham, Phan Dinh Phung, Hang Cot, Hang Luoc, Luong Van Can, Bo Ho

HANOI'S OLD QUARTER
AND WALKING TOUR

MASON FLORENCE

Top: Hardware store with everything from wire to washboards.

Bottom: Now that the work is done and the display arranged, the staff can have a five minute break before starting to pack it away again.

Title Page: A shady spot in the Old Quarter (photograph by Mason Florence).

Inset photograph by Mason Florence

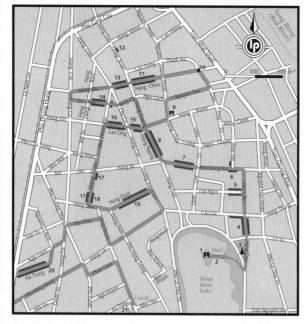

1 Ngoc Son Temple
2 The Huc Bridge
3 Martyrs' Monument
4 Shoe Shops
5 Flower Market
6 Gravestones
7 Jewellery Shops
8 Clothing Shops
9 Bach Ma Temple
10 Cua O Quan Chuong
   (Old East Gate)
11 Straw Mats & Rope
12 Don Xuan Market
13 'Ghost Money'
14 Blacksmiths
15 Towel Shops
16 Herb Sellers
17 Tin Box Makers
18 Mirrors
19 Buddhist Altars
   & Statues
20 Leather Shops
21 St Joseph's Cathedral

HANOI'S OLD QUARTER

The 36 streets (36 Pho Puong) of Hanoi's Old Quarter, with over a thousand years of history, are one of Vietnam's most lively and unusual places to visit. Here you can buy anything from a gravestone to silk pyjamas.

Hanoi's commercial quarter evolved beside the Red River and the smaller To Lich River, which once flowed through the city centre to create an intricate network of canals and waterways. Waters could rise as high as 8m during the monsoon, so dikes, which can still be seen today along Tran Quang Khai, were constructed to protect the city.

Exploring the maze of back streets is fascinating; some streets open up while others narrow down into a warren of smaller alleys. The area is known for its tunnel, or tube, houses – so called because their small frontages hide very long rooms. These tunnel houses were developed to avoid taxes based on the width of their frontage. By feudal law, houses were also limited to two storeys and, out of respect for the king, could not be taller than the Royal Palace. These days there are taller buildings (six to eight storeys) but no high rise buildings.

In the 13th century, Hanoi's 36 guilds established themselves here with each taking a different street. Hang in Vietnamese means merchandise and is usually followed by the name of the product that was traditionally sold in that street. Thus, Hang Hanh translates as Onion Street. These days the street name may not correspond to what is sold there – Hang Hanh is now known as 'coffee street' because it is lined with bars and cafés.

As you wander around the 36 streets you'll find wool clothes, cosmetics, fake Ray-Ban sunglasses, luxury foods, printed T-shirts, musical instruments, plumbing supplies, herbal medicines, gold and silver jewellery, religious offerings, spices, woven mats and much, much more (see the Shopping chapter). Some of the more specialised streets include Hang Quat, with red candlesticks, funeral boxes, flags and other temple items, and Hang Gai which has silk, embroidery, lacquerware, paintings and water puppets – silk sleeping bag liners and elegant Vietnamese *ao dai* are very popular.

Of course, you could keep your money in your pocket and just drink in the atmosphere of a part of Vietnam that has retained an essence of life from centuries past. Either way, the following tour will give you a fascinating insight into Hanoian culture and history.

A stroll through the historic Old Quarter can last from minutes to the better part of a day. A logical starting point is the **Ngoc Son Temple** at the northern end of Hoan Kiem Lake. After crossing back over bright red **The Huc Bridge**, stop for a quick look at the **Martyrs' Monument**, erected to those who died fighting for Vietnam's independence. Head north on Hang Dau past the Water Puppet Theatre (see the 'Puppetry in a Pool' boxed text in the Things to See & Do chapter) and you'll be surrounded by **shoe shops** selling every shape, size and style. Crossing over Pho Cau Go, pop into the colourful **flower market** which occupies the narrow eastern terminus of Pho Gia Nhu. Back on Hang Be, continue north to Hang Bac, where a left turn will soon put you at an intersection where intricate **gravestones** are carved by hand. Stay on Hang Bac past a strip of snazzy **jewellery shops**, and head right onto Hang Ngang past a row of **clothing shops** and turn right again onto Hang Buom; this will take you past the small **Bach Ma Temple** (White Horse Temple). As you pass the pagoda, with its red funeral palanquin, look for its white-bearded temple guards, who spend their days sipping tea. Legend has it that Ly King used the pagoda to pray for assistance in building the city walls because they persistently collapsed no matter how many times he rebuilt them. His prayers were finally answered when a white horse appeared out of the temple and guided him to the site where he could safely build his walls. Evidence of his success is still visible at **Cua O Quan Chuong**, the quarter's well-preserved Old East Gate on Tran Nhat Duat, at the eastern end of Hang Chieu. Head west, back along Hang Chieu past a handful of shops selling **straw mats and rope** (here you might consider a detour north to the enormous **Dong Xuan market**), to reach one of the most interesting streets, Hang Ma (literally 'counterfeit street'), where imitation **'ghost money'** is sold for burning in Buddhist ceremonies – it even has US$5000 bills! Loop around and follow your ears to the sounds of **blacksmiths** pounding away on metal on the corner of Lo Ren and Thuoc Bac. Moving south on Hang Duong, head right past the **towel shops** onto Lan Ong, a fantastic row of traditional medicine pharmacies selling **herbs** which fill the street with succulent aromas.

Finally, head south past the **tin box makers** on Hang Thiec, then left toward the interesting shops selling **Buddhist altars and statues** along Hang Quai. Time permitting, loop around and zigzag west to check out the **leather shops** along Ha Trung, working east again to end the walk at the superb, neo-Gothic **St Joseph's Cathedral**.

Mason Florence & Juliet Coombe

MASON FLORENCE

Left: The best way to get around the Old Quarter is on foot or by bicycle. Scooter, moped and cyclo are other options, but these are increasingly being banned from its narrow streets.

CAR & MOTORBIKE
The discomfort and unreliability of Vietnam's public transport makes renting a vehicle a popular option. The major considerations are costs, safety, the mechanical condition of the vehicle and the reliability of the rental agency. Car hire always includes a driver, as foreigners are generally not permitted to drive cars in Vietnam.

The labels 'Regular' or 'Super-Unleaded' on pumps at petrol stations actually mean nothing, but petrol does have an octane rating – 86 would be low lead and 95 would be high octane leaded, with several gradations in between.

One for the Road

Russian 4WDs, based on the latest 1950s technology, are still being manufactured and widely used in northern Vietnam. There has been absolutely no change in design for the past 40 years, with the exception of the door handles – the new ones are made of plastic and break more easily than the old metal ones. Obviously intended for the Russian climate, the windows do not even open (a horror in summer). You can get a nice breeze if you put the top down, but it's quite a complex procedure, not to mention the dust you'll end up engulfed in. By contrast, with a spanner and a screwdriver you could disassemble the whole vehicle – it's a wonder of simplicity.

Although the Russian 4WDs lack seat belts and roll bars, they are otherwise pretty safe – they negotiate the mud at least as well as (or better than) the fancy Japanese-made 4WDs.

Renting one is easy in Hanoi – this is an excellent, exciting and, split between a few friends, affordable way to tour the rugged north-west. If you'd like to buy one, a new Russian 4WD can be had for US$21,000. They easily exceed the 20kg weight limit imposed by Vietnam Airlines, so you'll have to find another way to get it home.

Black-market petrol *(xang)* is sold – along with oil *(dau)* – in soft drink bottles at little roadside stalls. Most charge around US$0.40 per litre. Be warned that black-market petrol is often mixed with kerosene (it's cheaper), which can cause engine problems – use it in an emergency only.

Leaving an unattended vehicle parked out on the street overnight is not wise. If travelling by motorbike you can usually bring it right inside the hotel. If travelling by car, it's necessary to find a hotel with a garage or fenced-in compound (many hotels are so equipped). There are also commercial non-hotel garages.

Road Rules
Basically, there aren't any. A good rule of thumb is always give way to anything bigger than you and anything in front of you. If there is an accident, the law says that whoever is the larger vehicle must hold responsibility. The reality, unfortunately, is that the foreigner is assumed to be at fault, and language barriers do not help the situation. If you get angry and make a scene, expect an even harder time. Even if you're completely in the right, helping the other person off the road and producing some 'compensation money' is usually the best ticket to a speedy exit.

Vehicles are supposed to drive on the right-hand side of the road, but you cannot turn right on a red light. You will be fined for this offence. Another rule to watch out for applies only to the circular road around Hoan Kiem Lake – it's illegal to turn left onto this road from any side street.

Honking at all pedestrians and bicycles (to warn of your approach) is considered a basic element of safe driving – larger trucks might as well have a permanent siren attached.

When Vietnamese have an accident, the two drivers will usually stand in the street and argue for 30 minutes about whose fault it was. Whoever tires of the argument first hands over some money to pay for damages and it's all settled. As a foreigner, you're at a disadvantage in these negotiations. You might feign some injury (to gain sympathy) but offer to pay for the other driver's minor damages. If none of this works and you are being asked to pay excessive damages, you could always say you want to call the police. As a foreigner, they might just believe you're crazy enough to do that, and the negotiations will probably be concluded quickly.

Car

Self-drive rental cars have yet to make their debut in Vietnam, but cars with drivers can be hired from a variety of sources. Given the low cost of labour, renting a vehicle with a driver and guide is a realistic option even for budget travellers.

A car with driver can be rented by the day or by the hour. A 'day' is defined as up to eight hours with a total distance travelled of up to 100km. It costs about US$25 per day (or US$4 per hour) for a Russian-built vehicle, US$35 per day (US$5 per hour) for a small Japanese car, and from US$40 per day (US$6 per hour) for a larger, late model Japanese car. Air-conditioned cars often cost more to rent.

Renting a van is worth considering if your group is large, and can work out even cheaper than a car.

Renting cars from private individuals can sometimes be successful as some of these self-proclaimed guides with cars offer very low prices. However, they have no insurance and by law are not permitted to transport tourists. It's often better to rent from a reliable company. Foreigners with resident certificates can purchase a car.

Motorbike

Motorbike wrecks are the number one cause of death in Vietnam – for both Vietnamese and foreigners – so don't become a statistic. Safety is paramount, and trouble is real trouble in a Third World country like Vietnam. Anticipate gravel on the roads, bolting dogs across your path and sudden incoming traffic from all directions. Always drive with maximum defensiveness, and remember that there are no ambulances in Vietnam; if you crash, no matter how badly, understand that within minutes hordes of people will gather around you,

and, incredibly, do nothing. Check that your travel insurance policy doesn't exclude motorbike accidents.

To legally drive a motorbike over 50cc in Vietnam you need a sponsored visa (eg a business visa) and an address registered with the local police. If you satisfy these conditions you can apply for a Vietnamese driving licence. Unfortunately, applications take at least three weeks to process and there is no such thing as a short-stay licence for tourists.

The best option for tourists is to carry an international driving permit and the motorbike's registration card. Although the police do not officially recognise international driving permits, it's better than nothing when you are dealing with the police.

You will only run into problems with the police when there is an accident, or if you do something wrong like run a red light. In the latter case you can expect a fine of at least US$20 and your bike may have to spend the night in the pound. They will ALWAYS want to see the motorbike's registration documents – without them you won't get your bike back.

Motorbike Warning

Self-drive motorbiking is neither practical nor recommended in the inner city, and is hazardous in the suburbs and farther afield. Before embarking on a self-drive motorbike trip, read the Motorbike section in this chapter carefully.

If you are worried about your legal status as a motorbiker, it is worth noting that a strict reading of Vietnamese law states that any foreigner travelling by any mode of transport anywhere in Vietnam is the responsibility of the visa's sponsor (whether that be their office, company or the overseas Vietnamese embassy which issued the tourist visa). When travelling, the foreigner technically must do so with backup (guide, transport etc) from the sponsor.

Renting or Buying Renting a motorbike is now possible from a wide variety of sources – cafés, travel agencies, motorbike shops, hotels etc. If you don't want to drive yourself, you can hire a driver as your personal motorbike chauffeur and guide for around US$6 per day. Renting a 50cc moped is cheap at around US$7 per day, usually with unlimited mileage. Regular motorbikes start from about US$8, and there might be an additional distance charge.

A deposit or some other security may be required. New motorbikes cost about US$2000, so a sizeable deposit would be required. Some renters may prefer to hold your visa or passport until you return the bike. There have not been any huge problems with renters losing or refusing to return these items, though you are placing yourself in their hands. You should definitely sign some sort of agreement in a language you understand clearly stating what you are renting, how much it costs, the extent of compensation you must pay if the bike is stolen etc. Also check the condition of the bike. Rental businesses are usually equipped with a standard rental agreement.

Most cities have parking lots *(giu xe)* for bicycles and motorbikes – usually just a roped-off section of sidewalk – which charge US$0.20 to guard your vehicle (bike theft is a major problem). Don't lose your reclaim chit; without it, getting your wheels back may be a real hassle, especially if you come back after the workers have changed shifts.

Insurance Locals are required to have liability insurance on their motorbikes, but foreigners are not covered and there is currently no way to arrange this. If you want to insure yourself against injury, disfigurement or death, you'll need travel insurance with a foreign company (check that your policy doesn't exclude motorbike accidents!) – arrange this before you come to Vietnam. As for liability insurance, consider burning some incense at a local temple.

Registration Documents The bike's registration card is the most important piece of

documentation, so make sure you get the card when you buy or rent a bike. This laminated card gives the name of the original buyer, a description of the bike and number on the rear plate. It is the only documentation which confirms the bike is yours, not stolen. You'll need the card to get the bike back should it be impounded after an accident.

Driving Licence Any bike smaller than 50cc (technically a moped) needs no licence to drive. To legally ride any bike up to 175cc requires a Vietnamese A1 licence; anything over 175cc calls for a Vietnamese A2 licence. You can only get these licences if you a registered resident of Vietnam (eg you have a business visa). Vietnam is a signatory to the International Driving Convention, but the police generally do not recognise international driving permits. However, driving without a proper licence will only become an issue should you crash, and usually attracts a fine.

An international driving permit can be transferred into a Vietnamese licence so long as the you can obtain a stamp from the office/NGO/sponsor you are working for ie. if you have a work visa.

To do the test, go to 83A Ly Thuong Kiet in Hanoi and enter the office marked "Trung Tam Dao Va Ky Thuat Oto". It will cost you at least 600,000d. To transfer an overseas licence into a Vietnamese licence go to 310

In Hanoi motorbikes are like children – they look so peaceful when they're asleep.

Ba Trieu street, office #5, 2nd floor. It will cost you about US$20. In both cases the process will take at least three weeks. The police are aware that tourists on short-term visas do not have time to make Vietnamese versions of their licence and generally leave foreigners alone.

Safety Motorcycle touring in Vietnam is a serious venture. Needless to say, always wear a helmet (technically required by law), protective clothing and footwear, and be aware of the potential dangers on the road.

Security-wise, you'll find that your bike will be around you most of the time, so there is little need to worry about it being stolen. Bikes can be parked inside hotels overnight, although you may be charged a few thousand dong for the privilege. If you do leave the bike alone – say to stroll down to the river's edge for a swim – either pull the cap off the spark plug, or disconnect one of the essential wires under the tank.

Vietnamese motorists drive fast and recklessly, but at the same time appear totally relaxed. Whether riding in the city or along the Chinese border, remember that Vietnamese road rules and traffic patterns are like nothing you've ever seen before (unless of course you're coming from India). Driving on the opposite side of the road for many (Aussies, Brits, Kiwis, etc) creates a whole other challenge. Even if you're a veteran rider, spend a bit of time riding on the back of one before venturing out on your own; at least to get a feel for the logic (or lack thereof) of Vietnam's traffic patterns. If you are an inexperienced rider, do not just assume you'll acclimatise; consider hiring a driver.

Sound your horn whenever approaching people (pedestrians, cyclists or fellow motorbikers) or animals. Beware of bikes which are slowing down and look like they may be about to turn; turn signals are rarely used. Most bikes' rear-view mirrors are removed or turned around so that they don't get broken in the handlebar-to-handlebar traffic. This might make sense in Hanoi, but have the mirrors properly installed if you're going out on the highway. It's rather important to know when a big truck is bearing down on you from behind.

Be particularly aware of children on the road, as well as cattle and water buffalo (especially if a calf is on one side of the road and the mum is on the other). Don't get freaked out by chickens on the road; the best way to proceed is to keep a straight line, accelerate, and should you hit one do not stop unless you want to invite a heated and potentially overcostly negotiation with the owner. Pigs are smarter, and generally not a problem.

See the Motorbiking in Northern Vietnam appendix following the Excursions chapter for more on motorbiking.

Honda Om

The *Honda om* is a motorbike taxi on which you ride seated behind the driver. Don't expect to find one with a meter – negotiate the price beforehand. The fare is a fraction more than a cyclo for short trips and about the same as a cyclo for longer distances. Getting around this way is quite respectable as long as you don't have a lot of luggage.

You'll see plenty of Honda om drivers hanging around looking for customers. If you can't find one, though, just stand by the roadside and try to flag one down or ask a Vietnamese to find a Honda om for you.

TAXI

Hanoi boasts more taxi companies than any other city in Vietnam. All charge similar rates. Flagfall is US$1.10, which takes you 2km, and every kilometre thereafter costs between US$0.45 and US$0.60 depending on which company you choose. Companies include:

A Taxi	(☎ 832 7327)
City Taxi	(☎ 822 2222)
Duong Sat Taxi	(☎ 864 5645)
Five Star Taxi	(☎ 855 5555)
Fuji Cap	(☎ 825 5452)
Hanoi Taxi	(☎ 853 5252)
Red Taxi	(☎ 856 8686)
Taxi 25	(☎ 825 2525)
Taxi 52	(☎ 852 5252)
Taxi CP	(☎ 824 1999)

Taxi CP2	(☎ 826 2626)
Taxi PT	(☎ 856 5656)
Taxi Thu Do	(☎ 831 6316)
V Taxi	(☎ 821 5668)
Viet Phuong Taxi	(☎ 828 2828)

Taxis perpetually hang around the Vietnam Airlines booking office. These drivers of course intend to take you to the airport, but you could hire them to take you to other destinations.

CYCLO

The cyclo *(xich lo)*, or pedicab, is the best invention since sliced bread. The cyclo, short for the French *cyclo-pousse*, offers easy, cheap and aesthetic transportation around Hanoi. Riding these clever contraptions will also give you the moral superiority that comes with knowing you're being kind to the environment – much kinder than all those whining, smoke-spewing motorbikes.

Cyclo drivers typically hang out near major hotels and markets. To make sure the driver understands where you want to go, it's useful to bring a city map with you.

Cyclo drivers (all male) vary in age from around 15 to perhaps 60 years old. Many of

One of Hanoi's 6,000 cyclos. For about US$10 it's yours for the day.

the younger ones are transients from the countryside, coming to Hanoi to seek their fortune – some may even sleep in their cyclo.

Hanoi cyclos are wider than the Saigon variety, making it possible for two people to fit in one vehicle and share the fare. Have your money counted out and ready before getting on a cyclo. It also pays to have the exact money – drivers may claim they cannot change a 20,000d note.

Rapacious cyclo drivers often bump up their rates to several times the Vietnamese price, but you should be able to get to most places around the city centre for about US$1.

Cyclos are cheaper by time rather than distance. US$0.80 is standard for a short trip in town, or about US$1 per hour. You can also hire a cyclo for a full day for around US$10. Bargaining is almost always necessary. Settle on a fare *before* going anywhere or you're likely to be asked for some outrageous quantity of dong at the trip's end. Misunderstandings over fares are sometimes sincere, though, not always attempts to cheat you. It may sometimes help to write things down. It is always best to be pleasant in negotiating the fare – getting hot-headed rarely helps.

BICYCLE

Perhaps the best way to get around Hanoi is by bicycle. Many hotels and café/travel agents rent bikes for about US$1 per day.

During rush hours, streets approach gridlock as rushing streams of cyclists and motor traffic force their way through intersections without the benefit of traffic lights. Riders frequently crash into each other and get knocked down, but they are rarely going fast enough to be injured. Although you will often see two Vietnamese riding on a single bike, this is generally *not* a good idea.

Bicycles are utility vehicles in Vietnam. To see a bike carrying three pigs or 300kg of vegetables is not unusual. One has to marvel at how people manage to load all these items on the bike and ride it without the whole thing tipping over.

GETTING AROUND

Using parking sites in the city (for a small fee of about US$0.04) gives you the security of knowing your bike will be there when you return. See the Motorbike section earlier for more details.

Mountain bikes and 10-speed bikes can be bought at a few speciality shops in Hanoi, but you're probably better off bringing your own if you plan to travel long distance by pedal-power. Mountain bikes are definitely preferred – big potholes or unsealed roads can be rough on a set of delicate rims.

Basic cycling safety equipment is hardly available in Vietnam, so bring along all the equipment, spare parts and tools you might need. A bell is required equipment – the louder the better.

The innumerable roadside bicycle repair stands in every city and town in Vietnam usually consist of no more than a pump and a few bolts and wrenches.

If you want to purchase your own set of wheels, Pho Ba Trieu and Pho Hué are the best places to look for bicycle shops. Many travellers buy a cheap bicycle and, at the end, either sell it or give it away. Locally produced bicycles are available but are of truly inferior quality. A fairly decent, one-speed, Chinese-made bicycle costs about US$60 to US$80. Taiwanese and Japanese-made mountain bikes average from US$150 to US$400.

WALKING

Exploring Hanoi on foot is an excellent way to see many of the sites in the city centre.

If you don't want to wind up like a bug on a windshield, you need to pay attention to a few pedestrian survival rules. Foreigners frequently make the mistake of thinking that the best way to cross a busy Vietnamese street is to run quickly across it. Sometimes this works and sometimes it can get you creamed. Most locals cross the street slowly – very slowly – giving motorbike drivers sufficient time to judge their position so they can pass to either side of you. They will *not* stop or even slow down, but they *will* try to avoid hitting you. Just don't make any sudden moves. Good luck.

ORGANISED TOURS

If you decide to rent a car with driver and guide, you'll have the opportunity to design your own itinerary for what amounts to a private tour for you and your companions.

The cost varies considerably. At the high end, a tour booked with travel agencies is about US$60 a day for one person (cheaper for two or more people). Backpacker cafés often charge around half this price.

When you settle on your itinerary, get a written copy from the travel agency. If you later find that your guide feels like deviating from what you paid for, that piece of paper is your most effective leverage.

A good guide can be your translator and travelling companion and can save you as much money as they are costing you. A bad guide can ruin your trip. If possible, meet your guide before starting out and make sure that this is someone you can travel with. Agree on the price before beginning the journey; for a private guide, US$5 to US$15 per day is a typical range and it's proper to throw in a bonus at the end of your trip if your guide proved helpful.

With private guides, ask whether you will be responsible for their travel expenses. If you can gather up a small group of travellers, you can share the cost of hiring a guide. If you are travelling solo, your guide may be able to drive you around on a motorbike, but you should pay for the petrol and parking fees.

Travel Agencies

There are plenty of travel agencies in Hanoi, both government and privately owned, which can organise tours, cars, air tickets and visa extensions. Many hotels also peddle tours, though most are farmed out to the agencies listed below. Many of these agencies are selling exactly the same tour (same bus, same boat etc) at vastly different prices, so you will save money, and have a better tour experience, if you shop around. Best of all, talk to other travellers who have just arrived back from a tour.

Consider the following places (all on map 5 unless otherwise stated):

Budget Agencies

A to Z Queen Café (☎ 826 0860, fax 826 0300, queenaz@fpt.vn) 65 Pho Hang Bac

Green Bamboo (☎ 826 8752) 42 Pho Nha Chung

Kim Café (☎ 826 6901) 135 Pho Hang Bac

Lotus Café (☎ 826 8642) 42V Pho Ly Thuong Kiet

Love Planet (☎ 828 4864, fax 828 0913, loveplanet @hn.vnn.vn) 25 Pho Hang Bac

Meeting Café (☎ 825 8812) 59B Pho Ba Trieu

Orient Café (☎ 824 7390) 53 Pho Tran Hung Dao

Real Darling Café (☎ 826 9386, fax 825 6562) 33 Pho Hang Quat

Sinh Café (☎ 828 7552, fax 822 6055) 18 Pho Luong Van Can
  (☎ 934 0535) 56 Pho Hang Be
  (☎ 926 0038) 52 Pho Hang Bac

TF Handspan (☎ 828 1996, fax 926 0270, tfhandspn@hn.vnn.vn) 116 Pho Hang Bac

Mid-Range & Top-End Agencies

Ann's Tourist (☎ 822 0018, fax 832 3866, anntours @yahoo.com) 26 Pho Yet Kieu

Best Service Travel (☎ 826 2386, fax 826 9285) 72 Pho Ba Trieu

Buffalo Tours (☎ 828 0702, fax 826 9370, buffalo @netnam.org.vn) 11 Pho Hang Muoi

ECCO Voyages (☎ 825 4615, fax 826 6519) 50A Pho Ba Trieu

Ecomtour (☎ 825 4935) 15 Pho Trang Thi

Especen (☎ 826 6856, fax 826 9612) 79E Pho Hang Trong

Exotissimo Travel (☎ 828 2150, 828 2146) 26 Pho Tran Nhat Duat

Hanoi Toserco (☎ 978 0004, fax 822 6055) Map 4; 8 Pho To Hien Thanh

Hanoi Tourism (☎ 826 6714, fax 825 4209) 18 Pho Ly Thuong Kiet

Red River Tours (☎ 826 8427/923 0396, fax 828 7159, redrivertours@netnam.org.vn) 73 Pho Hang Bo

Vietnam Tourism (☎ 826 4154, fax 825 7583) 30A Pho Ly Thuong Kiet

Things to See & Do

HIGHLIGHTS

Exploring the ancient '36 streets' of the bustling Old Quarter, both by day and night, is a top priority for a Hanoi visit. Architecture buffs will also enjoy strolling through the embassies area near Ba Dinh Square. In the same area the Ho Chi Minh Mausoleum and Museum, as well as the One Pillar Pagoda, are highly popular spots, as are the city's myriad parks and lakes.

Hanoi boasts countless temples and pagodas, including the spectacular Temple of Literature, Vietnam's first university, and Tran Quoc Pagoda near West Lake (Ho Tay).

Days could be spent in Hanoi's intriguing museums. Particularly notable are the Fine Arts Museum, History Museum and Museum of Ethnology, which depicts the life of Vietnam's 54 different ethnic groups. (In addition to the requisite two hour lunch break, and the fact that you should always arrive *at least* 30 minutes before closing time, it's worth noting that most of Hanoi's museums are closed on Monday.)

Hanoi has developed into a top-notch shopping city, and offers a wide range of handicrafts and fine art to take home. Finally, sample both the local and international culinary delights, cafés and nightlife of modern Hanoi. You also won't want to miss a performance of the city's famed water puppets.

This chapter groups Hanoi's sights by district and it is advisable to similarly plan your sightseeing by district. A bare minimum of one full day is necessary to see the main sights in the central Hoan Kiem district. Ditto for the Ba Dinh district (including a visit to the Temple of Literature).

Many of Hanoi's major sights are within walking or cycling distance of the city centre; some visitors opt to hire a cyclo for a full day to explore them.

WALKING TOURS

Both TF Handspan and the A to Z Queen Café (see the Travel Agencies listing in the Getting Around chapter) run walking tours of the Old Quarter. For an intriguing self-guided walking tour, see Hanoi's Old Quarter and Walking Tour special section.

HOAN KIEM DISTRICT (MAP 5)
Hoan Kiem Lake

Hoan Kiem Lake is an enchanting body of water right in the heart of downtown Hanoi. Every morning, around dawn, local residents can be seen doing their traditional morning exercises, jogging and playing badminton around this lake.

The forlorn **Turtle Tower** (Thap Rua) or **Tortoise Pagoda**, topped with a red star and situated on an islet in the middle of the lake, is often used as an emblem of Hanoi. Barring a swim, there is no access to this pagoda.

The **Hoa Phong Tower**, on the east bank of the lake, is across from the main post office.

Pagoda or Temple?

Travelling around Hanoi, one continually encounters the terms 'pagoda' and 'temple'. The Vietnamese use these terms somewhat differently from the Chinese and, as a result, there is a bit of confusion (particularly if you've just come from China).

To the Chinese, a pagoda *(bata)* is usually a tall eight-sided tower built to house the ashes of the deceased. A Chinese temple *(miao* or *si)* is an active place of worship.

The Vietnamese regard a pagoda *(chua)* as a place of worship (primarily Buddhist), and it's by no means certain that you'll find a tower to store the ashes of the dearly departed. A Vietnamese temple *(den)* is not really a place of worship, but rather a communal house (tied more closely to Confucianism or Taoism) built to honour some great local or national historical figure (Confucius, Tran Hung Dao or even Ho Chi Minh).

This four-sided tower once marked the entrance to the enormous 19th century Bao An Pagoda, a vast complex of buildings which used to occupy the site of the post office. Inspired by Indian stupa architecture, the tower is all that remains today.

Near the western bank of the lake is the modest **Le Thai To Temple** dedicated to Emperor Le Loi, founder of the Later Le Dynasty in the 15th century. There is a statue here in his likeness.

Ngoc Son Temple

Ngoc Son (Jade Mountain) Temple, founded in the 18th century, is on an island in the northern part of Hoan Kiem Lake. Surrounded by water and shaded by trees, it is a delightfully quiet place to rest. The temple is dedicated to the scholar Van Xuong, General Tran Hung Dao (who defeated the Mongols in the 13th century) and La To, patron saint of physicians.

Ngoc Son Temple is reached via the red painted, wooden The Huc (Rising Sun) Bridge, which was constructed in 1885. To the left of the gate stands an obelisk whose top is shaped like a paintbrush. The temple is open daily from 7.30 am to 6 pm and the entrance fee is US$0.90.

Indira Gandhi Park

In the late 19th century the pagoda compound which blessed this rectangular expanse was razed by the French to make room for the colonial Governor's Headquarters and garden. Following the death of Minister General Paul Bert in 1886, his cronies named the garden after him, and installed a statue in his likeness.

Following the August Revolution in 1945, Vietnamese nationalists removed the white guy icon, renaming the garden Chi Linh Park (after the high country region where King Le Loi led the uprisings which drove Chinese imperialists from Vietnamese territory in the 15th century).

The park was again renamed in 1984, this time to honour India's first female prime minister, Indira Gandhi, in the year of her assasination. Indira Gandhi was a longtime supporter of Vietnam. Today it is a pleasant place to read or enjoy a picnic (or perhaps escape the postcard sellers around Hoan Kiem Lake). There is a Chinese-style gazebo in the centre of the park, where traditional music and theatre is occasionally performed.

The park is on the west side of Hoan Kiem Lake, just north of the GPO.

The Tortoise Pagoda on Hoan Kiem Lake with Hanoi Post Office in the background and Hoa Phong Tower hidden by the trees.

THINGS TO SEE & DO

Cua O Quan Chuong (Old East Gate)

Near the bank of the Red River (Song Hong), on Pho Hang Chieu in the Old Quarter, stands the impressive 1749 Cua O Quan Chuong, also known as the 'Passage of the Regiment Commander'. It is the sole remaining from a legion of approaches into the original Hanoi Citadel. The brick structure underwent repairs in the early 19th century, though the original watchtower still sits atop the relic. The formal name of the gate, *Dong Ha Mon*, is engraved over the entryway in Chinese.

Bach Ma Temple

Bach Ma Temple, or 'White Horse Temple', is located at 40 Pho Hang Buom in the Old Quarter. This impressive Chinese-style temple dates from the 9th century, and is steeped in myth and lore. Legend has it that in the 11th century King Ly used the pagoda to pray for assistance in building the city walls, which persistently collapsed no matter how many times he rebuilt them. His prayers were finally answered when a white horse appeared out of the temple and, by leaving a trail of footprints, guided him to where he could safely build his walls.

As you approach the temple, with its red funeral palanquin, look for its white-bearded temple guards, who spend their days sipping tea.

Memorial House at 48 Pho Hang Ngang

The Memorial House at 48 Pho Hang Ngang (☎ 825 2622) is north of Hoan Kiem Lake in the Old Quarter. This is where Ho Chi Minh drafted Vietnam's Declaration of Independence in 1945. It has been preserved as a museum, and is well worth stopping in for a look.

Opening hours are Monday to Saturday from 8 to 11.30 am and 2 to 4.30 pm. Entry is free.

Hanoi Opera House

The magnificent 700 seat Hanoi Opera House (☎ 825 4312), a short walk from Hoan Kiem Lake, faces east up Pho Trang Tien. It was built by the French in 1911 – modelled on Paris' Palais Garnier – and with the aid of the French government recently saw the completion of a painstaking three year renovation. It was from a balcony of this building that a Viet Minh-run committee of citizens announced that it had taken over the city on 16 August 1945.

Periodically, performances are held here in the evenings. In late 1998 the conductorless Orpheus Chamber Orchestra became the first American philharmonic to perform in Vietnam since the end of war in 1975.

The theatre's Vietnamese name, *Nha Hat Lon*, appropriately translates to 'House Sing Big'.

History Museum

The History Museum (Bao Tang Lich Su), once the museum of the École Française d'Extrême Orient, is one block east of the Municipal Theatre at 1 Pho Pham Ngu Lao. It is housed in one of Hanoi's most impressive buildings, completed in 1930.

Exhibits include artefacts from Vietnam's turbulent history including some from prehistory (Palaeolithic and Neolithic periods); proto-Vietnamese civilisations (1st and 2nd millennia BC); the Dong Son culture (3rd century BC to 3rd century AD); the Oc-Eo (Funan) culture of the Mekong Delta (1st to 6th century AD); the Indianised kingdom of Champa (2nd to 15th century); the Khmer kingdoms; various Vietnamese dynasties and their resistance to Chinese attempts at domination; the struggle against the French; and the history of the Communist Party.

The museum is open Friday to Wednesday from 8.15 to 11.45 am and 1.30 to 5 pm; entry is US$0.80.

Revolutionary Museum

The Museum of the Vietnamese Revolution (Bao Tang Cach Mang), at 216 Pho Tran Quang Khai, creatively presents the history of the Vietnamese Revolution, and the country's struggle for independence from 1858 to 1975. Prior to 1911, this stately building served as the headquarters of the

Indochinese Taxation Department, and was converted into a museum in 1959.

The exhibits begin on the second storey with pre-1954 displays, mostly relating to the armed resistance against French colonial domination. The first storey takes visitors from 1954 to 1975, largely focusing on the conflict with America. Displays include a large number of period photographs, assorted weaponry and other artefacts.

Towards the end of the exhibition are two rooms chock-full of gifts presented over the years to both Ho Chi Minh and the Communist Party of Vietnam. These include a cigarette case from a Japanese woman (1959), a zebra pelt from the Peoples' Movement for the Liberation of Angola (1982), and Ho Chi Minh's Doctorate of Law degree and graduation robe from the University of Rangoon in Myanmar (Burma).

The museum is open Tuesday to Friday from 8 to 11.30 am and 1 to 4 pm, and Saturday mornings from 8 to 11.30 am. Admission costs US$0.80. It is close to the History Museum.

Geological Museum
The Geological Museum (Bao Tang Dia Chat) at 6 Pho Pham Ngu Lao details the whole story behind the geologic processes that created such breathtaking spots as Halong Bay; however, most of the explanations are in Vietnamese. It's technically open from 8 am to noon and 1.30 to 4.30 from Monday to Saturday, but don't be surprised to find the doors shut. Entry is free.

Border Guard Museum
The Border Guard Museum (Bao Tang Bien Phong) at 2 Pho Tran Hung Dao, dedicated to those friendly boys in uniform you encountered at the airport or border crossing, is of limited interest to most travellers. It is supposed to be open from 8 to 11 am Monday to Saturday, but is often closed. Entry is free.

St Joseph's Cathedral
Stepping inside the massive neo-Gothic St Joseph's Cathedral (inaugurated in 1886) is like being instantly transported to medieval Europe. The cathedral is noteworthy for its square towers, elaborate altar and stained-glass windows.

The awe-inspiring building faces up Pho Nha Tho (or Church Street), the sole remaining stretch of the 400km road which led to the 14th century Bao Thien Pagoda. St Joseph's Cathedral, a scaled down version of Paris' famed Notre Dame, was constructed upon the original foundation stones of the ancient pagoda's tower.

The main gate to St Joseph's Cathedral is open daily from 5 to 7 am and 5 to 7 pm, when Masses are held. Guests are welcome at other times of the day, but must enter the cathedral via the compound of the Diocese of Hanoi, the entrance to which is a block away at 40 Pho Nha Chung. After walking through the gate, go straight and then turn right. When you reach the side door to the cathedral, ring the small bell high up to the right-hand side of the door to call the priest to let you in.

Maison Centrale
This provocative site (☎ 934 2253, 1 Pho Hoa Lo) near the corner of Pho Hai Ba Trung is all that remains of the former Hoa Lo Prison, affectionately referred to as the 'Hanoi Hilton' by US POWs during the American War (one of whom, Pete Peterson, became the first US Ambassador to Vietnam following the re-establishment of diplomatic ties between USA and Vietnam in 1995).

The vast prison complex itself was built by the French in 1896. Originally intended to house around 450 inmates, records indicate that by the 1930s there were close to 2000 prisoners incarcerated here. The prison was recently razed to the ground to make room for a modern skyscraper, though the building at the front of the site has been thoughtfully preserved and restored as a museum.

The bulk of the exhibits relate to the prison's use up to the mid-1950s, focusing on the Vietnamese struggle for independence from France. Some notable objects on display in the dark chambers include an ominous guillotine and other tools of torture. You may be able to find an English-speaking guide on site. It's open from 8 to 11 am and 1 to 4 pm; entry is US$0.80.

Vietnamese Women's Museum

Opened to the public on Women's Day, 20 October 1995, the excellent Vietnamese Women's Museum (Bao Tang Phu Nu Viet Nam, ☎ 825 9937) is located at 36 Pho Ly Thuong Kiet, about 1km south of Hoan Kiem Lake. It gets good reviews from travellers. There's the inevitable adoration of women soldiers, but, fortunately, there's plenty on social equality, development and peace.

The collection is divided into four themes: Vietnam's mothers; female historical figures; women's unions; and the various ethnic groups in Vietnam. There are thoughtful recreations of a typical rural kitchen, an underground meeting room, and plenty of photographs. All of the exhibits have informative English and French explanations.

On central display in the 1st floor foyer is a larger-than-life statue of a mother and her baby, covered head-to-toe in gold leaf. Upstairs are three more floors of historical exhibits, including tributes to heroines like the triumphant Trung sisters (Hai Ba Trung), beloved martyr Vo Thi Sau, and the mother of all Vietnamese mothers, Au Co. Other exhibits focus on more contemporary figures and issues.

On the 4th floor you can see different costumes worn by the 54 minority groups in Vietnam. If this display whets your appetite, consider visiting the superb Museum of Ethnology (described later in this chapter).

The Women's Museum is open daily from 8 am to 4 pm (a no-lunch-break anomaly among Hanoi's museums). Entry costs US$0.80 and all bags should be checked in at the ticket office. A guided tour is included in the ticket price and well worth taking advantage of. Inquire inside the main building.

Ambassadors' Pagoda

The Ambassadors' Pagoda (Quan Su, ☎ 825 2427) at 73 Pho Quan Su is the official centre of Buddhism in Hanoi, attracting quite a crowd – mostly old women – on holidays. During the 17th century, there was a guest-house here for the ambassadors of Buddhist countries. Today there are about a dozen monks and nuns. Next to the pagoda is a store selling Buddhist ritual objects.

The Ambassadors' Pagoda is open to the public daily from 7.30 to 11.30 am and 1.30 to 5.30 pm.

Memorial House at 5D Ham Long

This modest little one storey house (☎ 826 3982) was chosen in 1928 as the secret headquarters of the Revolutionary Youth Association, considered to be the predecessor of Vietnam's Communist Party. It became a gathering place for radical reformers, who in March 1929 resolved to form a communist clique that quickly spread to other parts of Vietnam. There is a small plaque on the building's façade marking the event.

In 1959 the forlorn building underwent repairs to recreate its original humble decor, and it was dedicated as a public museum. The house can be visited from Monday to Saturday from 8 to 11.30 am and 2 to 4.30 pm. Entry is free.

Nearby, at the corner of Pho Ham Long and Pho Ngo Thi Nham is the **Ham Long Catholic Church**. A daily sermon and Mass are held at 5.30 am, and 7 pm on Saturday and Sunday.

HAI BA TRUNG DISTRICT (MAP 4)
Hai Ba Trung Temple

The Hai Ba Trung Temple, founded in 1142, is 2km south of Hoan Kiem Lake on Pho Tho Lao. A statue here shows the two Trung sisters (1st century AD) donning hibiscus hats and kneeling with their arms raised, as if to address a crowd. Some people say the statue shows the sisters, who had been proclaimed queens of the Vietnamese, about to dive into a river. They are said to have drowned themselves rather than surrender following their defeat at the hands of the Chinese.

Lenin Park

At over 50 hectares, Lenin Park is one of Hanoi's largest parks. It's a pleasant place to join the hundreds of Hanoians for early morning callisthenics or a run. There is a small amusement park with rides.

Every year, following the Tet Lunar New Year holiday, a large spring flower festival is held in the park.

Boats can be hired to potter around **Bay Mau Lake**, which prior to 1958 served as a garbage dump. Over a two year period the city effectively mobilised the citizens of Hanoi to voluntarily transform the rubbish heap into 'Unity Park'. In 1980 the area was renamed Lenin Park in commemoration of the 110th anniversary of Lenin's birth.

The main entry gates to the park are on Đ Le Duan and Pho Tran Nhan Tong (near the Central Circus).

Just north of Lenin Park lies **Thien Quang Lake**, with several pagodas near the west bank.

Lien Phai Pagoda

The Lien Phai Pagoda (1726), on Pho Bach Mai, is notable for an assemblage of nine ancient towers in the rear of the complex. The most significant is the Cuu Sinh ('life-saving') Tower, said to contain the remains of Trinh Thap (1696-1733), a prince of the Trinh nobility. After unearthing a stone in the shape of a lotus flower one day, he converted his palace into a Buddhist pagoda and served as the endowing monk until his death at the age of 37.

DONG DA DISTRICT
Dong Da Mound (Map 2)

The Dong Da Mound was the site of the decisive battle (during the Ky Dau Tet Festival in 1789) in which Emperor Quang Trung defeated a 200,000 strong Chinese invasion force near Thang Long (Hanoi).

According to historical accounts, the corpses of the dead intruders were piled high into a dozen giant heaps and covered with layers of dirt. Of these large artificial hillocks just one remains today, with a grove of banyan trees and a stone carving at the summit.

Quang Trung (Nguyen Hue) was one of the three brothers who led the Tay Son rebellion. His plans to forge north and invade China were cut short by an untimely death in 1792 at the age of 39. There is an enormous statue of him at the rear of the mound. At the time of writing, a museum dedicated to Quang Trung was being built there. The front wall of the building features stone relief work portraying scenes of Quang Trung's triumphant campaign against the Chinese. Every year, following Tet, a festival on the mound commemorates the Dong Da victory.

Stone relief on the wall of the Quang Trung Museum at Dong Da Mound, depicting Emperor Quang Trung's victory over Chinese invaders in 1789.

The Dong Da Mound is a few kilometres south-west of the Temple of Literature, near the intersection of Đ Nguyen Luong Bang and Pho Dang Tien Dong.

Temple of Literature (Map 3)

The Temple of Literature (Van Mieu) is 2km west of Hoan Kiem Lake and is a pleasant retreat from the streets of Hanoi. The temple constitutes a rare example of well-preserved traditional Vietnamese architecture and is a highlight of the city's sites (see Van Mieu special section for a history and walk-through).

It is open daily from 7.30 am to 6 pm (8 am to 5 pm from November to March). The entrance fee is US$1. English, French and Chinese-speaking tour guides can be hired for US$1.50 per group (not including tip).

Performances of traditional music and dance are put on near the main sanctuary from 8.30 am to noon, and 1.30 to 4.30 pm. There is no charge, but tips are appreciated.

THANH XUAN DISTRICT (MAP 4)
Air Force Museum

Seldom visited by foreigners, the Air Force Museum (Bao Tang Khong Quan) on Đ Truong Chinh makes a worthwhile stop for many. Many of its exhibits are outdoors including a number of Soviet-built MiG fighters, reconnaissance planes, helicopters and anti-aircraft equipment. There is also an impressive bonsai garden where shrubbery and large ceramic pots are sold.

Inside the drab museum hall are other weapons, including mortars, machine guns and some US-made bombs (hopefully defused). The highlight here is a partially truncated MiG with a stepladder – you are permitted to climb up into the cockpit, fiddle around with the Russian-labelled control panels and joystick, and even have your photo taken.

Another interesting display is the landing hold of the 37 Link Spacecraft, which carried famed Vietnamese astronaut Pham Tuan and his Russian counterpart Gorbatco in the summer of 1980. Except for being Day-Glo orange, it looks remarkably like a oversized tank of *bia hoi* (draught beer). Incidentally, Tuan was an air force fighter pilot and is remembered for his bravery in shooting down the first American War B-52 bomber, Super Flying Fortress (mislabelled 'Supper Flying Fortress'), over Hoa Binh 1972. The MiG 21-F96 he flew is the first exhibit inside the museum gate. According to the placard, 'All the US crew was fired'.

Other war memorabilia on display includes war-era photographs, paintings of obvious Soviet design, and portraits of Ho Chi Minh, as well as the red velvet chair of the MI4 helicopter (which rests just outside in the yard) in which Uncle Ho made frequent 'business journeys'.

The Air Force Museum is in the far south-west of the city. It's almost 5km from the train station, near the terminus of Pho Ton That Tung; it's a rather long cyclo ride, so you might consider getting there by bicycle or motorbike. The museum is open daily from 8 to 11 am and 1 to 5 pm. Admission costs US$0.40, plus another US$0.40 to take photos inside.

BA DINH DISTRICT
Fine Arts Museum (Map 3)

The building housing the Fine Arts Museum (Bao Tang My Thuat), at 66 Pho Nguyen Thai Hoc (on the corner with Pho Cao Ba Quai), was built in 1937 as *Famille de Jeanne d'Arc*, a Catholic residence house for the daughters of French colonialists and later served as the Indochinese Ministry of Information.

It was turned in a museum in 1962 after undergoing extensive restoration (including adding an Asian flair to the otherwise purely French façade). Today, the building houses a superb collection of both traditional and contemporary Vietnamese fine arts.

The 1st floor features several large Buddhist statues, including an impressive Bodhisattva with 1000 eyes and arms. There are also excellent examples of 9th to 12th century stone sculpture unearthed in and around the capital. One room is dedicated to the Bronze Age, and has displays of ancient drums, jars and tools.

MASON FLORENCE

MASON FLORENCE

Tran Quoc Pagoda

MASON FLORENCE

Buddhist temple gate

Gate to Ngoc Son Temple, Hoan Kiem Lake

MASON FLORENCE

Tran Quoc Pagoda stands on Ca Vang (Goldfish) Islet near the south-eastern shore of Ho Tay (West Lake).

Le Thai To Temple

Coffin fragments in a wall in Phu Lang Village

Chua Mot Cot (The One Pillar Pagoda)

The 6th century Chua Tran Quoc is the oldest pagoda in Vietnam.

MASON FLORENCE

St Joseph's Cathedral, built in 1886, is one of the oldest buildings in the French Quarter.

BETHUNE CARMICHAEL

The Hanoi Opera House

BETHUNE CARMICHAEL

Cau Long Bien was originally called Doumer Bridge.

BETHUNE CARMICHAEL

Plaque on the much bombed Long Bien Bridge.

Architectural relief with tree motif

The Old Jail

Simple architectural relief

Mosaic celebrating women in Vietnamese industry.

The Dong Xuan Market

On the 2nd floor are traditional folk paintings, as well as wood sculptures produced by both ethnic Vietnamese and minority groups. Other paintings are of the nationalist propaganda genre, and there is also an eerie sequence depicting the 10 Courts of the Kings of Hell.

The top floor of the museum features a large gallery of contemporary paintings, many by famous Vietnamese artists like Nguyen Tu Nghiem, Bui Xuan Phai and Nguyen Sang, and some patriotic bronze sculpture.

Adjacent to the main building is the new wing, built in the 1970s, which houses a worthy collection of ultramodern painting and sculpture. There is also a gift shop in this building selling paintings and some reproduction antiques (be sure to ask for a certificate which will clear any 'new antiques' through customs when you leave Vietnam).

The Fine Arts Museum is across the street from the north end of the Temple of Literature. It is open Tuesday to Sunday from 8 am until noon and 1 to 4 pm. Entry costs US$0.80.

Elephant guarding the Fine Arts Museum.

Hanoi Citadel (Map 3)

Just to the west of the Old Quarter is the Hanoi Citadel, constructed by Emperor Gia Long in 1805 on the site of the old Thang Long Citadel. The original square fortress covered a far larger area than the walls today and featured five main entry gates.

The Citadel is now a military base and also the residence of high-ranking officers and their families – in other words, closed to the public. There is no longer much to see because it was largely destroyed by French troops in 1894 – US bombing took care of the rest. Other than the walls surrounding the central section and the Flag Tower (see the Army Museum entry following), all that can be seen today is the **Cua Bac Mon** (North Gate) on Pho Phan Dinh Phung. Cannonball holes still remain here from the French siege of the citadel in April 1882.

Across from the gate, on the corner of Pho Phan Dinh Phung and Pho Nguyen Bieu, is the Gothic (yet Vietnamese accented) **Cua Bac Catholic Church**. Sermons and Mass are held here on Sunday at 6.30 am.

Army Museum (Map 3)

The Army Museum (Bao Tang Quan Doi, ☎ 823 4264) is on 28A Pho Dien Bien Phu. Outside, Soviet and Chinese weaponry supplied to the North are displayed alongside French and US-made weapons captured in the Franco-Viet Minh and American wars.

The centrepiece is a Soviet-built MiG-21 jet fighter, triumphant amid the wreckage of French aircraft downed at Dien Bien Phu, and a US F-111. Displays include scale models of various epic battles from the long military history of Vietnam, including Dien Bien Phu and the capture of Saigon.

The museum is open Tuesday through Sunday from 8 to 11.30 am and 1.30 to 4.30 pm; entry costs US$0.80. There is a camera fee of US$0.16, or US$0.80 for video.

On the grounds of the museum is the hexagonal **Hanoi Flag Tower**, constructed

The hexagonal Cot Co Flag Tower, in the grounds of the Army Museum, is one of the symbols of Hanoi. The museum itself has fascinating displays covering the decades from 1930 onwards.

between 1805 and 1812 (during the Nguyen Dynasty). Over 33m tall (counting all three tiers), the tower is considered one of the symbols of Hanoi. It is also a rare example of 19th century architecture which was *not* razed by French administration (1894-97). It is well worth the climb up into the steeple, offering one of the best bird's-eye views of the city.

Chi Lang Park & Lenin Statue (Map 3)

This small triangular park, just across the street from the Army Museum, was originally a large swimming hole called Elephant Lake where soldiers from the nearby Hanoi Citadel would bathe. When the French destroyed the fortress in the late 19th century, the lake was filled in and turned into a park. Today it features palm trees and a 5m-high statue of Lenin dating from 1985.

Ho Chi Minh's Mausoleum (Map 3)

In the tradition of Lenin and Stalin before him and Mao after him, the final resting place of Ho Chi Minh is a glass sarcophagus set deep in the bowels of a monumental ed-

ifice that has become a site of pilgrimage. Ho Chi Minh's Mausoleum – built despite the fact that his will requests he be cremated – was constructed between 1973 and 1975 of native materials gathered from all over Vietnam; the roof and peristyle are said to evoke either a traditional communal house or a lotus flower – to many tourists it looks like a cold concrete cubicle with columns. While reviewing parades and ceremonies take place on the grassy expanses of Ba Dinh Square (partitioned into 79 pieces to represent the age at which 'Uncle Ho' died), high-ranking party and government leaders stand in front of the mausoleum.

Ho Chi Minh's Mausoleum is open from 8 to 11 am Tuesday to Thursday and weekends, and entry is free. The mausoleum is closed for three months a year (usually from 5 September to early December) while Ho Chi Minh's embalmed corpse goes to Russia for maintenance. Unlike the Vietnamese, foreigners do not have to queue but can go directly to the registration desk at 5 Pho Ngoc Ha.

Photography is permitted outside the building but not inside. All visitors must register and leave their bags and cameras at a reception hall in the block next to Pho Chua Mot Cot; if possible, bring along your passport for identification. Warning: despite what the clerk may say, you do *not* have to pay anything for this service. Soundtracks for a 20 minute video about Ho Chi Minh are available in Vietnamese, French, English, Khmer, Lao, Russian and Spanish.

Honour guards will accompany you as you march in single file from the reception area to the mausoleum entrance. Inside the building, more guards in snowy-white bleached military uniforms are posted at intervals of five paces, giving an eerily authoritarian aspect to the macabre spectacle of the embalmed, helpless body with its wispy white hair. The whole place has a very spooky 'sanitised for your protection' atmosphere.

The following rules are strictly applied to all visitors to the mausoleum:

- People wearing shorts, tank tops etc will not be admitted.
- Nothing (including day-packs and cameras) may be taken into the mausoleum.
- A respectful demeanour must be maintained at all times.

- For obvious reasons of decorum, photography is absolutely prohibited inside the mausoleum.
- It is forbidden to put your hands in your pockets.
- Hats must be taken off inside the mausoleum building.
- Although the rules do not explicitly say so, it is suggested that you don't ask the guards 'Is he dead?'.

Many of the visitors are elderly VC comrades who make the pilgrimage decked out in uniform to pay a tearful respect to Uncle Ho. The mausoleum also attracts groups of students and it's interesting too to watch their reactions to seeing Ho. Though the Vietnamese as a whole are mostly disappointed with communism, most show deep respect and admiration for the man; few show any hostility or bitterness towards Ho himself. He is seen as the liberator of the Vietnamese people from colonialism, and Vietnam's subsequent economic and political mismanagement are viewed as the misdoings of Ho's comrades and successors. Of course, this view is reinforced by the educational system which only emphasises Ho's deeds and accomplishments.

If you're lucky, you'll catch the 'Changing of the Guard' outside the mausoleum – the pomp and ceremony displayed here rivals the British equivalent at Buckingham Palace.

Ho Chi Minh's Stilt House (Map 3)

Behind Ho Chi Minh's Mausoleum is a stilt house (Nha San Bac Ho) where Ho lived on and off from 1958 to 1969. The house is built in the style of Vietnam's ethnic minorities, and has been preserved just as Ho left it. It's set in a well tended garden next to the carp-filled **Peace Pond**. Just how much time Ho actually spent here is questionable – the house would have made a tempting target for US bombers had it been suspected that Ho could be found here (although there is a 10m-square underground bomb shelter, closed to visitors, beside the stilt house).

There is a US$0.25 entry. Free guides are available at the ticket office, which is on the narrow side street on the north side of the

MASON FLORENCE

Ho Chi Minh's Mausoleum

mausoleum; tips (around US$1 per person) are appreciated.

Between the entrance and the stilt house, stop for a look at the one storey **54 House**; Ho's modest bedroom (complete with a white chair he received as a gift from Fidel Castro), dining room, and study can be viewed through glass from outside. Close by in the garage are two antique cars (one French and one Russian) Uncle Ho used to ride in.

The lime-green building (with 60cm-thick concrete walls) at the back of the stilt house was where Ho died on 2 September 1969.

Just inside the entry gate to Ho's stilt house is the **Presidential Palace**, a beautifully restored colonial building designed by two German architects and constructed between 1900 and 1906 as the palace of the governor general of Indochina. Until 1945 it was the office and living quarters for 23 successive Indochinese governor generals. From 1945 to 1954 it housed the French High Commissioner and from 1954 to 1969 it was the office of Ho Chi Minh. Currently it serves as the offices of the president, and is used for official receptions.

The 200m-long, 5m-wide 'mango alley' leading from the back of the Presidential Palace to the stilt house is said to have been a favourite strolling place of Ho Chi Minh. At the end of the path, on the edge of the Peace Pond, is a South American pine tree whose roots rise up from the ground like small Buddhist statues.

Ho Chi Minh Museum (Map 3)

The Ho Chi Minh Museum (Bao Tang Ho Chi Minh), in the huge cement structure next to Ho Chi Minh's Mausoleum, is divided into two sections, 'Past' and 'Future'. You start in the past and move to the future by walking in a clockwise direction downwards through the museum, starting at the right-hand side of the top of the stairs. The displays are very modern and all have a message (eg peace, happiness, freedom).

It's probably worth taking an English-speaking guide since some of the symbolism is hard to figure out (did Ho Chi Minh have a cubist period?). The 1958 Ford Edsel bursting through the wall (a US commercial failure to symbolise their military failure) is a knockout.

Photography is forbidden, and all bags and cameras must be left at reception upon entry. The museum is open daily from 8 to 11 am and 1.30 to 4.30 pm.

One Pillar Pagoda (Map 3)

Hanoi's famous One Pillar Pagoda (Chua Mot Cot), on Pho Ong Ich Kiem near Ho Chi Minh's Mausoleum, was built by the Emperor Ly Thai Tong, who ruled from 1028 to 1054. According to the annals, the heirless emperor dreamed that he had met Quan The Am Bo Tat (Goddess of Mercy), who, while seated on a lotus flower, handed him a male child. Ly Thai Tong then married a young peasant girl he met by chance and had a son and heir by her. To express his gratitude for this event, he constructed the One Pillar Pagoda in 1049.

The One Pillar Pagoda, built of wood on a single stone pillar 1.25m in diameter, is designed to resemble a lotus blossom, symbol of purity, rising out of a sea of sorrow. One of the last acts of the French before quitting Hanoi in 1954 was to destroy the One Pillar Pagoda; the structure was rebuilt by the new government.

Dien Huu Pagoda (Map 3)

The entrance to Dien Huu Pagoda is a few metres from the staircase of the One Pillar Pagoda. This small pagoda, which surrounds a garden courtyard, is one of the most delightful in Hanoi. The old wood and ceramic statues on the altar are very different from those common in the south. An elderly monk can often be found performing acupuncture on the front porch.

Bach Thao Park & Botanical Gardens (Map 3)

Just north of Ho Chi Minh's stilt house is the site of Bach Thao (literally 'hundreds of different trees') Park, originally the hamlet of Khan Xuan. It was here that the celebrated 18th century Ho Xuan Huong poetry was composed. In the late 1800s, the French displaced the residents of the village to build a garden and animal farm. In 1954 the park was turned into the Hanoi Botanical Gardens.

Perhaps Hanoi's most scenic natural enclosure, the 20 hectare area boasts two large lakes and is home to a wide variety of old-growth trees, flowers and other plant life. On a small hillock in the north-west of the park is an ancient temple dedicated to Huyen Thien Hac De, a young boy who is said to have helped expel Chinese invaders during the Ly Dynasty.

Thu Le Park & Zoo (Map 2)

On the western edge of the Ba Dinh District (about 6km west of Hoan Kiem Lake) is the Thu Le Park and Zoo (Bach Thu Le means 'hundreds of different animals').

The park boasts expanses of shaded grass and the Bo ('cow') Earth Mound on the shore of Ling Lang lake. The Ly Dynasty (11th century) Voi Phuc ('Kneeling Elephant') Temple here is steeped in legend and surrounded by shrubbery and ficus trees.

The zoo, with resident elephants, monkeys, lions, tigers, reptiles and birdlife, is open daily from 6 am to 6 pm. The entrance is on Đ Buoi a few hundred metres north of Pho Ngoc Khanh.

TAY HO DISTRICT
West Lake (Map 2)

Two legends explain the origins of West Lake (Ho Tay), also known as the Lake of Mist and the Big Lake. According to one, West Lake was created when the Dragon King drowned an evil nine-tailed fox in his lair, which was in a forest on this site. Another legend relates that in the 11th century, a Vietnamese Buddhist monk, Khong Lo, rendered a great service to the emperor of China, who rewarded him with a vast quantity of bronze from which he cast a huge bell. The sound of the bell could be heard all the way to China, where the Golden Buffalo Calf, mistaking the ringing

for its mother's call, ran southward, trampling on the site of West Lake and turning it into a lake.

In reality, the lake was created when the Red River overflowed its banks. Indeed, the Red River has changed its course numerous times, alternately flooding some areas and causing silt build-up (which creates new land). The flood problem has been partially controlled by building dikes. The highway along the east side of West Lake is built atop such a dike.

The lake was once ringed with magnificent palaces and pavilions. These were destroyed in the course of various feudal wars. The circumference of West Lake is about 13km.

On the south side of the lake is a popular strip of outdoor seafood restaurants (see the Places to Eat chapter) while the north side has been earmarked for the development of luxurious villas and hotels.

Tran Quoc Pagoda (Map 3)

The Tran Quoc Pagoda (the 'National Defence' pagoda), on the east shore of West Lake, was originally built in the 6th century and is considered to be the oldest pagoda in Vietnam. A stele here dating from 1639 tells the history of this site. The pagoda was rebuilt in the 15th century and again in 1842. There are a number of monks' funerary monuments in the garden.

Truc Bach Lake & Quan Thanh Temple (Map 3)

Truc Bach (White Silk) Lake is separated from West Lake by Đ Thanh Nien, originally a 17th century dike that today is lined with flame trees. During the 18th century, the Trinh lords built a palace on this site; it was later transformed into a reformatory for deviant royal concubines who were condemned to weave a very fine white silk.

The Quan Thanh Temple (Den Quan Thanh) is on the shore of Truc Bach Lake shaded by huge trees. It was established during the Ly Dynasty (1010-1225) and was dedicated to Tran Vo (God of the North), whose symbols of power are the tortoise and the snake. A bronze statue and bell here date from 1677. Entry costs US$0.40.

Ngu Xa Pagoda (Map 3)

Built on a small peninsula in Truc Bach Lake, this 18th century pagoda is dedicated to Nguyen Minh Khong, a monk who is believed to have discovered the craft of the bronze metal casting. The pagoda houses a 4m-tall, 10 tonne copper statue of the Amida Buddha cast in 1952.

Tay Ho Pagoda (Map 2)

The Tay Ho Pagoda (Phu Tay Ho) is the most popular spot for worship in Hanoi. Throngs of people come here on the first and 15th day of each lunar month in the hopes of decreasing risk and receiving good fortune.

CAU GIAY DISTRICT (MAP 2)
Museum of Ethnology

The superb Vietnam Museum of Ethnology (☎ 756 2193), on Đ Nguyen Van Huyen, was designed with the help of the Musée de l'Homme in Paris. It is well worth the trip to observe the depth of Vietnam's cultural diversity. The museum features an astounding collection of art and everyday objects with some 15,000 artefacts gathered from throughout Vietnam.

It has excellent maps and the displays are well labelled in Vietnamese, French and English. Interesting dioramas portray a typical village market, the making of conical hats and a Tay shamanic ceremony, while videos show the real life contexts. Visitors can also enter a traditional Black Thai house reconstructed within the museum. There is a centre for research and conservation and staff regularly collaborate with ethnographers and scholars from Japan, France, the Netherlands, Canada, USA and other countries. On display outdoors at the rear of the museum building is an interesting collection of minority tombs.

A gift shop here – affiliated with Craft Link, a fair-trade organisation – sells books,

postcards and arts and crafts from ethnic communities.

The museum is about a 20 minute drive west of the city centre. It can be reached in under an hour by bicycle. It is open Tuesday to Sunday from 8.30 to 12.30 am and 1.30 to 4.30 pm; entry is US$0.80.

Keeping the same hours, the **Handicraft Village Museum**, 1.5km away, presents an array of traditional crafts produced in the Hanoi region (see the Handicraft Villages section in the Excursions chapter).

WHAT'S FREE

Many of Hanoi's greatest attractions require little or no outlay of dong.

Days alone could be spent just wandering the streets of the Old Quarter, discovering architectural masterpieces and exploring the city's parks, lakes, temples and pagodas.

Hanoi's bustling markets (see the Shopping chapter) provide a colourful close-up look at how local merchants vend their wares. The city's myriad art galleries provide even more places to explore.

Perhaps Hanoi's most intriguing freebie of all is the chance to view (in the flesh) the embalmed corpse of Vietnam's beloved 'Uncle Ho', at the Ho Chi Minh Mausoleum.

ACTIVITIES
Health Clubs

The Vietnamese government strongly promotes gymnastics, which is a mandatory subject from elementary school to university. Other popular sports include tennis, badminton, table tennis and handball. Jogging is popular among Hanoians and the city's lakes and parks have several excellent routes.

A number of international hotels open their exercise centres to the public for a fee. The Clark Hatch Fitness Centre (☎ 826 6919 ext 8881) in the Sofitel Metropole Hotel (Map 5) charges US$15 per visit. Similar rates prevail at the Guoman Hotel health club (Map 5; ☎ 822 2800). Day passes at the Daewoo Hotel Fitness Centre (Map 2; ☎ 831 5000) cost US$20.

Prices are cheaper at Hanoi Private Club (Map 4; ☎ 852 9108) at 8 Pho Chua Boc. One-time visitors pay just US$4.

Long-termers with fat bank accounts might check out the exclusive Hanoi Club (Map 2; ☎ 823 8115), at 76 Đ Yen Phu.

Swimming
The Sofitel Metropole and Meritus Westlake hotels have swimming pools, but for hotel guests' and members' use only.

For the general public, the Ho Tay Villas (Map 2; ☎ 825 8241) out by West Lake has the best deal, charging US$3 per day for use of their facilities. Also by West Lake is the Thang Loi Hotel (Map 2), which has tennis courts and a swimming pool open to the public for US$10 per day.

Closer to the city centre, the Army Hotel (Map 5) on Pho Pham Ngu Lao charges just US$4 for day use of the pool, which is large enough to swim laps.

Hash House Harriers
Founded in Malaysia in the mid-1930s, this organisation has slowly spread around the world. Hash House Harriers is a loosely organised international club that appeals mainly to the young or young at heart. Activities typically include a weekend afternoon jogging session followed by a dinner and beer party which can continue until the wee hours of the morning.

The Hash is very informal. There is no club headquarters and no stable contact telephone or address. Nonetheless, finding the Hash is easy. Some embassy or consulate employees know about it; otherwise look for announcements in *The Guide*, *Time Out* and expat bars like the Verandah Bar or Polite Pub.

There is a mandatory US$5 donation which entitles you to a free T-shirt and refreshments. All excess funds are donated to local charities.

Golf
Mark Twain once said that playing golf was 'a waste of a good walk' and apparently Ho Chi Minh agreed with him. When the French departed Vietnam, Ho's advisers declared golf to be a 'bourgeois practice'. In 1975, after the fall of South Vietnam, golf was banned and all courses were shut down and turned into farming cooperatives. However, times have changed – golf was revived in 1992 and now even government officials can often be seen riding around in electric carts over hills and fields in hot pursuit of a little white ball.

King's Valley (☎ 034-834666) is a nine hole golf course just 45km west of Hanoi, close to the base of Ba Vi Mountain. Membership is a whopping US$5000, but the club is open to visitors.

On the western side of Hanoi, but still within the city limits, is the Lang Ha Golf Club (Map 2; ☎ 835 0909), at 16A Pho Lang Ha. Basically, this is just a driving range, open daily from 9 am to 9.30 pm. One-time visitors pay US$10 (including a bucket of 60 balls). One and three-month all-you-can-drive member cards cost US$110 or US$275 respectively.

Tennis
There are tennis courts (☎ 823 7530) in the Van Phuc Diplomatic Quarter, and also out by West Lake at the Thang Loi Hotel (Map 2).

Billiards
Pool playing has swept Hanoi recently and hard-core local shooters typically gather at pool halls as opposed to foreigner-dominated pubs. These places are reasonably priced (about US$1 an hour for regular tables, or US$2 for snooker) and are good places to meet young Vietnamese.

Bida Tu Do (Map 3; ☎ 828 2838) at 67 Pho Duc Chinh is pure pool hall – no décor, just 10 tables and a snooker table. It's open from 9 am to 1.30 am.

Tu Do (Map 4; ☎ 978 0513) at 250 Pho Ba Trieu is one of Hanoi's largest and most popular billiards places, with tables on all five storeys of the building.

A third possibility is Cau Lac Bo Billiards (Map 4; ☎ 821 0693) at 9A Pho Hoa Ma), just down the street from the popular Apocalypse Now bar.

Bowling

A few years ago there were none, but now Hanoi boasts not one, not two, but *three* giant bowling alleys! They are:

Cosmos Bowling Centre
  (☎ 831 8668) Map 2; 8B Pho Ngoc Khanh
Hanoi Starbowl Centre
  (☎ 574 1614) Map 4; 2 Pho Pham Ngoc Thach
Hanoi Superbowl
  (☎ 831 3333) Map 2; Fortuna Hotel, 6B Lang Ha

Other Sports

There are a number of expat amateur sport teams which organise occasional games in Hanoi. A current sampling includes **rugby** (men's and women's), **football/soccer**, **basketball** and **ultimate Frisbee**. For details and current contact numbers, check the recreation listings in *The Guide* or *Time Out*.

You may be able to join in a football game with local Vietnamese at the Quan Thanh Soccer Stadium (Map 3; near Quan Thanh Temple by West Lake).

Massage

The government has severely restricted the number of places licensed to give massages because of the concern that naughty 'extra services' might be offered. At the present time, you should be able to get a good legitimate massage at the Hoa Binh Hotel, Planet Hotel, Dan Chu Hotel and Thang Loi Hotel for about US$6 per hour. The Hanoi Hotel and Saigon Hotel charge around US$8 per hour for this service.

You can also be massaged at the upmarket fitness centres in the Guoman Hotel (US$12 per hour), the Clark Hatch Fitness Centre (US$16 per hour) and the Daewoo Hotel Fitness Centre (US$27 per hour).

There is also the women-only Eva Club on the 2nd floor of the Hom Market, at the intersection of Pho Hué and Pho Tran Xuan Soan.

Gambling

Following the lifting of the 14 year ban imposed by the communists, gambling, that most bourgeois capitalist activity, is staging a comeback. Vietnam's first casino since liberation opened in 1994 at Do Son Beach near Haiphong (see the Excursions chapter). Slot machines, now semi-legal as 'entertainment devices', have popped up inside many karaoke clubs and game centres.

It's easy to ignore the casino and slot machines if you don't want to play, but you'll have a hard time escaping the state lottery. Street vendors sell lottery tickets for a scant commission of just 12% of the face value of each ticket sold; 1% goes to the wholesaler and the other 87% goes to the government.

While your chances of winning are minuscule, hitting the jackpot in the state lottery can make you a dong multimillionaire. The smallest denomination lottery ticket is 2000d (US$0.16), while the largest prize is 100 million dong (US$8000).

The official state lottery has to compete against an illegal numbers game *(danh de)* reputed to offer better odds. Popular forms of illegal gambling are cards *(ta la)*, paper dice *(xoc dia)*, Chinese dominoes *(tu sac)* and cock fighting.

COURSES

Language

If you'd like to learn to speak Vietnamese, several courses are offered in Hanoi. To qualify for student visa status, you need to study at a bona fide university (as opposed to a private language centre or with a tutor). Universities require that you study at least 10 hours per week. Lessons usually last for two hours per day, for which you pay a tuition fee of around US$5.

The most popular place to study the Vietnamese language is at Hanoi National University (Map 2; ☎ 858 1468). The Vietnamese Language Centre is actually within the Polytechnic University with entrances on Đ Gai Phuong and Pho Dai Co Viet. There is a dormitory at the Polytechnic University (Map 3) for foreign students (Nha A-2 Bach Khoa) and this is a good place to inquire about tuition. If you enrol, you can stay in this dormitory (rooms cost around US$150 to US$250 per month).

Another other place to study is the Hanoi Foreign Languages College, Vietnamese Language Centre (☎ 826 2468). The main campus (Map 2) is 9km from central Hanoi, but there is a smaller campus closer to the city centre at 1 Pho Pham Ngu Lao. Tuition here varies depending on class size, but should be no more than US$5 per hour for individual tutoring.

Martial Arts

Kung Fu Martial Art (Thieu Lam Son Dong) at 100 Pho Ba Trieu is a kung fu training dojo. Most foreigners practising here both live in Hanoi and speak at least rudimentary Vietnamese, but it may be possible for newcomers to participate. There is a fee of about US$4 a session. Contact Mr Quang (☎ 822 6148) for details.

Places to Stay

The tourist boom at first created a shortage of hotel space, but overbuilding, the recent economic crisis in Asia and a decline in tourist arrivals has now produced a glut. What this means is that travellers now are in a better negotiating position, whether you stay at a grungy guesthouse or a top-notch hotel. Some of these top end hotels are operating at 20% occupancy rate and offer rooms for as little as US$88!

Even at the fanciest hotels it's possible to get discounts if you're staying long term (three days or more). Booking through some foreign or domestic travel agencies can also net you a discount. The rates quoted in this book are the short term, walk-in rates.

Another factor to take into account is taxes. There is a value added room tax of 10% imposed by the Vietnamese government (in cheaper places this is typically figured into the room price), and higher end hotels often tack on a 5% service fee.

HOTELS
Most of the large hotels *(khach san)* and guesthouses *(nha khach* or *nha nghi)* are government-owned or joint ventures. There is also a rapidly increasing number of foreign joint-venture hotels and small private hotels. Sadly, with the number of fantastic old French colonial buildings in Hanoi, scant few have been renovated for tourist lodging, and those that have remain out of the budget for many travellers. The city's potential for charming bed and breakfast type inns is unrealised.

It's always a good idea to take a look at the room to make sure that you're getting what you want and are not paying extra for something you don't need.

HOTEL SECURITY
Hotel security can be a problem. Some rooms come equipped with a closet which can be locked – if so, use it and take the key with you. You would be wise to bring a chain with a padlock – this can be used to lock the closet and you won't have to worry about the employees having keys. If your room or the hotel has a safe, make use of it.

POLICE REGISTRATION
Back in the old days when the Soviets told the Vietnamese how to run their country, all hotel guests had to deposit their passports and/or visas with reception – the staff then had to take these valuable documents over to the police station and register their guests.

The good news is that the government no longer requires police registration of hotel guests. The bad news is that some hotels make up their own rules. Some places still may insist on keeping your papers for security, but the bottom line is you are *not* required to. You may, however, need to show your passport upon checking in.

RESERVATIONS
Even during the busiest season, there is seldom much need for reservations in Hanoi – you can always find a place to stay and moreover a reservation usually nullifies any chance of negotiating the room tariff.

If you do book ahead by fax or email, most hotels (including budget guesthouses) can arrange airport pick-up for as cheap as US$8 or US$10.

DORMITORIES
While there are dormitories *(nha tro)* in Hanoi, most of these are officially off-limits to foreigners. In this case, the government's motives are not to charge you more money for accommodation – there is a significant chance of getting robbed while sleeping in a Vietnamese dormitory and by western standards many of these places are considered substandard.

Luckily, the concept of a relatively up-market, foreigner-only dormitory has caught on. Many of these 'dormitories' are actually regular hotel rooms with just two or four beds; you can find these in some backpacker hotels in the Old Quarter.

CAMPING

Despite the vast acreage of parks in Hanoi, camping is not a viable option. The biggest problem is finding a remote spot where curious locals and the police won't create difficulties for you. Some innovative private travel agencies in Hanoi do, however, offer organised camping trips to nearby national parks and small villages (see the Organised Tours section in the Getting Around chapter).

PLACES TO STAY – BUDGET

The vast majority of popular budget accommodation is found scattered in and around the Old Quarter within 1km of Hoan Kiem Lake (the following are all on Map 5).

The friendly *TF Handspan Hotel* (☎ 828 1996, ☎/fax 926 0270, tfhandspn@hn.vnn.vn, 116 Pho Hang Bac) has dorm beds for US$3 and clean air-con doubles (some with bath) costing US$10. On the ground floor is the popular Whole Earth Vegetarian Restaurant.

A short walk from TF is the *A to Z Queen Café* (☎ 826 0860, fax 826 0300, queenaz@fpt.vn, 65 Pho Hang Bac). Dorm beds here cost US$2.50 and very basic doubles with fans are US$6 to US$8. The same folks at Queen Café run the 27-room *Binh Minh Hotel* (☎ 826 7356, fax 824 7183, 50 Pho Hang Be). Rates here are US$4 for a dorm bed, and US$8 to US$15 for doubles. A couple of the rooms have enormous balconies with views.

Just across from the Binh Minh, the *Anh Sinh Hotel* (☎ 824 2229, 49 Pho Hang Be) recently underwent renovation. It has dorm beds for US$3 to US$4, and basic doubles from US$8 to US$12.

The *Real Darling Café* (☎ 826 9386, fax 825 6562, 33 Pho Hang Quat) advertises itself as 'probably the best tourist café in Hanoi'. Dorm beds cost US$3. Singles/doubles cost US$6/8.

The *Tong Dan Hotel* (☎ 825 2219, fax 826 5328, 17 Pho Tong Dan) is a welcoming place that comes highly recommended by travellers. Doubles cost US$10 to

US$30. It's east of Hoan Kiem Lake, close to the Red River (Song Hong). There is a second entrance around the block at 210 Pho Tran Quang Khai.

Lotus Guesthouse (☎ 826 8642, fax 826 8642, 42V Pho Ly Thuong Kiet) is a friendly, quiet and cheap place. There are six dorm beds for US$4 each, singles with shared bath for US$6 to US$8 (US$10 with bath inside), and double rooms with private bath for US$12 to US$20.

The small but friendly *Mai Phuong Hotel* (☎ 826 5341, 32 Pho Hang Be) charges US$8 to US$10 for doubles or US$12 to US$15 for triples.

The *Bodega Café* (☎ 826 7784, fax 826 7787, 57 Pho Trang Tien) was originally named in French during colonial times, though some have mistakenly taken the name to mean beef-goat-chicken – or *bo-de-ga* – in Vietnamese. It has 18 good clean rooms costing US$10 to US$20.

The *Trang Tien Hotel* (☎ 825 6115, fax 825 1416, 35 Pho Trang Tien) is on a busy central shopping street near the Opera House. Doubles are priced from US$15 to US$30.

There are several decent places to put up on Pho Hang Ga, or 'chicken street'. *Thuy Lam Hotel* (☎ 828 1788, fax 825 0468), at number 17, is run by a very friendly family who charge between US$10 and US$20 for respectable rooms. *Nam Hoa Hotel* (☎ 825 7603), at 49, is a bit worn, but a casual and friendly place charging US$8 to US$15. *Thanh Ha Hotel* (☎ 824 6496, fax 828 2248), at 34, has air-con rooms with satellite TV for US$13 to US$20. Ditto for the nearby *Prince Hotel* (☎ 828 1332, fax 828 1636) at 78.

Travellers arriving from Ninh Binh with the Sinh Café open tour may be deposited at the state-run Hanoi Toserco *Dong Xuan Hotel* (☎ 828 4474, fax 928 0124, 26 Pho Cao Thang). Fan/air-con doubles cost US$6 to US$8/US$10, while triples/quads cost US$12 to US$20.

The *Van Xuan Hotel* (☎ 824 4743, fax 824 6475, 15 Pho Luong Ngoc Quyen) is another Hanoi Toserco place with air-con doubles for US$16. A room with private bath,

PLACES TO STAY

balcony and breakfast included pushes the tariff up to US$20 to US$25. There is also an in-house sauna and massage service.

Next door is the popular 26-room *Camilla Hotel* (☎ *828 3583, fax 824 4277, 13 Pho Luong Ngoc Quyen)* where doubles cost US$15 to US$25.

The *My Kinh Hotel* (☎ *825 5726, fax 828 0514, 72-74 Pho Hang Buom)* has livable rooms starting from US$10.

The *Hotel 30/4* (Khach San 30/4, ☎ *826 0807, fax 822 1818, 115 Pho Tran Hung Dao)* is named after 30 April 1975, the date when the North Vietnamese entered Saigon. Not surprisingly, it's state-owned. The hotel is opposite the train station. Large echo-chamber rooms cost US$7 to US$10, or US$20 with private bath. This place is old and run-down, but has character and the staff proved friendly.

Especen Hotel (☎ *826 6856, fax 826 9612, 79E Pho Hang Trong)* operates several budget hotels around central Hanoi (all bear creative names such as Especen-1, Especen-2 etc) with rates from US$10 to US$25. This office can give you a map and call ahead to book a room.

The *Nam Phuong Hotel* (☎ *825 8030, fax 825 8964, 16 Pho Bao Khanh)* is on a small side street west of Hoan Kiem Lake. Staff are cordial and rooms cost US$10 to US$30 – all with air-con and satellite TV. There is a second *Nam Phuong Hotel* (☎ *824 6894, 26 Pho Nha Chung)* offering similar rates.

The *Anh Dao Hotel* (☎ *826 7151, fax 828 2008, 37 Pho Ma May)* is a friendly place with reasonable rooms and satellite TV. Windowless rooms cost US$15, or US$20 to US$25 with a window and balcony, respectively.

The *Cuu Long I Hotel* (☎ *823 6741, fax 824 7641, 2 Pho Cua Nam)* is a friendly place charging from US$15 to US$25, including breakfast. It's just across from the Metal Nightclub. The *Cuu Long II Hotel* (☎ *823 3541, fax 823 6393, 6 Pho Dinh Ngang)* nearby costs slightly more.

The *Kim Tin Hotel* (☎ *825 3740, fax 825 3741, 8 Pho Hang Bac)* is notable for its glitzy lobby (which doubles as a gold

jewellery shop) and the rooms are OK too. Doubles cost US$13 to US$30.

Another stylish cheapie is the *Fortuan Hotel* (Khach San Phu Do, ☎ *828 1324, fax 828 1323, 18 Pho Hang Bo)* where clean singles/doubles are US$15/20.

The *Time Hotel* (☎ *825 9498, fax 824 2348, 6 Pho Cau Go)* is a newish place in the busy 'shoe land' part of the Old Quarter. Doubles cost US$15 to US$25.

The *Asia Hotel* (☎ *826 9007, fax 824 5184, 5 Pho Cua Dong)* is a cosy 10-room place with very friendly staff who speak both French and English well. Comfortable singles/doubles rent for US$15/$20.

The *Mango Hotel* (☎ *824 3704, fax 824 3966, 118 Pho Le Duan)* is near the Hanoi train station. It has spacious grounds and the restaurant seems to have gained a reputation as a good place for Vietnamese wedding banquets. The price for rooms here ranges from US$16 to US$27.

PLACES TO STAY – MID-RANGE
Hoan Kiem Lake District (Map 5)

The *Quoc Hoa Hotel* (☎ *828 4528, fax 826 7424, quochoa@hn.vnn.vn, 10 Pho Bat Dan)* opened in 1991 as Hanoi's first privately owned hotel. Rooms are large and comfortable and rent from US$21 to US$65. There is an excellent Italian café-restaurant on the first floor.

The *Win Hotel* (☎ *826 7150, fax 824 7448, 34 Pho Hang Hanh)* is a friendly, family-run place amid the many local cafés on 'coffee street'. Rooms go for US$25 to US$35 (with a balcony), and have satellite TV and IDD phones.

The *Phu Long Hotel* (☎ *826 6074, fax 825 3124, 12 Pho Cau Go)* charges US$20 to US$35 for clean doubles.

The *Hoa Linh Hotel* (☎ *825 0034, fax 824 3886, 35 Pho Hang Bo)* is located north-west of Hoan Kiem Lake and is decorated with a Chinese motif. The 15 rooms here are priced according to size, from US$20 to US$40.

The 50-room *Phu Gia Hotel* (☎ *825 5493, fax 825 9207, 136 Pho Hang Trong)* is centrally located on the west side of Hoan

Kiem Lake. Dark rooms on the first floor cost just US$15, and get progressively more expensive as they move up. The best rooms (US$37) have nice little balconies overlooking the lake.

The plush *Army Hotel (Khach San Quan Doi, ☎ 825 2896, fax 825 9276, 33C Pho Pham Ngu Lao)* is indeed owned by the army but looks nothing like a barracks. This place has a gym and saltwater swimming pool with rooms from US$50 to US$198.

ATS Hotel (☎ 824 3428, fax 824 8152, 33B Pho Pham Ngu Lao), also brought to you by the boys in green, is just down from the Army Hotel. Rooms are a bit musty, but it's a quiet place and some rooms have views into the neighbouring army barracks. Rates are US$49 to US$89.

Trang An Hotel (☎ 826 8982, fax 825 8511, 58 Pho Hang Gai) is a good mini-hotel at the north-west corner of Hoan Kiem Lake. Singles/doubles cost US$20/30. There is also an in-house restaurant and cocktail lounge.

The *Binh Minh Hotel (☎ 826 6442, fax 825 7725, 27 Pho Ly Thai To)* is in the same building as the China Southern Airlines office. It is a welcoming place, and singles /doubles cost US$32/36.

The *Energy Hotel (Khach San Dien Luc, ☎ 825 0457, fax 825 0456, 30 Pho Ly Thai To)* belongs to the Ministry of Energy. This is the agency responsible for the frequent power blackouts that grip Hanoi. Rooms cost US$25 to US$35, including breakfast.

The *Prince Hotel (☎ 824 8316, fax 824 8323, 96A Pho Hai Ba Trung)* is a recommended place with nice rooms in the US$20 to US$45 range.

The *Hung Hiep Hotel (☎ 828 4922, fax 828 0092, 32 Pho Thuoc Bac)* has received a few good reports and prices range from US$15 to US$35. It is in the northern part of the Old Quarter near the Hanoi Citadel.

Travellers have also had good things to say about the old-world décor of the *Hong Ngoc Hotel (☎ 828 5053, fax 828 5054, 34 Pho Hang Manh)*. Rooms cost US$25 to US$45 and the staff speak English and French.

Chains First Eden Hotel (☎ 828 3896, fax 828 4066, 2 Pho Phung Hung) is near the Old Quarter to the west of the Long Bien bridge. This new, large business hotel has a health club, business centre, sauna, satellite TV, and Chinese-Vietnamese restaurant. Rooms cost from US$49 to US$99.

Very close is the *Galaxy Hotel (☎ 828 2888, fax 828 2466, 1 Pho Phan Dinh Phung)*, a fairly standard business hotel, with business centre, cocktail lounge, restaurant and satellite TV. Rooms here cost US$79 to US$105.

The *Thuy Nga Hotel (☎ 934 1256, fax 934 1262, 4 Pho Ba Trieu)* is centrally located near the south-west corner of Hoan Kiem Lake and receives good reports from guests. Rates are now US$75 to US$125, but 20% discounts are the norm.

The *Saigon Hotel (☎ 826 8505, fax 826 6631, 80 Pho Ly Thuong Kiet)* is near the Hanoi train station. The tariff here ranges from US$59 to US$89. There is a sauna and massage service, and the rooftop bar is a good hang-out on warm summer nights.

The *Thu Do Hotel (☎ 825 2288, fax 826 1121, 109 Pho Tran Hung Dao)* is also known as the *Capital Hotel*. It is just opposite the train station and the US$30 rooms are decent value.

The old *Dong Loi Hotel (☎ 825 5721, fax 826 7999, 94 Pho Ly Thuong Kiet)* is very near Hanoi's train station. The door attendants wear crisp, white uniforms and greet you with 'Hello sir' or 'Good morning madam.' All this courtesy costs US$25 to US$35.

The Eden Hotel (☎ 824 5273, fax 824 5619, 78 Pho Tho Nhuom) is on a quiet street south-west of Hoan Kiem Lake. Double rooms cost US$49 to US$99. On the ground floor are an Italian restaurant and the Pear Tree Pub.

The *Royal Hotel (☎ 824 4230, fax 824 4234, 20 Pho Hang Tre)* is proud of its Royal Palace nightclub. It's north-east of Hoan Kiem Lake and offers luxury business facilities. Rooms cost US$60 to US$75.

West Area (Map 2)

Just to the west of Ho Chi Minh's Mausoleum is the *Heritage Hotel (☎ 834 4727, fax 834 3882, 80 Pho Giang Vo)*. This very business-oriented Singapore joint-venture hotel also features a health club, restaurant and bar. Double rooms including breakfast cost from US$40 to US$75.

West Lake (Ho Tay) Area

The *Ho Tay Villas (Map 2; Khuy Biet Thu Ho Tay, ☎ 0804 7772, fax 823 2126, Đ Dang Thai Mai)* used to be the Communist Party Guesthouse. Now it's a 50-room tourist hotel. The well designed, spacious villas, set amid a beautifully landscaped area on West Lake, were once the exclusive preserve of top party officials, but now visitors bearing US dollars are welcome to avail themselves of the facilities. Even if you don't stay, it's instructive to visit to see how the 'people's representatives' lived in one of Asia's poorest countries. The hotel is 5.5km north of central Hanoi. Rooms cost US$40 to US$130.

The *Dragon Hotel (Map 2; ☎ 829 2954, fax 829 4745, 9 Pho Xuan Dieu)* is a relatively small place facing the lake. Singles/doubles are US$28/44 and there are also apartments for US$76.

The *Tien Thuy Hotel (Map 3; ☎ 733 1972, fax 733 1988, 38 Pho Yen Ninh)* is sparsely decorated with antique-like Chinese furniture. Rooms cost US$25 to US$35.

The *Anh Hotel II (Map 3; ☎ 843 5141, fax 843 0618, 43 Pho Nguyen Truong To)* is a small, private mini-hotel between the lake and the Old Quarter. Rates are US$25 to US$45.

The *Planet Hotel (Map 3; ☎ 843 5888, fax 843 5088, 120 Pho Quan Thanh)* has some rooms on the top floor with a view of West Lake. Facilities include a business centre, sauna, massage service and health club. Room rates are US$35 to US$60.

South Area

This is not an area of town that attracts many travellers, but there are some hotels here.

The *Queen Hotel (Map 2; ☎ 864 1238, fax 864 1237, 189 Đ Giai Phong)* is near the Giap Bat train station. Double rooms cost US$40.

The *Madison Hotel (Map 4; ☎ 822 8164/822 5533, 16 Pho Bui Thi Xuan)* is just east of Thien Quang Lake. The management advertises this as Hanoi's first 'boutique hotel' – a flaky description, but it's still quite nice. More significantly this is one of the few hotels in this class that has a lift. Rooms with breakfast are US$30 to US$50.

PLACES TO STAY – TOP END
Hoan Kiem Lake District (Map 5)

The attractive *De Syloia Hotel (☎ 824 5346, fax 824 1083, 17A Pho Tran Hung Dao)* is an elegant variation on the French theme. All rooms have a clean, Continental touch and cost US$109 to US$198. There is a fitness centre and sauna here, not to mention the respectable Vietnamese restaurant Cay Cau.

Sofitel Metropole Hotel (☎ 826 6919, fax 826 6920, 15 Pho Ngo Quyen) is one of Vietnam's great luxury hotels. This place has a French motif that just won't quit – close the curtains and you'll think you're in Paris. Facilities include a swimming pool, fitness centre, sauna and beauty parlour. Rooms cost from US$220 and it's US$550 for the 'Heritage Suite'.

The *Hoa Binh Hotel (☎ 825 3315, fax 825 4655, 27 Pho Ly Thuong Kiet)* is due south of Hoan Kiem Lake. This grand French colonial hotel was originally built in 1926 as *Le Splendide* (there is a top-notch French restaurant by the same name on the 1st floor). Service and facilities are spot-on, but the overall atmosphere of the rooms lacks charm. Room rates are US$60 to US$130.

The brand new *Hanoi Opera Hilton (☎ 933 0500, fax 933 0530, 1 Pho Le Thanh Tong)* commands a prime location beside the Opera House. The architecture was thoughtfully made to gel with its neighbour, save perhaps for the big modern sign plastered on the exterior. Rates range from US$139 for deluxe rooms to US$800 for a night in the Presidential Suite.

The *Melia Hanoi (☎ 934 3343, fax 934 3344, melia.hanoi@fpt.vn, 44B Pho Ly*

Thuong Kiet) is another recent addition to Hanoi's expanding number of luxury hotels. It is a gigantic sky-scraping eyesore just saved by a well done interior, wide range of facilities and good service. Introductory rates are being offered from US$88 to US$138.

The *Dan Chu Hotel (☎ 825 4937, fax 826 6786, 29 Pho Trang Tien)*, once called the *Hanoi Hotel*, was built in the late 19th century. Room rates have risen considerably since then, and now range from US$65 to US$129, but breakfast is thrown in. The Dan Chu also runs an attractive villa a few hundred metres away at 4 Pho Pham Su Manh.

Walking distance from the Hanoi train station, the stately *Guoman Hotel (☎ 822 2800, fax 822 2822, 83A Pho Ly Thuong Kiet)* is a sleek place with a health club, 24 hour café and two fine bars. Rates range from US$75 to US$200.

West Area (Map 2)

A good place to work on your swing, the *Capital Garden Hotel (☎ 835 0383, fax 835 0363, 48A Pho Lang Ha)* is close to the Lang Ha Golf Club and the hotel offers a 'golf workshop'. There are a few single rooms with queen-sized beds, but otherwise it's doubles from US$140.

The snazzy *Hanoi Horison Hotel (☎ 733 0808, fax 733 0688, 40 Pho Cat Linh)* is housed in a gigantic modern building with a towering brick smokestack out front (preserved from an old brick factory which once stood on the site). Rooms cost US$95 to US$105, and suites are US$200. It also has a health club and swimming pool.

For the price, and number of dignitaries who stay here, the *Hanoi Hotel (☎ 845 2270, fax 845 9209, D8 Pho Giang Vo)* is a somewhat lacklustre place. Rooms here cost US$88 to US$385, and facilities cover virtually everything from karaoke and disco to a beauty parlour and sauna.

The *Lakeside Hotel (☎ 835 0111, fax 835 0121, 6A Pho Ngoc Khanh)* is a Taiwanese joint venture by the shore of Giang Vo Lake. Most rooms have a lake view. Doubles cost US$70 to US$130, and facilities

include a café, Chinese restaurant, fitness room, karaoke lounge and nightclub.

The 411-room *Daewoo Hotel (☎ 831 5000, fax 831 5010, 360 Pho Kim Ma)* is the city's largest and most expensive hotel. The style at this South Korean joint venture is most definitely *not* French colonial. This 15-storey behemoth offers everything you could want in life, including a swimming pool, nightclub, health club, business centre and three fine restaurants. Budget rooms are only US$99, but suites go for up to a cool US$1500.

West Lake Area

An example of Hanoi's nouveau French colonial genre is the pleasant *Hang Nga Hotel (Map 3; ☎ 843 7777, fax 843 7779, 65 Pho Cua Bac)*. Rooms on the top floor have a view of West Lake. The price range here is from US$75 to US$125.

The *Meritus Westlake (Map 3; ☎ 823 8888, fax 829 388, 1 Đ Thanh Nien)* is a gigantic Singaporean joint venture boasting every possible amenity, including South-East Asia's first all-weather swimming pool (it has a retractable roof). Rates range from US$88 to US$1000 for the Presidential Suite.

The *Thang Loi Hotel (Map 2; ☎ 829 4211, fax 829 3800, Đ Yen Phu)* is nicknamed 'the Cuban Hotel' because it was built in the mid-1970s with Cuban assistance. The floor plan of each level is said to have been copied from a one-storey Cuban building, which explains the doors that lead nowhere. Around the main building are bungalows. The hotel is built on pylons over West Lake, and is surrounded by attractive landscaping. The hotel also boasts a swimming pool, tennis courts, a sauna and a massage service. Excepting the massage, all this cushy comfort will cost you US$90 to US$105.

South Area (Map 4)

Hotel Nikko Hanoi (☎ 822 3535, fax 822 3555, sale-nikko@hn.vnn.vn, 84 Pho Tran Nhan Tong), across from Lenin Park and the Hanoi Circus, is a brand new pleasure palace brought to you by the Japanese. Facilities include a fitness club, spa and sauna, pool, business centre and three restaurants (including a top-notch sushi bar). Rates range from US$90 to US$400.

A short walk from Lenin Park, the **Green Park Hotel** (☎ *822 7725, fax 822 5977, 48 Pho Tran Nhan Tong*) is done up in a pastel green motif. If you can handle the colour scheme, it's not a bad place to stay. There are fine views overlooking Lenin Park from the top floor restaurant. Rooms cost from US$60 to US$80, including breakfast.

LONG TERM RENTALS

Well heeled foreigners with big budgets typically live in fancy apartments which command high rents. As elsewhere in Vietnam, many expats wind up living in mini-hotels. Big discounts can be negotiated for long term stays. It's wise to first stay in the hotel for at least one night before agreeing to anything.

Aside from the backpacker guesthouses or mini-hotels, it's possible to find cheap housing in Hanoi's student quarters for around US$150 to US$250 per month. At any budget, agents advertise in the *Vietnam News* daily newspaper; you do not generally deal directly with landlords. Shop around for the best deal, and don't be afraid to negotiate.

Serviced Apartments

At the **Hanoi Towers** (*Map 5;* ☎ *934 2342, fax 934 2343, 49 Pho Hai Ba Trung*), a new sky-scraper built on the site of the former 'Hanoi Hilton' POW prison, you can rent short or long term. One, two and three bedroom flats go for between US$85 and US$135 per night – good value when you consider breakfast is included and guests have access to facilities including a pool, sauna and health club. The building also boasts an excellent restaurant-bar on the 4th floor.

Typical two-bedroom flats lease for US$1000 to US$5000 per month. Some new luxury apartments include **Oriental Park** (☎ *829 1200*), **Hanoi Lakes** (☎ *829 2998*), **Golden Lodge** (☎ *718 0098*), **Coco Flower Village** (☎ *845 6510*), **Regency West Lake** (☎ *843 0030*), **Thanh Cong Villas** (☎ *835 4875*) and the **Daeha Centre** (☎ *834 9467*).

'Com Binh Dan' style restaurant

Banh Chung; traditional Tet sticky rice cake

Fresh green vegetables at the market

A selection of fresh 'Com Binh Dan' ingredients.

Shrimp cakes *(banh tom)* – crunchy unshelled shrimps cooked in batter – yum!

Goose blood and peanuts

Something moved!

'Sear for onetwothree seconds.'

Sun-drying rice paper on woven bamboo mats.

Dog meat restaurant on Pho Nhat Tan

Places to Eat

In recent years Hanoi has undergone a miraculous transformation from a culinary wasteland to a premier world city for eating and drinking. The city boasts everything from cheap backpacker hang-outs to exquisite Vietnamese restaurants and a growing legion of chic cafés. Keep an eye out for inexpensive Sunday buffets. Many local eateries, including restaurants at top-notch hotels like the Nikko, Meritus and Daiwoo, offer tempting spreads where you can eat like a king, usually for under US$10.

Connoisseurs say the secret of Vietnamese cooking is in the delicate use of herbs. Northerners are known for not sparing MSG (often considered a 'seasoning' to replace salt and pepper) in food preparation – especially in *pho* noodle soup; they are also known for their heavy-handed use of garlic and onion. Hanoians seem to hold the Saigonese in contempt for their sweeter tastes, and frequent use of spicier treats like ginger and tameron. These days, however, tastes are changing, and more and more Hanoians are adapting somewhat to southern tastes, and blending cooking styles. One age-old delicacy among Hanoian women – young and old – are boiled snails.

Hanoi is almost completely self-sufficient when it comes to tasty ingredients, and although its cuisine has been subject to colonial influences from the French and Chinese, it retains a unique flavour. This is largely due to the use of uniquely Vietnamese *nuoc mam* (fermented fish sauce), an abundance of fresh vegetables and herbs, and the dominance of rice in the country. The proximity of Hanoi to the sea and Red River (Song Hong) Delta has also ensured the use of fish and seafood in many dishes.

UTENSILS

In a traditional Vietnamese home cooking was done over the hearth, considered to be the most important part of a house. There were no ovens as such, so food was prepared by boiling, steaming, grilling or frying. Thus a traditional kitchen would be equipped with terracotta cooking pots, bamboo chopsticks and utensils, woks and an essential rice cooker. A pestle and mortar would also be used to finely grind herbs and spices.

Nuoc Mam

Nuoc mam (pronounced 'nuke mom') is a type of fermented fish sauce – instantly identifiable by its distinctive smell – without which no Vietnamese meal is complete. Though nuoc mam is to Vietnamese cuisine what soy sauce is to Japanese food, many hotel restaurants won't serve it to foreigners, knowing that the odour may drive away their western customers. Nuoc mam actually isn't bad once you get used to it and some people even take a few bottles home with them in their luggage (God help you if the bottle leaks). The sauce is made by fermenting highly salted fish in large ceramic vats for four to 12 months.

The price of nuoc mam varies considerably according to the quality. Connoisseurs insist the high-grade rocket fuel has a much milder aroma than the cheaper variety. Most foreigners will find it hard to tell the difference though.

A more palatable version of fish sauce served in eateries throughout Vietnam is *nuoc mam cham*. This is basically nuoc mam with lime, vinegar, sugar, water, chilli and garlic added, which makes it much more agreeable to western tastes.

If, on the other hand, nuoc mam isn't strong enough for you, try *mam tom*, a powerful shrimp paste which American soldiers sometimes called 'Viet Cong tear gas'. It's often served with dog meat – foreigners generally find it far more revolting than the dog itself.

Most of these utensils are still regularly used in Vietnamese kitchens, although these days gas burners have replaced the hearth. Some restaurants have retained the tradition of serving food in terracotta pots that resemble samovars, with their tops cut off and live coals in the centre, to keep the food hot.

EATING ETIQUETTE

Eating plays a huge role in Vietnamese society and there is certain etiquette involved in the dining experience. Although your hosts will be too polite to actually point out your mistakes, it is worth abiding by certain customs. When invited out to dine, it is polite to bring along a small gift – flowers are suitable but should never be white as this is a death sign.

Unlike the western practice of each person ordering their own plate of food, dining in most Asian countries is a communal affair. That is, a selection of dishes are put on the table to be shared by a small group. People generally use their own chopsticks to serve themselves from a communal plate of food, although serving spoons or chopsticks may be supplied. Sharing dishes with three or four people ensures that you get to sample several different types of dishes and is a fun and very sociable way to eat – many foreigners come to prefer it over western individualism. If you eat with a group of Vietnamese, you may find that some of your fellow diners pick out the best-looking pieces of food with their chopsticks and put them into your rice bowl – a way of honouring you as a distinguished guest.

No one will be offended if you ask for a knife and fork, although in some places this may not be an option. Fortunately spoons will usually be provided alongside chopsticks – although it's worth noting that the Vietnamese sip their food from the spoon and never place it directly into their mouth.

The proper way to eat Vietnamese food is to take rice from the large shared dish and put it in your rice bowl. Once you have the rice, use your chopsticks to take meat, fish or vegetables from the serving dishes (never pour dipping sauces directly into your bowl).

Transfer all food to your rice bowl before eating it and never use the chopsticks to pierce food on communal plates. Hold the rice bowl near your mouth, using your chopsticks to eat. Leaving the rice bowl on the table and conveying your food, precariously perched between chopsticks, all the way from the table to your mouth strikes Vietnamese as odd, though they will be more amused than offended. When passing or taking something always use both hands and it is polite to acknowledge the transaction with a small nod.

All good hosts must feed their guests, even if they're not hungry. In most cases they will feed you till you are unable to move, and then they will continue to try and stuff more food into you. It's a good idea to make sure you are really hungry before arriving somewhere to eat and then start feigning satisfaction from the earliest point possible. This way you may only be force-fed an extra one or two helpings over your limit.

DINING OUT

You'll never have to look very far for food in Hanoi – restaurants *(nha hang)* of one sort or another seem to be in every nook and cranny. Unless you eat in exclusive hotels or aristocratic restaurants, Vietnamese food is very cheap. The best bargains can be found at street stalls, most of which are limited to the amount of ingredients they can carry so tend to specialise in a couple of particular dishes. Wander around until something takes your fancy – a bowl of noodles costs around US$0.50.

Basic restaurants with bamboo and cardboard walls have rice, meat and vegetable meals costing around US$1. Most cafés and decent restaurants can fill your stomach for US$2 to US$5. With the relaxation of laws governing joint ventures, there has been a recent surge of classier Vietnamese restaurants popping up. Traditional Vietnamese dishes taste all the better for being consumed in ambient French-style courtyards or riverside terraces. However, in classy restaurants the bill can add up fast.

Western restaurants are increasing in number and the cooks are slowly learning to cater for western tastes. Plus there is a growing wave of expat chefs, notably Italians and French, offering up savoury delights from their home countries.

As a general rule of thumb, cafés (especially travellers cafés) are open most of the day and into the night. Street stalls are open from very early in the morning till late at night. Restaurants will usually open for lunch from about 11 am to 2 pm and dinner from 5 to 10 pm.

EXOTIC MEATS

Disturbing to animal lovers is the fact that Fido can wind up on the menu; however, it is a speciality item. Dog meat is most popular in the north where its consumption is believed to bring good fortune as long as it is only eaten during the second half of the lunar month. To find (or avoid) a restaurant serving dog meat, look for a sign saying *thit cho* or *thit cay*.

Though it may be exotic to try wild meat such as muntjac, bat, frog, deer, sea horse, shark fin and snake, many of these are endangered, and eating them will indicate your support and acceptance of such practices, and consequently add to the demand for these products.

Fortunately, new laws regarding the capture and sale of endangered animals has made these meats much harder to find. But you will probably still see snake, which is believed to have various medicinal properties and is widely touted as an aphrodisiac. The more poisonous the snake, the worthier its reputation (and the higher the price charged).

If your stomach (and conscience) can handle it, there is a list of places to sample snake meat and wine at Le Mat (see the Excursions chapter).

THE BILL

Many foreigners are surprised to find that most local Vietnamese restaurants do not display prices on the menu at all. This is normal. Vietnamese typically eat out in groups and are charged by the amount ordered to feed the whole group. In the case of no-price menus, you should definitely ask the total price when you place your order. Vietnamese diners know this and will always ask, so don't be shy about speaking up unless you want a shock when the bill finally comes. To get the bill, politely catch the attention of the waiting staff and write in the air as if with a pen on an imaginary piece of paper. Once you have it, check it very carefully – overcharging or simple human error is not uncommon when more than one person orders food or when many items are listed on the bill.

The moist hand towels sealed in plastic which you'll be given at many restaurants are occasionally free, but typically you'll be charged from US$0.04 to US$0.20 for the pleasure of using them (a small price to pay depending on how dirty your hands are). It is advisable not to wipe your face with these – people have complained of eye irritation, though it's hard to say if this is from bacteria or the chemicals used to clean the towels.

SNACKS

Vietnamese spring rolls are called *nem ran* in the north. They are made of rice paper filled with minced pork, vermicelli, *moc nhi* (a kind of edible fungus), onion, mushroom and eggs, and are fried until the rice paper turns a crispy brown. *Nem cua be* are made with the above ingredients and crab meat, and *nem rau* are a vegetarian version.

A variation on the theme is the larger spring rolls called *banh da*. With these you put the ingredients together yourself and roll your own. The outer shell is a translucent rice crêpe. It's excellent, but pass on the shrimp paste – it's horrible.

Other snacks available throughout Vietnam include:

banh cuon – a steamed rice pancake into which minced pork and moc nhi is rolled. It is served with *nuoc mam cham* (see the boxed text 'Nuoc Mam').

oc nhoi – snail meat, pork, chopped green onion, nuoc mam and pepper rolled up in ginger leaves and cooked in snail shells.

gio – lean, seasoned pork pounded into paste before being packed into banana leaves and boiled.

cha – pork paste fried in fat or broiled over hot coals.

cha que – cha prepared with cinnamon.

chao tom – grilled sugar cane rolled in spiced shrimp paste.

dua chua – bean sprout salad that tastes vaguely like Korean kimchi.

There are also a number of western-style foods available. French bread is available everywhere – it's best in the morning when it's warm and fresh. Imported French cheese spread can be bought from street stalls for around US$1.50 per pack and sometimes salami is available.

Vietnamese-made biscuits are not too good, though they're slowly improving. Biscuits imported from China are truly awful, except for one brand labelled 'Coconut Crackers'.

MAIN DISHES

Some common dishes you might try include:

cha ca – filleted fish slices broiled over charcoal. Often served with noodles, green salad, roasted peanuts and a sauce made from nuoc mam, lemon and a special volatile oil.

ech tam bot ran – frog meat soaked in a thin batter and fried in oil; usually served with nuoc mam cham and pepper.

rau xao hon hop – fried vegetables.

bo bay mon – sugar-beef dishes.

com tay cam – rice with mushrooms, chicken and finely sliced pork flavoured with ginger.

RICE

The staple of Vietnamese cuisine is plain white rice *(com)*, dressed up with a plethora of vegetables, meat, fish and spices. Rice's various by-products include rice wine and noodles.

NOODLES

Vietnamese noodle dishes *(pho)* are eaten at all hours of the day, but are a special favourite for breakfast. Most westerners would prefer their noodles for lunch, though, and fortunately you can get bread, cheese and eggs in the morning. Noodles are usually eaten as a soup rather than 'dry' like spaghetti.

The noodles served with Vietnamese soups are of three types: white rice noodles *(banh pho)*, clear noodles made from rice mixed with manioc powder *(mien)* and yellow,

wheat noodles *(mi)*. Many noodle soups are available either with broth *(nuoc leo)* or without *(kho*, literally 'dry'). Most pho shops also serve *quay*, a kind of deep-fried rice powder doughnut, which is put in soup to soften before eating. Prices average from around US$0.40 to US$0.80 for a bowl of noodles, and some of the more popular dishes include:

pho bo – standard beef noodle soup.

pho ga – standard chicken noodle soup.

xup rau – vegetable soup.

lau – fish and vegetable soup.

mien luon – vermicelli soup with eel seasoned with mushrooms, shallots, fried eggs and chicken.

bun thang – rice noodles and shredded chicken with fried egg and prawns on top; served with broth made by boiling chicken, dried prawns and pig bones.

canh kho hoa – a bitter soup said to be especially good for the health of people who have spent a lot of time in the sun.

VEGETARIAN FOOD

Because Buddhist monks of the Mahayana tradition are strict vegetarians (at least they are supposed to be), Vietnamese vegetarian cooking *(an chay)* has a long history and is an integral part of Vietnamese cuisine. Because it does not include many expensive ingredients, vegetarian food is unbelievably cheap.

On a full moon (the 15th day of the lunar month) or sliver moon (the last day of the lunar month), many Vietnamese and Chinese avoid eating meat or even nuoc mam. On such days, some street stalls, especially in the markets, serve vegetarian meals. To find out when the next sliver or full moon will be, consult any Vietnamese calendar.

DESSERTS

Sweets *(do ngot)* and desserts *(do trang mieng)* you are likely to have an opportunity to sample include the following:

banh chung – square cake made from sticky rice and filled with beans, onion and pork which is boiled in leaves for around 10 hours – a traditional Tet favourite (see the boxed text 'The Tet Festival').

banh deo – cake made of dried sticky rice flour mixed with a boiled sugar solution and filled with candied fruit, sesame seeds, fat etc.

banh dau xanh – mung bean cake – served with hot tea it melts on your tongue.

mut – candied fruit or vegetables made with carrot, coconut, kumquat, gourd, ginger root, lotus seeds, tomato etc.

banh bao – filled Chinese pastry that can most easily be described as looking like a woman's breast, complete with a reddish dot on top. Inside the sweet, doughy exterior is meat, onions and vegetables. It's often dunked in soy sauce.

banh it nhan dau – a traditional Vietnamese treat, it is a gooey pastry made of pulverised sticky rice, beans and sugar. It is steamed (and sold) in a banana leaf folded into a triangular pyramid.

banh it nhan dua – a variation of banh it nhan dau made with coconut instead of beans.

kem dua or kem trai dua – a delicious mix of ice cream, candied fruit and the jelly-like meat of young coconut served in a baby coconut shell.

yaourt – sweetened frozen yoghurt, available from ice cream stalls.

FRUIT

Plenty of fresh fruit *(qua or trai)* is available in Hanoi year-round, but many of the most interesting specialities have short seasons.

green bananas – sold in markets and usually ripe enough to eat and, in fact, taste better than the yellow ones.

avocado – often eaten in a glass with ice and sweetened with either sugar or condensed milk.

cinnamon apple – also known as custard apple, sugar apple and sweetsop, it is ripe when it's very soft and the area around the stem turns blackish.

coconuts – in their mature state eaten only by children or as jam. The Vietnamese prefer the soft jelly-like meat and fresher milk of young coconuts.

jackfruit – an enormous watermelon-sized fruit, has bright orange segments with a slightly rubbery texture.

pomelo – looks like a huge orange or grapefruit. The skin is greenish and the flesh often has a purple tinge.

papaya or pawpaw – has bright orange flesh that tastes melon-like. The black seeds are said to act as a contraceptive for women.

DRINKS
Non-Alcoholic Drinks

Coffee Vietnamese coffee is fine stuff. Particularly notable are the beans grown in the Central Highlands area. The Vietnamese prefer their coffee so strong and sweet that it will turn your teeth inside out. Ordering 'white coffee' usually results in about 30% of sweet condensed milk being added. Ovaltine and Milo, which are regarded as desserts rather than drinks, will also be served this way. Those restaurants accustomed to foreigners will be prepared with thermos bottles of hot water so you can dilute your coffee (or Ovaltine etc) as you wish. However, restaurants which deal with a mainly Vietnamese clientele will probably be dumbfounded by your request for hot water. You'll also need to communicate the fact that you need a large glass – ultra-sweet coffee is often served in a tiny shot glass, thus leaving you no room to add any water.

Instant coffee *(ca phe tan* or *ca phe bot)* made its debut in 1996 – a disaster! Many cafés just assume that westerners prefer instant coffee because it's 'modern' and comes from the west. You need to let them know that you want fresh-brewed Vietnamese coffee *(ca phe phin)*, not imported instant powder.

Rather than prepare coffee in a pot, the Vietnamese prefer to brew it right at the table, French-style – a dripper with ground coffee is placed over the cup and then hot water is poured in. If you prefer iced coffee, the same method is applied, but a glass of ice is placed under the dripper.

Both the drippers and packaged coffee make for inexpensive and practical souvenirs.

Tea Vietnamese tea in the south is cheap but tastes disappointing, whereas tea grown in the north is much better, but also much stronger – be prepared for a caffeine jolt. The northern tea is similar to Chinese green tea and is almost always sold in loose form rather than tea bags. The Vietnamese never put milk or sugar into green tea and will think you're a loony if you do.

Imported tea (in tea bag form) can be found almost everywhere. The price is perfectly reasonable so there's no need to bring it from abroad. Most restaurants can dig up some lemon and sugar for your tea, although milk is not always available.

Mineral Water High-quality mineral water *(nuoc suoi)* in large plastic bottles is readily available for under US$1 (see the boxed text 'C'est la Vie'). If you prefer your mineral water with fizzy bubbles, it's normally mixed with ice, lemon and sugar (outstanding!) and is called *so-da chanh*.

Coconut Milk There is nothing more refreshing on a hot day than fresh coconut milk *(nuoc dua)*. The Vietnamese believe that coconut milk, like hot milk in western culture, makes you tired. Athletes, for instance, never drink it before a competition.

Soft Drinks An excellent domestic soft drink with a pleasant fruit flavour is *nuoc khoang kim boi*; a bottle costs US$0.20.

When the US economic embargo was lifted in 1994, Pepsi beat Coca-Cola into the Vietnamese market – a major coup. However, Coke hit back hard with a high-pitched sales campaign and seems to have the dominant market share now. Sprite and 7 Up are also widely available. Diet drinks sweetened with the usual suspected carcinogens can sometimes be found in the supermarkets of large cities, but they're expensive.

The usual fruit juices are available throughout Vietnam.

Alcoholic Drinks

Beer Hanoi Beer and Halida are two local brands of beer costing about two-thirds the price of the imported brands in cans and about half the price of bottles. Other 100% Vietnamese brands include Bi Vina, Castel, Huda, and 333.

There are a number of foreign brands which are brewed in Vietnam under licence. These include Fosters, BGI, Carlsberg, Heineken and Vinagen.

Finally, God created Vietnam's ubiquitous *bia hoi* (see the boxed text 'Bia Hoi').

Wine Vietnam produces over 50 varieties of wine *(ruou)*, many of them made from rice. The cheapest rice wines *(ruou de)* are used for cooking – drink them at your peril.

Another Vietnamese speciality is snake wine *(ruou ran)*. This is basically rice wine with a pickled snake floating in it. This elixir is said to have some tonic properties and is claimed to cure everything from night blindness to impotence (see Exotic Meats earlier in this section).

A variation on the theme is to have the snake killed right at your table and the blood poured into a cup. To get the full health benefits, the Vietnamese recommend that you drink the snake's blood mixed with rice wine and eat the gall bladder raw. Connoisseurs of this cuisine also recommend that you put the snake's still-beating heart into a glass of rice wine and 'bottoms up'. This cocktail is believed to work as an aphrodisiac. For the less adventurous, the imported wine and champagne situation is constantly improving.

C'est la Vie

The Vietnamese are the world's best copy-cats; nobody does it better. The prevailing trend in business is to imitate thy neighbour, rather than create an original niche. This tendency is displayed by restaurants, hotels, street names and tour programs, but perhaps the best example is the bottled water market.

In 1989, La Vie, the famed French mineral water maker, was the first foreign outfit to set up bottling plants in Vietnam. Since then, strikingly close variations on the trademark red, white and blue label design, and the name La Vie, have appeared in all corners of the country. At last count there were as many as 20 spin-offs, including those with nonsense names like La Viei, La Vu, La Vi and La Ve. The best, perhaps, are the those which have meaning (in their masculine form) in French: slurp down a cold bottle of 'the quick' (La Vif), 'the empty' (La Vide) or, brace yourself, 'the rape' (La Viole).

Hard Liquor Alcoholic beverages *(ruou manh)* from China are very cheap, taste like paint thinner and smell like diesel fuel. Russian vodka is one of the few products the former USSR has left to export. Locally produced Hanoi Vodka is also available, and one brand worth trying, Nep Mui, is flavoured with young sticky rice.

As in the rest of Asia, the Hanoian elite prefer foreign name brands like Johnny Walker Black.

Bia Hoi

Avid beer-drinkers on a tight budget should memorise the words *bia hoi*, Vietnam's version of draught beer. Since its appearance in the early 1990s, bia hoi has swept the nation like a plague and, particularly in the north (where beer starts flowing in the early morning!), has become a social institution.

Bia hoi quality varies from lukewarm and flat to chilled and bubbly, depending on whether it is siphoned through a rubber hose from large petrol drums (the most common variety) or drawn out of pressurised kegs. Either way, most bia hoi in Hanoi is generally OK, and it is always cheap – about US$0.25 per litre! Places that serve bia hoi usually also have good, cheap food to help soak up the alcohol.

Most bia hoi spots are indoor-outdoor and offer the comfort of small plastic tables and six-inch stools. Don't expect English menus or air-conditioning, but what bia hoi places lack in décor is dutifully made up for in price and local atmosphere.

So where to find it? There are signs advertising bia hoi all over the city (notably along Pho Phan Chu Trinh, running south from the Opera House), and some cafés even have it on the menu.

For bia hoi virgins, we can recommend a few places to help get initiated. Look for the unnamed bia hoi at 24 Pho Tong Dan (a short stumble north from the Opera House), easy to spot by the yellow façade advertising 'Bia Hoi Viet Hai' brand beer. Another no-name place worth seeking out is the 'bia hoi on the dike' north of the Old Quarter on Ð Yen Phu. In the Old Quarter at 40 Pho Bat Dan, look for Bia Hoi Ha Chau Quan, a small bia hoi-cum-restaurant.

VIETNAMESE
Vietnamese – Budget

Banh My Hué *(Map 4;* ☎ *971 5914, 9 Pho Hoa Ma)* is a hugely popular Hué-style beefsteak place, open from 7 am to 11 pm. The house speciality is *banh my bittet xiu mai opla*, a high cholesterol hot plate of sizzling beef with fried eggs, potatoes, a fried pork ball and vegetable garnish (pickled cucumber on the side) – all for US$1.10. Other selections include *banh khoai*, a kind of Vietnamese crêpe (US$0.50), *banh my cari opla*, curry with pork, chicken and beef (US$0.90), and *bun bo gio heo Hué*, beef and pig's feet soup (US$0.60). You can watch the food being prepared in pools of flaming grease near the entrance. Incidentally, watch your step inside this place – the floor is as slippery as an ice skating rink!

Another popular local steak place is the ***Hoang Long Restaurant*** *(Map 4;* ☎ *826 1991, 70 Pho Hoa Ma)*, just up the road from Banh My Hué. You might try ***Thanh Thuy*** *(Map 5;* ☎ *828 2052, 15 Hang Cot)*, a popular little beefsteak restaurant just next to Van Xuan Restaurant – tasty steaks here cost under US$1.

Bun Bo Nam Bo *(Map 5;* ☎ *828 5229, 65 Pho Hang Dieu)* serves up delicious bowls of *bun bo* (beef and vegetable noodle soup) for under US$1. Just next door at No 67 is an identical spin-off restaurant, equally good.

Lau De Nhat Ly *(Map 5;* ☎ *927 1434, 1 Pho Hang Cot)* specialises in goat meat barbecued over coals at your table. Intrepid eaters might try the house rice wine, mixed with goat's blood or, better yet, gall bladder.

There are two more popular goat meat restaurants, ***Dung Lau de Quan*** *(Map 4;* ☎ *971 1059, 5 Pho Hoa Ma)* and ***Lau de Thong*** *(Map 4;* ☎ *971 0492, 9B Pho Hoa Ma)*, both

PLACES TO EAT

located between the above-mentioned Banh My Hué and Apocalypse Now bar.

Khoa *(Map 5; ☎ 824 2206, 77 Pho Hai Ba Trung)* is a popular goose *(ngan)* speciality restaurant. It serves savoury goose soup with vegetables and a choice of fresh rice noodles *(bun ngan)* or dry noodles *(mien ngan)* for about US$0.40. For about US$1, consider sampling grilled goose *(ngan nuong)*, boiled goose *(ngan luoc)* or fried goose *(ngan xao lan)*; all go down well with a side of cherry-red fresh goose blood topped with grated peanuts and goose liver (US$0.40). Khoa is open from 7.30 am to 10 pm, and is clean, friendly and always packed.

The sign at ***Restaurant 75 Tue Tinh*** *(Map 4; ☎ 821 8363, 75 Pho Tue Tinh)* reads simply 'Com' (or rice), but inside this tidy little hideaway awaits a positively fresh daily selection of meats, seafood and vegetables. In addition to orthodox offerings, you can choose from exotic dishes like frog, snail, chicken testes and bull penis, all of which you simply point to and it will be cooked to order. Expect to spend about US$1.60 per plate.

Restaurant 3 Dien Bien Phu *(Map 3; ☎ 828 7833, 3 Pho Dien Bien Phu)* is a classic little enter-through-the-kitchen place which sits right beside the railway tracks (keep your arms inside the window!). It serves standard Vietnamese fare, including excellent spring rolls and whole fish, plus things like frog, turtle and pigeon (all kindly illustrated on the menu).

On Pho Cha Ca in the Old Quarter, ***Tuyet Nhung*** *(Map 5; ☎ 828 1164)* is an excellent place to sample *banh cuon*. A set meal costs US$1, but you may need more than one to fill up.

If you want to try something *very* local, ***Ba Luy*** *(Map 5; ☎ 822 5537, 54 Pho Tran Xuan Soan)* has a 70 year history in preparing *gio* and *cha*. *Banh gio* is ground pork inside a salted rice cake wrapped and steamed in banana leaf; *cha* is a pork paste cooked with cinnamon powder around a thick length of bamboo; and *cha com* is silver dollar pork pies made with young sticky rice. You can fill up here for under US$1. The restaurant

(actually just a few tiny stools in an alley-way) is open daily from 7 am to 7 pm.

Pho *Pho* noodle soup is Vietnam's ubiquitous breakfast of champions, and Hanoi has no shortage of places to sample it. Most pho shops are open from early in the morning until late afternoon, and charge between US$0.40 and US$0.80 a bowl.

For a great bowl of beef noodle soup, try ***Pho Bo Dac Biet*** *(Map 5; 2B Pho Ly Quoc Su)*. This place is a bit filthy, but the food is delicious – look for the line out front in the morning.

Pho Cuong *(Map 5; 23 Pho Hang Muoi)* in the Old Quarter opens at 4 am and is one of Hanoi's most popular beef noodle soup places.

Tiem Pho *(Map 5; 48-50 Pho Hué)* serves up Hué-style chicken noodle soup and keeps late hours.

Mai Anh *(Map 5; ☎ 825 8492, 32 Pho Le Van Huu)* dishes up excellent chicken noodle soup served with a raw egg which slow-cooks as you eat.

At 48 Pho Hang Be (next door to the Binh Minh Hotel) in the Old Quarter is an unnamed *pho ga* place with excellent chicken noodle soup prepared with ground pork and mushrooms *(bun moc)*.

Speciality Streets A trip to one of Hanoi's many speciality food streets is a must. From street stalls with pint-size plastic stools to hole-in-the-wall restaurants featuring the remnants of the last customer's meal scattered on the floor, you'll find an astounding variety of food, great local atmosphere and low prices. Some places do have English menus, but it is best to go with a Vietnamese friend who can help you decide what to eat and make sense of the fact that most places do not show prices on the menu.

The speciality streets are highly popular with locals, and the level of competition is evident by the aggressive touts who will go to any length to extol the virtues of their particular restaurant. These daredevils will literally grab the handlebars of passing motorbikes or leap out in front of oncoming traffic to steer you to their tables!

Cam Chi (Maps 3 & 5) is about 500m north-east of Hanoi train station. It's a very small street – basically an alley – crammed full of lively street stalls serving budget priced, delicious food. Only a few places have English menus and don't expect comfortable seating. Still, where else can you have a small banquet for US$1 or less? The derivation of 'Cam Chi' (meaning forbidden to point), dates from centuries ago. It is said that the street was named as a reminder for local residents to keep their curious fingers in their pockets when the King and his entourage made their way through this neighbourhood.

Pho Mai Hac De (Map 4), in the south-central area, has several blocks of restaurants running south from the northern terminus at Pho Tran Nhan Tong.

Bun Cha – Nem Cua Be (38 Pho Mai Hac De) serves delicious BBQ pork, and pork and crab filled spring rolls.

Quyen (☎ 943 0431, 63 Pho Mai Hac De) dishes up bowls of *bun ngan* and *mien ngan* (noodle soups) for about US$0.50. Overlooking the tables is an enormous, antique, wood-carved statue of a legendary local doctor.

Đ Thuy Khue (Map 3), on the south bank of West Lake (Ho Tay), features a strip of 30-odd outdoor seafood restaurants (called Quan Ca in Vietnamese) with pleasant lakeside seating. You can eat well around here for about US$7 per person.

Pho To Hien Thanh (Map 4) runs in an east-west direction, and also specialises in small seafood restaurants. It's to the south of the city centre, just east of Bay Mau Lake.

Man's Best Friend Approximately 10km north of central Hanoi are about 60 dog meat restaurants all concentrated in a 1km stretch of Đ Nghi Tam (Map 2). This street runs along the embankment between West Lake and the Red River. Hanoians believe that eating dog meat *(thit cho)* in the first half of the lunar month brings bad luck – consequently, these restaurants are deserted

at that time and most shut down. Business picks up in the second half of the lunar month and the last day is particularly auspicious – the restaurants are packed.

In the same area there are also several places to feast on snails *(oc)*, but don't expect the hygienic preparation standards of a French restaurant.

Vietnamese – Mid-Range

Hanoi has a legion of reasonable-priced Vietnamese restaurants which offer a higher level of hygiene than street stalls, but where you can eat well without breaking the bank.

Soho Café (Map 5; ☎ 826 6555, 57 Pho Ba Trieu) is in an attractive villa and serves excellent Vietnamese and Asian dishes, most costing between US$2 and US$4. Order from the menu (try the house speciality, Franco-Vietnamese bouillabaisse), or check the daily specials board. Upstairs you can sit outside on the pleasant veranda. Soho also offers take-away and free delivery.

Dinh Lang Restaurant (Map 5; ☎ 828 6290, 1 Pho Le Thai To) is another inexpensive place for good Vietnamese food. It hosts traditional music nightly. The restaurant is right above the busy *Thuy Ta Café (Map 5; ☎ 828 8148)*, overlooking Hoan Kiem Lake.

Trong Dong (Map 5; ☎ 934 0604, 2 Pho Le Thach) serves good Vietnamese dishes, free tea and also has live traditional music. The restaurant faces Indira Gandhi Park, just behind the main post office. It's open from 6 am to 10 pm daily.

There are several restaurants all in a cluster calling themselves *Hué Restaurant*. Hué food is justifiably famous, and it's worth seeking these places out. Consider trying *Quan Hué Restaurant (Map 5; ☎ 824 4062, 6 Pho Ly Thuong Kiet)*. On the opposite side of the street is *Huong Giang (Map 5; ☎ 824 1515, 11 Pho Ly Thuong Kiet)*. The slogan here is 'Our food is more Hué than Hué'.

Cung Dinh Quan (Map 5; ☎ 825 4400, 15 Pho Tran Quoc Toan) serves Hué-style cuisine in a delightfully kitschy, bright yellow and red replication of a royal banquet hall.

Vietnamese – Top-End

Hanoi has several top-notch Vietnamese restaurants, many housed in elegant French villas. Most are excellent, not overpriced for the quality of the food, boast a romantic atmosphere, and feature live traditional music.

Seasons of Hanoi (Map 3; ☎ 843 5444, 95B Pho Quan Thanh) is one of the city's best choices for authentic Vietnamese food. This thoughtfully restored villa has a hint of art deco and some interesting antiques on display. It serves classical Vietnamese fare, blending tastes of both north and south. The banana flower salad and sautéed aubergines (eggplant) are both superb.

Indochine (Map 5; ☎ 824 6097, 16 Pho Nam Ngu) is housed in a restored villa and features authentic southern Vietnamese cuisine. Wait staff dress in colourful formal wear and there is also live traditional music nightly.

Another elegant setting for authentic Vietnamese cuisine is *Nam Phuong* (Map 5; ☎ 824 0926, 19 Pho Phan Chu Trinh). Housed in a charming colonial villa, Nam Phuong has traditional in-house music and an impressive wine list to complement the stunning southern Vietnamese fare.

Countryside Restaurant (Map 4; ☎ 821 9487, 9 Pho Nguyen Cong Tru) also serves good southern Vietnamese fare and boasts an attractive ethnic décor.

Com Duc Vien (Map 4; ☎ 943 0081, 13 Pho Ngo Thi Nham) is yet another classic villa (with beautiful French doors) in which to sample fine Vietnamese food.

Also recommended is the pleasant *Cay Cau* (Map 5; ☎ 824 5346, 17A Pho Tran Hung Dao) on the ground floor of the De Syloia Hotel. The name means betel nut in Vietnamese.

A stylish spot to try Hué-style dishes is *Van Xuan* (Map 5; ☎ 927 2888, 15A Pho Hang Cot). Traditional folk music is performed here nightly from 7.15 to 8.45 pm.

Hanoi Specialities

One of Hanoi's most famous food specialities is *cha ca*, perhaps best thought of as sumptuous fish hamburgers. The best known cha ca place in town is *Cha Ca La Vong* (Map 5; ☎ 825 3929, 14 Pho Cha Ca)*, a true Hanoi institution. Other worthy (and slightly cheaper) places to try this local delicacy include *Cha Ca 66* (Map 5; ☎ 826 7881, 66 Pho Hang Ga) and *Thang Long* (Map 5; ☎ 824 5115, 40 Pho Hang Ma).

VEGETARIAN

An excellent vegetarian option in the Old Quarter is *The Whole Earth Vegetarian Restaurant* (Map 5; ☎ 828 1996, 116 Pho Hang Bac).

The atmospheric, smoke-free *Com Chay Nang Tam* (Map 5; ☎ 826 6140, 79A Pho Tran Hung Dao) is known for delicious vegetarian creations which are named and look remarkably like meat dishes (an ancient Vietnamese tradition intended to make guests feel at home). Try the superb 'fried snow balls'.

Thanh Tam (Map 3; ☎ 828 1252, 204 Pho Pho Duc Chinh) is a bit out of the way (north of the Old Quarter), but the food is commendable and prices are reasonable.

SEAFOOD

The excellent *Sam Son Seafood Market Restaurant* (☎ 825 0780, 77 Pho Doc Bac Co) is right on the banks of the Red River. This huge, new fish market-cum-restaurant is named after the small fishing village, about 175km south of Hanoi, where they get all their fresh sea creatures. Here you can buy fresh seafood and have it cooked to your liking. Prices are reasonable.

One of the best upmarket seafood restaurants in Hanoi is *San Ho Restaurant* (Map 5; ☎ 822 2184, 58 Pho Ly Thuong Kiet), set in an attractive French villa. Also consider the creatively named *Seafood Restaurant* (Map 5; ☎ 825 8759, 22A Pho Hai Ba Trung).

The *Shrimp Cakes Restaurant* (Map 3; Nha Hang Banh Tom Hotay, ☎ 825 7839, 1 Ð Thanh Nien) has a number of great dishes on the menu, including (surprise?) shrimp cakes. Weather permitting, you can sit outside and admire the view of Truc Bach Lake. The food is excellent, though we've been hearing recent complaints about inflated prices for foreigners.

INTERNATIONAL

The Red Onion Bistro (Map 5; ☎ 934 2342 ext 6218, Hanoi Towers, 49 Pho Hai Ba Trung) is one of Hanoi's newest gems. Californian chef Bobby Chinn has mastered the art of orgasmic fusion cooking, while keeping prices in the realm of foreplay (most dishes cost between US$2 and US$6). Eclectic selections include superb salads, authentic Thai curries and decadent desserts (try the warm chocolate pudding). They are open for breakfast, lunch and dinner from 6.30 am to midnight.

Cyclo Bar & Restaurant (Map 5; ☎ 828 6844, 38 Pho Duong Thanh) is worthy of a plug for creative design alone. Here they serve up respectable Vietnamese and French food to customers seated in actual cyclos (cleverly transformed into tables). There is also a pleasant outdoor courtyard.

Delightful for lunch is the open-air *Hoa Sua (Map 5; ☎ 824 0448, 81 Pho Tho Nhuom)*, a Hanoi institution which takes in and trains a steady stream of needy street children for culinary careers (it has already turned out more than 300 professional chefs). There is good French and Vietnamese food and the French pastries from the bakery here are excellent.

Al Fresco's (Map 5; ☎ 826 7782, 23L Pho Hai Ba Trung) is a casual Aussie-run restaurant serving up pizzas, ribs, salads and the like. Prices are reasonable and the portions are gigantic. Come hungry. The same folks run *Pepperonis Pizza & Café (Map 4; ☎ 976 0088, 71 Pho Mai Hac De)*. Pizzas range from just US$1.25 to US$4 and pasta dishes cost US$1.60.

Another casual spot for simple pizzas and pastas is *Mama Rosa (Map 5; ☎ 825 8057, 6 Pho Le Thai To)*, just across from Hoan Kiem Lake.

The British-run *Verandah Bar & Café (Map 5; ☎ 825 7220, 9 Pho Nguyen Khac Can)* is a popular café-restaurant in a stylish French villa with bistro-style cooking. It's open daily from 8 am to midnight, and serves Sunday brunches. The menu includes such things as chicken enchiladas and smoked salmon and quiche. Besides the dining room, you can sit by the bar or out on the verandah.

Another popular expat hang-out is *Mekki's Bar (Map 5; ☎ 826 7552)* and the *Lan Anh Restaurant*. This bar-restaurant is run by an Algerian man and his Vietnamese wife and offers a wide variety of French, Middle Eastern and Vietnamese dishes. It also has satellite TV behind the bar.

There are pool tables and straightforward Vietnamese fare at the *Pear Tree Pub (Map 5; ☎ 825 7812, 78 Pho Tho Nhuom)*, just south-east of the Ambassadors' Pagoda.

Just 30m in front of the Hanoi Hotel is the *Latino Pub (Map 2; ☎ 846 0836, 102 C8 Pho Giang Vo)*. The menu includes Tex-Mex food and other Latin American dishes. The Vietnamese owner lived abroad for a while and speaks fluent Spanish.

The *Met Pub (Map 5; ☎ 826 6919 ext 8857)* is in an annexe of the Sofitel Metropole Hotel. It's a lovely place with fine food and Hanoi's best beer selection, but it's very expensive.

Les Flamboyants (Map 5; ☎ 824 5581, 37A Pho Hang Thung) may be the only place in Vietnam to sample authentic Creole cuisine. Chef Richel brings to Hanoi the flavours and spices of his native Reunion Island. Recommended are his salads, black pudding, and rougail sausages. Most dishes cost between US$1.50 and US$4.

The *Wild Horse Saloon (Map 5; ☎ 824 0607, 82 Ly Thuong Kiet)* is done up in honky-tonk cowboy décor. Here local beefsteaks sell for US$4.50, or imported US Angus beef for around three times the price. It serves a decent selection of American wines – a relative rarity in Hanoi.

In the creative naming category, there is *Five Royal Fish (Map 5; ☎ 824 4368, 16 Le Thai To)*, overlooking Hoan Kiem Lake and serving Vietnamese and European food. Close by, the modern *Rendezvous Café (Map 5; ☎ 828 9705, 136 Pho Hang Trong)* is open for breakfast, lunch and dinner. It offers Asian and western selections, and has an in-house bakery.

Also near the lake, *Green Ho Guom (Map 5; ☎ 828 8806, 32 Pho Le Thai To)* is a spacious and funky place with live music and karaoke. It serves Vietnamese and western dishes at reasonable prices.

ITALIAN

Perhaps the best all-round ristorante in town is the family-style *La Dolce Vita*, aka Bat Dan Café *(Map 5; ☎ 828 6411, 10 Pho Bat Dan)*, right in the heart of the Old Quarter. The friendly photographer/chef Gino makes excellent pastas and salads at reasonable prices.

Il Grillo (Map 4; ☎ 822 7720, 116 Pho Ba Trieu) is a classy upmarket option which stocks the best selection of Italian wines in Hanoi.

Equally good, *Il Padrino (Map 5; ☎ 828 8449, 42 Pho Le Thai To)* commands a great location across from Hoan Kiem Lake and may just serve the perfect coffee.

For the best pizza this side of Bangkok try *Mediterraneo (Map 5; ☎ 826 6288, 23 Pho Nha Tho)*, a few steps from St Joseph's Cathedral.

Attached to the Pear Tree Pub is Hanoi's first Italian restaurant, *A Little Italian (Map 5; ☎ 825 8167, 78 Pho Tho Nhuom)*.

FRENCH

The romantic *Le Splendide (Map 5; ☎ 826 6087, 44 Pho Ngo Quyen)* is Hanoi's *crème de la crème* for French cuisine. The restaurant is in the historic Hoa Binh Hotel, which was built by the French as Hotel Le Splendide in 1926. The menu offers savoury, authentic south-western French cooking and fine wines.

Another elegant upmarket option for fine French fare is *Le Beaulieu (Map 5; ☎ 826 6919 ext 8028, 15 Pho Ngo Quyen)*, in the Sofitel Metropole Hotel.

Le Café des Arts (Map 5; ☎ 828 7207, 11B Pho Bao Khanh) is a more casual affair. This artsy expat/Vietnamese-run place is modelled on a Parisian brasserie and serves up good 'anytime food' at moderate prices.

Other choices for French food include the *President Garden Restaurant (Map 5; ☎ 825 3606, 14 Pho Tong Dan)* and, very close to the Opera House, *Gustave Eiffel Restaurant (Map 5; ☎ 825 0625, 17 Pho Trang Tien)*.

ASIAN
Chinese

Despite the proximity to China, Chinese food in Hanoi tends to be pricey. The *Chau Giang Restaurant (Map 5; ☎ 822 2650, 18 Pho Yet Kieu)* is one possible exception.

The large Chinese restaurant on the ground floor of the *Hoa Long Hotel (Map 5; ☎ 826 9319, 94 Pho Hang Trong)*, near the west shore of Hoan Kiem Lake, is also worth checking out. Just next door at No 96 is another option, the *Thu Huong Chinese Restaurant (Map 5; ☎ 825 5490)*.

Thai

There is excellent Thai fare at *Sukiyaki (Map 5; ☎ 825 4613, 63 Pho Hang Trong)*, in the rear of a supermarket. Why it is named after a Japanese delicacy remains a mystery.

Tam Tu (Map 5; ☎ 825 1682, 84 Pho Ly Thuong Kiet) and *Baan Thai Restaurant (Map 5; ☎ 828 1120, 3B Pho Cha Ca)* are also good choices.

Japanese

Hanoi's resident Japanese seem to agree that *Benkay (Map 4; ☎ 822 3535)*, in the snazzy new Hotel Nikko, serves the best Japanese food in town. The closest upmarket contender is *Edo (Map 2; ☎ 831 5000)*, in the Daewoo Hotel.

Despite the cheesy name, *Saigon Sakura (Map 5; ☎ 825 7565, 17 Pho Trang Thi)* is nicely decorated, centrally located and affordable.

There are a couple of excellent choices on Pho Ba Trieu.

Ohan (Map 4; ☎ 821 6033) at number 322 has a Vietnamese owner who spent some years living in Japan. It has two Japanese chefs in-house and all of the sashimi is imported from Japan.

Farther down the road *Show (Map 4; ☎ 821 5701)*, at number 244, is another place with a resident Japanese chef.

Ky Y (Map 4; ☎ 978 1386, 29 Pho Phu Dong Thien Vuong) serves Japanese fare in a quaint French colonial villa just off Pho Hoa Ma.

Indian – Malay

Khazana (Map 5; ☎ 824 1166, 41B Pho Ly Thai To), literally 'a treasure', offers the most authentic Indian food and décor in Hanoi. Business lunch sets are good value at under US$5. *Tandoor Indian Restaurant (Map 5; ☎ 824 5359, 24 Pho Hang Be)* in the Old Quarter is another possibility.

Moca Café (Map 5; ☎ 825 6334, 14-16 Pho Nha Tho), in addition to being a full service café, has a good selection of Indian dishes and other fine foods.

Thu Thuy Asian Food (Map 5; ☎ 943 0413, 53 Pho Ba Trieu) is a good choice for authentic Malaysian and Singaporian food. It is open for breakfast, lunch and dinner, and also offers take-away and free delivery.

DELICATESSENS & SELF-CATERING

Many decide that the best cheap option is to pick up a loaf of delicious French bread, some salami, cheese and a Coke or beer, then take it to a quiet park or lakeside (or even back to their hotel room) to enjoy it.

No Noodles (Map 5; ☎ 828 6861, 51 Pho Luong Van Can) is a trendy sandwich joint which has mastered the art of applying avocado between the slices. There are only a few stools to sit on, so you might plan on takeaway, or pay a few thousand dong for delivery.

Both locations of *The Deli (Map 5; ☎ 846 0007, 18 Pho Tran Huy Lieu and ☎ 934 2335, 13B Hai Ba Trung)* whip up very tasty sandwiches for about US$1.20.

Independent of the above, there is a snazzy third place calling itself *The Deli (Map 5; ☎ 934 0888)* at *The Press Club*, an upmarket restaurant at 59A Pho Ly Thai To. This one too has both eat-in and take-away service.

Hanoi Gourmet (Map 5; ☎ 943 1009, 1B Pho Ham Long) is one of the chicest delis in town. It has fine imported meats and every European fix – at a price.

More determined self-caterers can buy fresh vegetables at the *Hom Market* (Map 4), just south of the city centre near the intersection of Pho Hué and Pho Tran Xuan Soan.

Supermarkets

Close to the Hanoi Opera House, new *Mini Mart Trang Tien (Map 5; ☎ 825 3602, 7 Pho Trang Tien)* has a good selection of local and imported goods. There is also a mini-mart worth a look in the Hanoi Towers building.

Western Canned Goods (Map 5; Cua Hang 66, ☎ 822 9217, 66 Pho Ba Trieu) sells imported staples, deli meats and cheeses, and is open from 8.30 am to 8 pm.

Cua Hang Thuc Pham 17 (Map 5; ☎ 934 3854, 17 Pho Hai Ba Trung) is smaller, but has a good selection of imported wines. It's open from 8 am to 10 pm.

The *Hanoi Star Mart (Map 4; ☎ 822 5999, 60 Pho Ngo Thi Nham)* is a good mini-supermarket, with a smaller branch next to the Energy Hotel at 30 Pho Ly Thai To.

Sieu Thi Nam Bo (Map 3; ☎ 843 9883, 5 Đ Le Duan) is a large, three-storey place selling a wide variety of food and consumer goods.

CAFÉS

When you're visiting St Joseph's Cathedral, stop into *Moca Café (Map 5; ☎ 825 6334, 14-16 Pho Nha Tho)*, a open-air Arcadia of *real* espressos, cappuccinos and lattes. They specialise in Arabian coffee, which is roasted and ground on the premises. On a chilly winter day, try one of the body-warming spiked espresso cocktails.

Café Lac Viet (Map 5; ☎ 828 9155, 46 Pho Le Thai To) is a sleek contender in Hanoi's prime java category, and is a good idea for a light lunch. The café is next to Fanny's ice cream shop.

Au Lac (Map 5; ☎ 825 7807, 57 Pho Ly Thai To) is a garden café and bar in the front courtyard of a lovely French villa just across from the Sofitel Hotel. It serves good light food and coffee. Just a few steps away from Au Lac is another Parisian-style place, *Diva (Map 5; ☎ 824 7579)*, run by a former Miss Vietnam.

The *Dak Linh Café (Map 5; ☎ 828 7043)* commands a prime location on the shore of Hoan Kiem Lake.

Café Pho (Map 5; ☎ 826 6862, 15 Pho Ly Thuong Kiet) is in an attractive villa with a cosy outdoor courtyard facing the street. Vietnamese and European foods are also served in the dining room. Prices are reasonable.

Café Lam (Map 5; 80 Pho Nguyen Huu Huan) is a Hanoi institution. This bohemian artists' hang-out has been around for nearly a half-century, and the walls are covered by the owner's rare collection of Vietnamese paintings.

Another atmospheric, old-world place in the Old Quarter is *Café Quyen (Map 5; 46B Pho Bat Dan)*.

Popular with teens and upwardly mobile young Hanoians are the cafés along Pho Hang Hanh (Map 5), known locally as 'coffee street' (despite the fact the name means 'onion street'). Many places stay open late and offer reasonable prices. Most popular is the five-storey *Café Nhan (☎ 826 9861, 39D Pho Hang Hanh)*. This place serves over 1000 customers a day! A bit quieter is the atmospheric *Old Quarter Café*, which is dimly lit (look for the red Chinese paper lanterns). Just across the street is the more modern *Café Xuan*.

Quan Cay Da (Map 5; ☎ 934 1217, 8 Pho Le Lai), or the 'banyon tree café', is a popular outdoor café in the spacious front courtyard of the Children's Theatre.

Among the trendy new Vietnamese cafés, look for *Ciao Café (Map 5; ☎ 934 1494, 2 Pho Hang Bai)* and *Friend Café (Map 5; ☎ 826 2588, 1 Pho Ba Trieu)*, both near the southern end of Hoan Kiem Lake, and the *Gallery Café (Map 5; ☎ 828 0905, 35 Pho Luong Ngoc Quyen)*, in the Old Quarter.

Finally, for some of the best yoghurt, French pastries and coffee in Vietnam, visit the friendly *Kinh Do Café (Map 5; ☎ 825 0216, 252 Pho Hang Bong)*, near the city centre. The breakfasts are outstanding.

TRAVELLERS' CAFÉS

The budget end of the food business is dominated by a handful of small cafés preparing a variety of Vietnamese and western dishes. Aside from the food, these are good places to look for cheap rooms, meet other travellers and arrange tours.

The Aussie-run *Kangaroo Café (Map 5; ☎ 828 9931, 18 Pho Bao Khanh)* is one of Hanoi's most recent arrivals. They serve up good local and western grub, including some vegetarian selections and down-under staples like Vegemite.

A well established backpacker mecca is *A to Z Queen Café (Map 5; ☎ 826 0860, 65 Pho Hang Bac)*. Food is light with plenty of baguettes, fried eggs and coffee. You can book tours and surf the Net here too. Queen Café has a second branch in the Binh Minh Hotel at 50 Pho Hang Be.

Love Planet Café (Map 5; ☎ 828 4864, 25 Pho Hang Bac) receives good reports for backpacker cuisine, tours and email service. On the second floor is the new *Lovely Pub*, serving cheap drinks and some interesting homemade fruit liquors.

Red River Café (Map 5; ☎ 826 8427, 73 Pho Hang Bo) is another contender in the tour-booking/cheap-eats business.

Tin Tin Bar & Café (Map 5; ☎ 826 0326, 14 Pho Hang Non) is another backpacker haven. The menu includes good pizza, juices, crêpes, fried rice, burgers and so on.

Old Darling Café (Map 5; ☎ 824 3024, 142 Pho Hang Bac), another Old Quarter backpacker hang-out, has respectable cheap eats.

Smiling Café (Map 5; ☎ 825 2750, 100 Pho Cau Go) is a great place to study the Hanoi traffic.

We can assure you that the *Lonely Planet Café (Map 5; ☎ 825 0974, 33 Pho Hang Be)* is in no way affiliated with a certain guidebook company. However, as Hanoi cafés go, the food is edible and prices reasonable.

The *Meeting Café (Map 5; ☎ 825 8812, 59B Pho Ba Trieu)* is a well established budget travellers' haven. Here you can find the usual backpacker cuisine (banana pancakes, milkshakes, cakes, coffee and spring rolls).

ICE CREAM SHOPS

Fanny's (Map 5; ☎ 828 5656, 48 Pho Le Thai To), on the Hoan Kiem lakefront, dishes up excellent 'Franco-Vietnamese' ice cream and tempting sorbets. (If the season is right, try the *com*, a delightful local flavour extracted from young sticky rice.)

The most popular ice cream with local Hanoians is at ***Kem Trang Tien*** *(Map 5; 54 Pho Trang Tien)*. Just look for the mob on the sidewalk lined up to take away sticks of the tasty treat (US$0.30). There is also an indoor place here where you can relax in air-con comfort.

Great ice cream sundaes can be found at ***Kem Tra My*** (Map 3), on Pho Nguyen Thai Hoc a few hundred metres from Ho Chi Minh's Mausoleum.

Kem Kiwi *(Map 5; ☎ 825 1906, 39 Pho Ly Thuong Kiet)*, strategically located adjacent to the New Zealand embassy, serves up real New Zealand-style ice cream for about US$0.40.

Hanoi also has branches of American ice cream kings ***Baskin Robbins*** *(Map 5; ☎ 825 2658, 20 Pho Ngo Quyen)* and ***Carvel*** *(Map 5; ☎ 828 7192, 32 Pho Ly Thai To)*.

If you don't feel like ice-cream try the fancy take-away cakes and pastries at ***Loc Tai*** *(Map 5; ☎ 826 1326, 76 Pho Hang Dieu)*.

PLACES TO EAT

Entertainment

WATER PUPPETS

There is perhaps no more typically Hanoian form of entertainment than a water puppet performance. This fantastic art form (see the boxed text 'Puppetry in a Pool') originated in northern Vietnam and Hanoi is *the* place to see it.

Just on the shore of Hoan Kiem Lake is the *Municipal Water Puppet Theatre (Map 5; Roi Nuoc Thang Long, ☎ 824 9494, 57B Pho Dinh Tien Hoang)*. Performances are held daily from 8 to 9.15 pm. Admission is US$1.60, or US$3.20 for the best seats and a take-home cassette of the music. There is a camera fee of US$0.80, or US$4 to shoot video.

TRADITIONAL THEATRE

The *Theatre of Traditional Arts (Map 4; Cau Lac Bo Nghe Thuat – Doan Cheo Ha Noi, ☎ 826 7361, 15 Pho Nguyen Dinh Chieu)* offers satirical performances of *cheo*. Shows are on

---

Puppetry in a Pool

The ancient art of water puppetry *(roi nuoc)* was virtually unknown outside of northern Vietnam until the 1960s. Depending on which story you believe, it originated with rice farmers who spent much of their time in flooded fields and either saw the potential of the water surface as a dynamic stage or adapted conventional puppetry during a massive flood of the Red River Delta. Whatever the true history, it is at least 1000 years old.

The farmers carved the puppets from water-resistant fig tree timber *(sung)* in forms modelled on the villagers themselves, animals from their daily lives and more fanciful mythical crea-

JULIET COOMBE/LA BELLE AURORE

Vietnamese water puppets during a performance at the municipal Water Puppet Theatre in Hanoi.

tures such as the dragon, phoenix and unicorn. Performances were usually staged in ponds, lakes or flooded paddy fields.

Ancient scholarly references to water puppetry indicate that during the Ly and Tran dynasties (1010-1400) water puppetry moved from being a simple pastime of villagers to formal courtly entertainment. The art form then all but disappeared, until interest was rekindled by the opening of the Municipal Water Puppet Theatre in Hanoi.

Contemporary performances use a square tank of waist deep water for the 'stage'; the water looks dirty, apparently by design to conceal the mechanisms that operate the puppets. The wooden puppets can be up to 50cm long and weigh as much as 15kg, they're painted with a glossy vegetable based paint. Each lasts only about three to four months if used continually, so puppet production provides one village outside Hanoi with a full-time industry.

Eleven puppeteers, trained for a minimum of three years, are involved in each performance. They stand in

Monday, Wednesday and Friday from 8 to 10 pm, and tickets cost US$4. The performances are interesting, but hard for many to follow. Fortunately an English pamphlet is provided.

The impressive French colonial style *Chuong Vang Theatre (Map 5; ☎ 825 7823, 72 Pho Hang Bac)* is right in the centre of the Old Quarter. Performances of contemporary *cai luong* are held here every Saturday and Sunday at 8 pm (shows last about two hours), for US$1.60.

DANCE

The *Hoan Kiem Cultural House (Map 5; Cau Lac Bo Vu Co Dien, ☎ 825 4620, 42 Pho Nha Chung)* hosts classical dance performances *(vo co dien)* on Tuesday, Thursday, Saturday and Sunday from 7 to 10 pm.

CLASSICAL MUSIC & OPERA

The *Central Cultural House (Map 5; Nha Van Hoa Trung Tam, ☎ 828 9664, 16 Pho Le Thai To)* recently established classical music performances. There is currently no fixed schedule, so you should call to find out if there is anything happening during your visit.

Ditto for the *Hanoi Opera House* (see the Things to See & Do chapter).

Puppetry in a Pool

the water behind a bamboo screen and have traditionally suffered from a host of water borne diseases – these days they reputedly wear waders to avoid this nasty occupational hazard.

Some puppets are simply attached to a long pole while others are set on a floating base which in turn is attached to a pole. Most have articulated limbs and heads, some also have rudders to help guide them. There can be as many as three poles attached to one puppet, and in the darkened auditorium it looks as if they are literally walking on water.

The considerable skills required to operate the puppets were traditionally kept secret and passed only from father to son; never to daughters through fear that they would marry outside the village and take the secrets with them.

The music, which is provided by a band, is as important as the action on stage. The band includes wooden flutes, gongs, cylindrical drums, bamboo xylophones and the fascinating single stringed *dan bau*. The body of the *dan bau* is made of the hard rind of the *bau*, a Vietnamese watermelon, and produces a range of haunting notes through the use of a 'whammy bar', a flexible bamboo stem attached to one end of the soundbox that alters the tension on the string.

The performance consists of a number vignettes depicting pastoral scenes and legends that explain the origins of various natural and social phenomena from the formation of lakes to the formation of nation states. One memorable scene is a wetly balletic depiction of rice farming in which the rice growing looks like accelerated film footage and the harvesting scenes are frantic and graceful. Another tells of the battle between a fisherman and his prey which is so realistic it appears as if a live fish is being used. There are also fire breathing dragons (complete with fireworks), a slapstick cat and mouse game between a Jaguar, a flock of ducks and the ducks' keeper, and a flute playing boy riding a buffalo.

The performance is entertaining and quite amusing, the water puppets are graceful and the water greatly enhances the drama, allowing the puppets to appear and disappear as if by magic.

Tony Davidson & Juliet Coombe

FOLK & TRADITIONAL MUSIC

Most of Hanoi's traditional Vietnamese music is limited to Hanoi's upmarket traditional Vietnamese restaurants. One place, however, where you can catch regular packaged-for-tourists performances is at the *Temple of Literature* (see the Things to See & Do chapter).

If you're keen on hearing tender Vietnamese folk songs on a peaceful boat ride on the Cau River, *TF Handspan (☎ 828 1996, 116 Pho Hang Bac)* can organise interesting day outings or overnight trips to the rice paper and alcohol village of Tho Ha (see Excursions chapter), famed for its local musicians.

ROCK & POP

There are no real clubs to hear live rock and roll, though discos occasionally feature live dance bands (usually a Filipino singer backed by a local band). Some bars and cafés also have a small stage where Vietnamese bands perform pop hits and lizardy lounge music.

JAZZ

The *Quan Nhac Jazz Club (Map 5; ☎ 826 6377, 16 Pho Le Thai To)*, better known as 'Jazz Club by Quyen Van Minh', is *the* place to catch live jazz in Hanoi. Bar owner Minh teaches saxophone at the Hanoi Conservatory and moonlights here, jamming with a wide variety of musicians from his students and his talented son (who is following in Dad's footsteps) to top-notch jazz players. The bar commands a prime second floor location overlooking Hoan Kiem Lake, with seating on a cool outdoor terrace as well in the bar. Bands play nightly from 8.30 to 11.30 pm.

PUBS & BARS

The majority of Vietnamese-style pubs tend to be karaoke lounges – you know you've been assimilated when you start enjoying these places.

However, with the influx of expats, Hanoi has experienced a boom in western-style pubs. Many of these are husband-and-wife joint ventures (typically a western husband

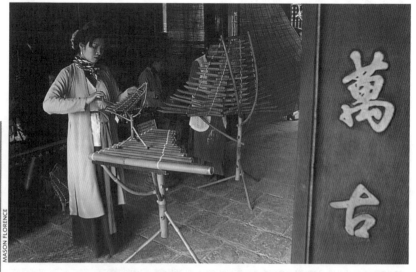

MASON FLORENCE

Traditional Vietnamese music at the Temple of Literature.

and Vietnamese wife). Aside from serving Halida beer, many of these places are indistinguishable from their counterparts in London, Berlin, New York or Melbourne. Darts, Mexican food, rock music and CNN can make you forget just where you are.

Bar Le Maquis (Map 5; ☎ 828 4402, ☎/fax 828 2598, 2A Pho Ta Hien) is a little speakeasy in the heart of the Old Quarter. It's run by French-Vietnamese motorcycle guide Fredo-Binh, who dubbed the place *Rung* (jungle) in Vietnamese as a place of escape. It is a popular after-hours hang-out of Hanoi's multinational biker contingent, and a good place to find information on motorbiking in northern Vietnam (see the Motorbiking in Northern Vietnam appendix for more).

Café-restaurant *La Dolce Vita*, aka Bat Dan Café *(Map 5; ☎ 828 6411, 10 Pho Bat Dan)*, also in the Old Quarter, is a relaxing place for drinks and features Hanoi's best selection of board games.

Fat Jacks (Map 5; ☎ 934 2342 ext 6218, Hanoi Towers, 49 Pho Hai Ba Trung), inside the popular Red Onion Bistro, has a dangerously long happy hour (1 to 8 pm!) and the best pool table in Hanoi. Tasty food can be ordered here from the tapas menu.

The *R&R Tavern (Map 4; ☎ 971 0498, 17 Pho Le Ngoc Han)* is run by mellow American Jay (with his Vietnamese wife), who can regale you with friendly conversation and South-East Asia's best selection of Grateful Dead classics.

The Spotted Cow (Map 5; ☎ 824 1028, 23C Pho Hai Ba Trung) is one of Hanoi's newest watering holes. This Aussie-run place is just a few doors down from Al Fresco's Restaurant, and features darts and late hours.

The legendary *Apocalypse Now (Map 4; ☎ 971 2783, 5C Pho Hoa Ma)* is known for loud and raucous music. Apocalypse opens at 5 pm and closes when the last customers trickle away. The DJ booth here was fashioned after a helicopter cockpit.

The unforgettably named *Golden Cock Bar (Map 5; ☎ 825 0499, 5 Pho Bao Khanh)* is an open-minded expat favourite. Next door to the 'GC' is the equally popular *Polite Pub (Map 5; ☎ 825 0959)*. Pho Bao

Khanh is near the north-west corner of Hoan Kiem Lake.

At the *Relax Bar (Map 5; ☎ 824 8409, 60 Pho Ly Thuong Kiet)* you can unwind from 9.30 am to 8 pm with a cold beer or cocktail while enjoying a US$2 head and face massage – US$4 gets you a shampoo and haircut to boot. The place is a bit on the seedy side and the bar, which stays open until midnight, is customarily full of intoxicated Aussies. Consequently, if you are looking to quell the munchies, look for the sidewalk stall just in front of the bar grilling up the tenderest chicken wings on the Asian continent!

The long-standing *Café de Paris (Map 5; ☎ 825 1659, 79E Pho Hang Trong)* is perhaps more café-restaurant than bar, but offers a little bit of everything. It's attached to the headquarters of the Especen Hotel chain.

Café Que Huong (Map 4; ☎ 971 1444, 42 Pho Tang Bat Ho) offers quiet indoor-outdoor villa surroundings and pool tables, and sees a good mix of foreigners and Vietnamese.

A short stroll from the Meritus Hotel, the *C & W Bar (Map 2; ☎ 829 2670, 6 Ð Thanh Nien)* has a cave-like basement bar and an outdoor rooftop café-bar overlooking West Lake.

DISCOS & CLUBS

Following reunification, ballrooms and discos were denounced as imperialist dens of iniquity and were shut down by the authorities. Since 1990 they have reopened, though certain forms of dancing (like Brazil's erotic dance, the lambada) remain banned. There are now even modern dance classes at public schools and formal ballroom dancing halls can be sought out.

Metal Night Club (Map 5; ☎ 824 1975, 57 Pho Cua Nam) is two blocks north-east of Hanoi train station. There is a live band every night and the music is *loud*. The cover charge is US$4. Opening hours are from 11 am to 2 pm and 7.30 pm to 2 am.

The Japanese-run *Magic Night-club (Map 2; ☎ 563 0257, 3 Pho Thai Thinh)* is a cool dance place, entered via a boardwalk of arcade games. There is a US$5 cover charge.

ENTERTAINMENT

The *Queen Bee Nightclub (Map 2; ☎ 835 2612, 42A Pho Lang Ha)* is a long way west of the city centre, but the disco is lively. It's open from 2 pm to 2 am.

If you want to see how Vietnamese yuppies 'do the hustle', the fashionable *Sparks Nightclub (Map 4; ☎ 971 7207, 88 Pho Lo Duc)* is as good as it gets.

Dai Dong Centropell (Map 5; ☎ 826 7703, 46 Pho Hang Cot) is a combination karaoke and disco. It's in the Old Quarter just east of the Hanoi Citadel. Opening hours are from 7 pm to 2 am, and admission is free.

The Hanoi Hotel near Giang Vo Lake is home to the *Volvo Discotheque (Map 2; ☎ 845 2270)*. This place is very expensive, so bring your Visa card or a wheelbarrow full of dong.

KARAOKE

Most westerners find karaoke as appealing as roasted gecko with shrimp paste. Nonetheless, karaoke has taken over Hanoi and you'll have a hard time avoiding it. The Vietnamese seem to only enjoy karaoke if it's played at over 150 decibels.

Warning – many karaoke joints double as *karaoke om* (holding bars), where young female hostesses cater to hormone-driven men in the smoky comfort of a dimly lit singing room.

Some places may also have hidden charges, so it is best is to go together with a local Vietnamese friend (and incidentally a great way to get to know someone better).

CINEMAS

Movie theatres *(rap chieu bong)* are common in Hanoi. These days films from the former Eastern Bloc have been mostly replaced by Hollywood movies, as well as many Hong Kong and Chinese films. Most popular among Vietnamese are kung fu films, love stories and tear-jerking dramas.

Foreign films are occasionally subtitled, but usually dubbed. Typically each film's voice-overs, male and female, are handled by just one person. Watching Arnold Schwarzenegger speaking in Vietnamese is

hard enough to swallow, but try to imagine when it's in a dainty woman's voice!

These days Vietnam also produces its own movies, the majority made for TV, though these tend to err more towards the tamer aspects of real-life circumstances. Vietnamese censors take a dim view of nudity and sex, but murder and mayhem are OK.

Prior to the recent signing of an intellectual copyright pact with the US, pirated Hollywood films (largely coming from China on CD-ROM) were a common option. The authorities have been seemingly successful at stamping out public showings, which ironically means there are far fewer Hollywood films shown now than in recent years.

Fanslands Cinema (Map 5; ☎ 825 7484, 84 Pho Ly Thuong Kiet) offers the best movies in town.

The recently completed *Vuon Dien Anh Cinema Complex (Map 2; ☎ 851 4716, 87 Pho Lang Ha)* shows foreign films nightly at 8 pm. Tickets cost US$1.60. This new multiscreen complex is several kilometres west of the city centre, near the Lang Ha Golf Club.

French speakers will find a range of films on offer at *Alliance Française de Hanoi (Map 5; ☎ 826 6970, 42 Pho Yet Kieu)*.

Other places in town with occasional foreign films are the *Thang 8 Cinema* (Map 5) and neighbouring *New Age Cinema (Map 5; 45 Pho Hang Bai)*.

Opposite the Daewoo Hotel is the 3D *(phim noi)* cinema *Ngoc Khanh (Map 2)*. Admission is a steep US$5.

CIRCUS

One Russian entertainment tradition which has survived and thrived in Hanoi is the circus. Many of the performers (gymnasts, jugglers, animal trainers etc) at the *Central Circus (Map 4; Rap Xiec Trung Uong, ☎ 825 3330)* were originally trained in Eastern Europe, though today's new recruits can now learn their skills from their Vietnamese elders. The circus has nightly performances from Tuesday to Sunday from 8 to 10 pm in a huge tent beside the northern entrance to Lenin Park (Cong Vien Le Nin). There is a special show staged for children on Sunday morning at 9 am. Entry is US$2.50.

SPECTATOR SPORTS

Football (soccer) is Vietnam's number one spectator sport and Hanoians are no less crazy for it than the rest of the country. When Vietnam plays in any international contest, people are glued to the TV. Victories typically result in masses of people taking to the streets to celebrate, race motorbikes, and whoop it up.

Tennis has considerable snob appeal – trendy Vietnamese like to watch and play.

Shopping

No longer is a shopping trip in Hanoi a journey to a large state-owned department store specialising in empty shelves. In recent years the city has blossomed into a shoppers' paradise, catering to both tourists and the local market. Today Hanoians, in particular the youth, have fully embraced the craze for material goods, demonstrated by the myriad of fashionable boutiques and shopping malls springing up around the city.

Whether or not you wish to buy anything, your first encounter will likely be with the 'Hello, where are you from?' children who sell postcards, books (mostly bootlegged photocopies) and maps. A reasonable amount of bargaining is called for. Somewhat dated postcard sets can be picked up for under US$1, while larger, higher quality postcards sell individually for about US$0.25.

In general, items sold with no visible price tags must be bargained for – expect the vendor to start the bidding at two to five times the real price. Tagged items may be negotiable, but more often than not the prices are fixed.

One annoying habit that you'll just have to get used to is the tendency of street vendors in touristy areas to start shoving one item after another into your face, practically forcing you to buy things. It's a self-defeating sales tactic, since many foreigners will get flustered and walk away.

HANDICRAFTS

Hot items on the tourist market include lacquerware, mother-of-pearl inlay, carved water puppets, ceramics, colourful embroidered items (hangings, tablecloths, pillow cases, pyjamas and robes), blinds made of hanging bamboo beads, reed mats, carpets, jewellery, leatherwork, bird cages and aromatic cinnamon wood boxes and toothpick holders.

With its proximity to the prolific hill tribes in the mountainous north-west, Hanoi also has an excellent selection of ethnic minority crafts and clothing for sale.

There are countless handicrafts shops in the Hoam Kiem Lake district, especially around the streets of the Old Quarter. Pho Hang Bac, Pho Hang Gai, Pho Hang Khai and Pho Cau Go are good areas for general souvenir hunting.

South of Hoan Kiem Lake, Pho Ham Long specialises in ceramics and glassware.

North of the lake is Pho Hang Buom, the closest Hanoi gets to having a Chinatown. The goods on sale here differ significantly from what you see elsewhere. It is, for example, the best place to get Chinese chops (seals) carved. If nothing else, it's a picturesque place to stroll around.

Near St Joseph's Cathedral, Deltadeco (Map 5; ☎ 828 9616) at 12 Pho Nha Tho sells an interesting selection of wood crafts and ceramics featuring original designs.

Delicate handmade bird cages make a reasonably priced and unique memento, though getting them home in hand luggage may prove tedious. There are several easy-to-spot shops selling bird cages on the road out to the airport and Museum of Ethnology.

Pho Hang Gai and its continuation, Pho Hang Bong, are a good place to look for embroidered tablecloths, T-shirts and wall hangings. Kim Dung (Map 5; ☎ 824 5462), at 12 Pho Hang Bong, is one such shop which comes expat-recommended, though there are many other shops in the area to choose from.

Fair Trade Craft Shops

Craft Link (Map 3; ☎ 843 7710, Lantt@ bdvn.vnmail.vnd.net), at 43 Pho Van Mieu, is a praiseworthy nonprofit organisation supporting local craftspeople. It sells a wide variety of traditional handicrafts, made by both Vietnamese and ethnic minorities. The attractive two-floor shop is open daily from 9 am to 6 pm. There is also an affiliated shop at the excellent Museum of Ethnology (see the Cau Giay District section in the Things to See & Do chapter).

Since 1995, Lan (Map 5; ☎ 828 9278, Lan.V.H.@bdvn.vnmail.vnd.net) has providing productive training, education and employment to aid physically challenged and disadvantaged youths in becoming self-reliant. The shop specialises in quilts, and also has an interesting selection of handmade pillows and affordable, adorable ethnic minority dolls. All proceeds are funnelled back into the community. Lan is open from 9 am to 5 pm, Monday through Saturday. The shop is at 28 Pho Au Trieu, the narrow street adjacent to St Joseph's Cathedral.

Ethnic Minority Crafts

Other shops in the Old Quarter specialising in hill tribe clothing and paraphernalia include: The Pan Flute (Map 5; ☎ 826 0493), 42 Pho Hang Bac; Vietnamese Craft Guild (Map 5; ☎ 828 9717), 1A Pho To Tich; The Culture of Vietnam Ethnic Groups (Map 5; ☎ 828 0509), 44 Pho Hang Ga; and Nha Quay (Map 5; ☎ 826 1141), 18B Pho Nha Tho, adjacent to the popular Moca Café.

CLOTHING

Hanoi has excellent silk clothes and accessories, which are cheap and abundant. Silk sleeping bags are popular items – good for mosquito cover on a hot night. These cost about US$4 to US$8, and come in single and double sizes as well.

Ao dais, the national dress of Vietnam, are another popular item, especially for women. Ready-made ao dais start at about US$20, while the custom-tailored sets are notably more. Prices vary by the store and material used. If you want to buy custom-made clothing for your friends, you'll need their measurements. As a general rule, you get best results when you're right there and are measured by the tailor or seamstress.

T-shirts are ever-popular items with travellers. A printed shirt costs around US$2 while an embroidered design will cost maybe US$3.50. However, don't believe sizes – 'large' in Asia is often equivalent to 'medium' in the west, and a tumble through a clothes dryer will instantly make it a 'small'.

There is a solid string of silk shops scattered along Pho Hang Gai in the Old Quarter, mainly around the intersection of Pho Le Van Can. Here you can find pre-made clothes (both traditional and modern in design), and also have just about anything you wish custom-tailored. The most famous shop for silk clothing is Khai Silk (Map 5; ☎ 825 4237), at 96 Pho Hang Gai (the proprietor is fluent in French and English), though by all means shop around.

HATS

Women all over the country wear conical hats to keep the sun off their faces (though they also function like umbrellas in the rain). If you hold a well-made conical hat up to the light, you'll be able to see that between the layers of straw material are fine paper cuts.

Another popular form of headgear in the north of Vietnam are army green VC helmets (also see the boxed text 'Mu Coi').

Around Pho Hang Bong and Pho Hang Gai are T-shirt shops and places selling Viet Cong headgear. Ho Chi Minh T-shirts (printed or embroidered) cost US$2 to US$4.

SHOES

There are plenty of inexpensive shoes for sale in Hanoi, though large sizes to fit western feet can be a problem. Make sure they are very comfortable before you purchase them – some tend to be poorly made and will likely give you blisters.

There is an outstanding shoe market along Pho Hang Dau at the north-east corner of Hoan Kiem Lake.

FINE ART

From simple greeting cards with silk paintings on the front (US$0.50) to wood-block prints, oil paintings and watercolours, Hanoi is a premier city for art hunters. Even much of the mass produced stuff, most of which is very affordable, looks great at home.

The cheaper stuff (US$10 to US$50) is sent to touristy galleries and hotel gift

Mu Coi

The most popular male headwear in Hanoi is dark green pith helmets known as *mu coi*. The North Vietnamese armed forces adapted the design from those of the early French colonialists. Initially a standard fixture of the military uniform, today mu coi are popular among civilians as well, in particular cyclo drivers and manual labourers.

The name is derived from *mu* meaning hat, and *coi*, traditional stone or clay-fired basins used for mashing vegetables in – the hats not only share the same shape, but like coi are known for their durability. Ho Chi Minh himself was frequently seen sporting one, and may have had something to do with their popularity. For obvious reasons, mu coi never caught on in the

RICHARD I'ANSON

south, though once you are past the toll booth north of Hué (where the attendants all don mu coi) they are seen throughout the north of Vietnam.

These days foreigners too, it seems, have taken a liking to mu coi, some preferring them over the classical conical straw hats as souvenirs. Be aware, however, that some Vietnamese may consider it strange (or even offensive) to see you wearing one. And should you be travelling south (or in some overseas Vietnamese communities for that matter), the VC fashion statement may not indeed be very well received.

Depending on your bargaining skills, mu coi can be picked up for as cheap as US$1.50. Normally, sellers ask for US$2.50 or US$3 – still a fair price to pay considering the quality. Mu coi, as well as other army paraphernalia (including complete generals' uniforms!), can be found at shops along Đ Le Duan, near the Hanoi train station.

shops. It's important to know that there are quite a few forgeries around – just because you spot a painting by a 'famous Vietnamese artist' does not mean that it's an original, though it may still be an attractive work of art. Higher-standard works are generally put on display in one of the city's higher-end galleries.

Published bi-monthly in Hong Kong, *Asian Art News* magazine (asianart@ netvigator.com) is an excellent source on what's happening in the Vietnamese art market. Several of Hanoi's top galleries advertise here. You might also like to take a look at the online Gallery Cyclo at www .destinationvietnam.com.

Galleries

Both well established and aspiring young artists display their work at myriad state-run and private art galleries in hopes of attracting a buyer. Most have English (and often French) speakers on staff and are open daily until 8 or 9 pm. Prices range from a few dollars into the thousands, and bargaining is the norm at most galleries.

There are countless galleries of every standard scattered throughout the city, with a high concentration in the following areas:

Pho Trang Tien, starting from the Opera House and its continuation Pho Hang Khan; Pho Hang Gai and its continuation Pho

Hang Buom (north of Hoan Kiem Lake, in the Old Quarter); and Pho Le Thai To (near the Phu Gia Hotel, on the west side of Hoan Kiem Lake).

Some of Hanoi's most popular upmarket galleries include:

Apricot Gallery (☎ 828 8965) Map 5; 40B Pho Hang Bong
Co Xanh Gallery (☎ 826 7116) Map 5; 51 Pho Hang Gai
Dong Son Gallery (☎ 821 8876) Map 4; 47 Pho Le Dai Hanh
Gallerie L'Atelier (☎ 091-216353) Map 5; 6 Pho Nha Tho
Hanoi Studio (☎ 943 1106) Map 5; 33 Pho Tran Quoc Toan
Mai Gallery (☎ 825 1225) Map 5; 3B Phan Huy Chu
Nam Son Gallery (☎ 826 2993) Map 5; 41 Pho Trang Tien
Opera Fine Art Gallery (☎ 090-439217) Map 5; 26 Pho Tran Tien
Salon Natasha (☎ 826 1387) Map 5; 30 Pho Hang Bong
Song Hong Art Gallery (☎ 822 9064) Map 4; 71A Pho Nguyen Du
The New Factory (☎ 091-216353) Map 5; 24 Pho Trang Tien
Trang An Gallery (☎ 826 9480) Map 5; 15 Pho Hang Buom

Keep an eye out in *The Guide* and *Time Out* magazines to see what special exhibitions are on during your stay.

ANTIQUES
There are quite a number of stores in Hanoi offering real and fake antique Vietnamese handicrafts. A Vietnamese speciality is the 'instant antique' with a price tag of around US$2 for a teapot or ceramic dinner plate. Of course, it's OK to buy fake antiques as long as you aren't paying genuine antique prices. However, a problem occurs if you've bought an antique (or something which looks antique) and didn't get an official export certificate:

When I was in the airport in Hanoi, a customs officer eyed out two porcelain vases I had bought and told me that I should go to the Department of Culture in Hanoi to have them assessed or pay a fine of US$20. Of course, there

was no representative of the Department of Culture at the airport to make such an evaluation, so getting them assessed would require me to miss my flight.

Anna Crawford Pinnerup

Just what happens to confiscated 'antiques' is a good question. Some say that the authorities sell them back to the souvenir shops. You might call it recycling.

Indochine House (Map 5; ☎ 829 4660) at 13 Pho Nha Tho is an charming shop specialising in early 20th century 'rescued relics' (most were produced during the period when much of Hanoi was built up by the French colonialists). It sells fine art and memorabilia, furniture, old photos and prints, plus some older Asian ceramics. It is open 9.30 am to 6.30 pm daily.

For Chinese, Japanese and Korean reproduction furniture, you might take a look at the state-run Culturimex (Map 5; ☎ 825 2226), at 22B Pho Hai Ba Trung. If this place whets your appetite, consider a visit to the woodcraft village of Dong Ky (see the Excursions chapter).

JEWELLERY
Vietnam produces some good jewellery, but there are plenty of fakes and flawed gems around. Don't think that you'll find a cut diamond or polished ruby for a fraction of what you'd pay at home. Some travellers have actually thought that they could buy gems in Vietnam and sell these at home for a profit. Such business requires considerable expertise.

There are plenty of jewellery dealers in the Old Quarter, particularly along Pho Hang Bac. Pho Hang Dao is known as 'Watch Street' and here you'll find every kind of timepiece from Swiss and Japanese to antique Russian-made pocket watches.

STAMPS
Postage stamps already set in a collector's book are readily available either in or near the post office, at some hotel gift shops and bookshops, and of course from the ubiquitous street vendors.

MUSIC

Hanoi has an astounding collection of CDs and audio tapes for sale, most of which are pirated. The official word is that this illegal practice will be 'cleaned up' by the authorities, but don't hold your breath waiting.

In addition to traditional and contemporary Vietnamese hits, you'll also find the latest pop songs from Hong Kong, Taiwan and Japan, and a growing and devoted core of avant-garde types who prefer rock and roll from the west.

WOW (Map 5; ☎ 828 9690), an acronym of 'we offer whatever you want', is a treasure chest of music and video CDs, and well as CD-ROMs. It is one of the few places where the merchandise is authentic, and it can special order anything from Sinatra to Phish. The shop is at 39 Pho Hang Trong.

For the best in bootleg CDs (usually about US$2), there are several shops along Pho Hang Bong, including Tu Lap (Map 5; ☎ 826 1974) at No 36A.

For traditional music tapes and CDs, check the bookshops on Pho Trang Tien. You can also find Vietnamese folk CDs selling for US$5 at the Temple of Literature.

ELECTRONICS

Electronic goods sold in Vietnam are actually not such a great bargain and you'd be better off purchasing these in duty-free ports such as Hong Kong and Singapore. However, the prices charged in Vietnam are really not all that bad, mainly due to the black market (smuggling), which also results in 'duty-free' goods. Only those items imported legally by an authorised agent will include a warranty card valid in Vietnam.

The best place to look for electronics is around the intersection of Pho Hai Ba Trung and Pho Hang Bai, one block south of Hoan Kiem Lake.

EYEGLASSES

In Hanoi you'll find plenty of opticians willing to sell eyeglasses for as little as US$10. Although the price is hard to beat, the budget glasses are just that. Ultra-cheap eyeglass frames made in Vietnam or imported from China are mostly rubbish – the frames easily rust and soon break. These same shops usually sell European-made frames for a much higher price, but beware of primitive equipment used for checking your prescription and grinding the lenses.

Hanoi Optic (Map 5; ☎ 824 3751) at 48 Pho Trang Tien has modern equipment and skilled English-speaking staff. This is where most expats in Hanoi go to get their eyes examined.

WAR SOUVENIRS

In places frequented by tourists it's easy to buy what looks like equipment left over from the American War. However, almost all of these items are reproductions and your chances of finding anything original are slim. Enterprising back-alley tailors turn out US military uniforms, while metalcraft shops have learned how to make helmets, bayonets, dog tags and 'Zippo' lighters engraved with 'soldier poetry'.

One thing you should think twice about purchasing are weapons and ammunition. Most of these items are either fake or deactivated, but you can occasionally find real bullets for sale with the gunpowder still inside. Real or not, it's illegal to carry ammunition and weapons on airlines and many countries will arrest you if any such goods are found in your luggage.

BOOKSHOPS

Hanoi's best book shops are concentrated along Pho Trang Tien, bstween the southeast corner of Hoan Kiem Lake and the Hanoi Opera House. At 55 Pho Trang Tien is the Thang Long Bookshop (Map 5; ☎ 825 7043), the biggest and best in town. Next door at No 53 is another good one, the Trang Tien Bookshop (Map 5; ☎ 934 2782).

The air-conditioned Hanoi Bookstore (Map 5; Hieu Sach Hanoi, ☎ 824 1616), 34 Pho Trang Tien, has a decent collection of local and imported books and news magazines. Down in the basement of the same building, the Foreign Language Bookshop (Map 5; ☎ 824 8914) carries books in English, French and other languages.

For French books, try the Librairie Vietnamienne Francophone (Map 5; ☎ 825 7376), at 64 Pho Trang Tien.

The office of The Gioi Publishers (Map 5; ☎ 825 3841) is at 46 Pho Tran Hung Dao. This place puts out a few useful books in English about Vietnam, and maintains some small bookstalls all around town.

There are small second-hand bookshops at 80B Pho Ba Trieu and 42 Pho Hang Bo.

Xunhasaba (Map 5; ☎ 825 2313, fax 825 9881) operates a small bookshop, though that's not its main function. Anyone wishing to import books, movies, CDs etc into Vietnam can only do so by contacting this organisation first. The main office-cum-bookshop is at 32 Pho Hai Ba Trung.

The philatelic counter at the GPO (in the main postal services hall) is run by the government philatelic corporation, Cotevina (Cong Ty Tem Viet Nam).

MARKETS

The three-storey **Dong Xuan Market** (Map 5) is 900m north of Hoan Kiem Lake. The market burned down in 1994, killing five people (all of whom had entered the building after the fire started to either rescue goods or steal them). The market has now been rebuilt and is a tourist attraction in its own right. There are hundreds of stalls here, employing around 3000 people.

Hom Market (Map 4) is on the north-east corner of Pho Hué and Pho Tran Xuan Soan. It's a good general purpose market with lots of imported food items.

Hang Da Market (Map 5) is relatively small, but good for imported foods, wine, beer and flowers. The 2nd floor is good for fabric and ready-made clothing. The market is very close to St Joseph's Cathedral.

Cua Nam Market (Map 5) is a few blocks north of the Hanoi train station. The market itself is of no great interest (except maybe for the flowers), but Ð Le Duan between the market and the train station is a treasure trove of household goods, including electronics, plasticware and the like. It's a particularly good shopping area if you're setting up a residence in Hanoi.

Mo Market (Map 2) is far to the south of the central area on Pho Bach Mai and Pho Minh Khai. It's not a place for tourism, as the main products are fresh meat, fish and vegetables, but may be of interest to expats who prefer to do their own cooking.

Buoi Market (Map 2) out in the far northwest part of town is notable for live animals (chickens, ducks etc), but also features ornamental plants. You can probably find better quality ornamental plants for sale at the gardens in front of the Temple of Literature and at the Air Force Museum.

Excursions

Hanoi offers countless excursion options ranging from half a day to a weekend outing. Try to make the day trip out to the outstanding pilgrimage site of the famed Perfume Pagoda. Further afield, trips to Mai Chau and the Ninh Binh area prove popular with many travellers. A particular highlight is the spectacular geological displays of Halong Bay and Cat Ba Island.

Another day or two could easily be spent visiting the fascinating handicraft villages dotting Hanoi's rural outskirts. They each specialise in a particular cottage industry, and can make for a rewarding day trip, though you'll need a good guide to make the journey worthwhile. TF Handspan (☎ 04-828 1996), at 116 Pho Hang Bac, is one outfit in Hanoi specialising in handicraft villages, but by all means shop around and see what's being offered elsewhere. It is possible to organise a day-long outing combining several villages and other sites such as pagodas. In the more commercial villages, such as Bat Trang and Dong Ky, you can arrange to have custom-made goods exported directly to your address abroad.

A sampling of villages is included in this chapter, but there are *plenty* more to seek out.

South of Hanoi

PERFUME PAGODA
The Perfume Pagoda (Chua Huong) is about 60km south-west of Hanoi by road. The pagoda is a highlight of the Hanoi area and should not be missed. Getting to the pagoda requires a journey first by road and then by river. The boat trip along the scenic waterways takes about three hours and is good fun.

The Perfume Pagoda itself is a complex of pagodas and Buddhist shrines built into the limestone cliffs of Huong Tich Mountain (Mountain of the Fragrant Traces). Among the better known sites here are Thien Chu (Pagoda Leading to Heaven); Giai Oan (Purgatorial Pagoda), where the faithful believe deities purify souls, cure sufferings and grant offspring to childless families; and Huong Tich Chu (Pagoda of the Perfumed Vestige).

Great numbers of Buddhist pilgrims come here during a festival that begins in the middle of the second lunar month and lasts until the last week of the third lunar month – usually in March and April. Pilgrims and other visitors spend their time here boating, hiking and exploring the caves. Despite the occasionally large number of visitors, this place has a peaceful and perhaps holy atmosphere.

If you want to do the excellent river trip to the pagoda, you need to travel from Hanoi by car for two hours to My Duc, then take a small boat rowed by two women for 1½ hours to the foot of the mountain. From where the boat lets you off, you have about a 4km (two hour) walk up to the main pagoda area. The scenery is comparable to Halong Bay, though here you are on a river rather than the sea. The combined fee for the return boat journey and general admission ticket is US$7.

Nearly all tour operators in Hanoi book inexpensive day trips to the Perfume Pagoda.

THAY PAGODA
Thay Pagoda (the Master's Pagoda), also known as Thien Phuc (Heavenly Blessing), is dedicated to Thich Ca Buddha (Sakyamuni, the historical Buddha) and 18 *arhats* (monks who have attained Nirvana); the latter appear on the central altar. On the left is a statue of the 12th century monk Tu Dao Hanh, the 'Master' after whom the pagoda is named; on the right is a statue of King Ly Nhan Tong, who is believed to be a reincarnation of Tu Dao Hanh. In front of the pagoda is a small stage built on stilts in the middle of a pond.

EXCURSIONS

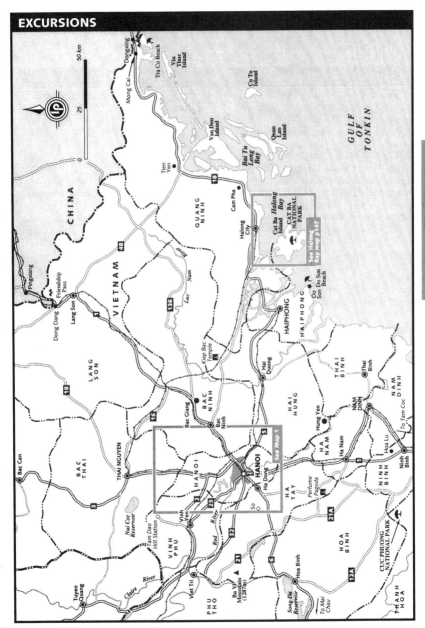

The pagoda's annual festival is held from the fifth to the seventh days of the third lunar month. Pilgrims and other visitors enjoy watching water puppet shows, hiking and exploring caves in the area.

Thay Pagoda is about 40km south-west of Hanoi in Ha Tay Province. Some of Hanoi's cafés catering to budget travellers offer combined day tours of the Thay and Tay Phuong (see next entry) pagodas.

TAY PHUONG PAGODA

Tay Phuong Pagoda (Pagoda of the West), also known as Sung Phuc Pagoda, consists of three parallel single-level structures built on a hillock said to resemble a buffalo. The 76 figures carved from jackfruit wood, many from the 18th century, are the pagoda's most celebrated feature. The earliest construction here dates from the 8th century.

Tay Phuong Pagoda is approximately 40km south-west of Hanoi in Tay Phuong hamlet, Ha Tay Province. A visit here can easily be combined with a stop at Thay Pagoda.

VAN PHUC

Van Phuc, 11km south-west of Hanoi in Ha Tay Province, is a silk making village. You can see silk cloth being produced on a loom. Many of the fine silk items you see on sale in Hanoi's Pho Hang Gai originate here.

SO

So is a village known for manufacturing the delicate *mien* noodles enjoyed throughout Vietnam. It is a northern custom to share a bowl of mien during the Tet holiday.

The village also produces the flour from which the noodles are made, and exports it to other noodle-making villages in the area. The flour is made from *rong gieng*, a root resembling ginger, which is widely harvested by the Muong and Thai highland minorities on the road from Hanoi to Mai Chau.

The flour is mixed with water in giant cement vats and poured onto a circular hot plate about 1½m in diameter. Covered, the mixture quickly steams into a rubbery crepe-like material about 1mm thick. It is then removed and stretched over a rectangular woven bamboo mat and left in direct sunlight.

When partially dry, the sheets are peeled off the bamboo and run through a machine which cuts them into tiny strips (about the thickness of angel hair pasta). The noodles are then draped over bamboo frames to dry completely (very photogenic), and finally wrapped into huge bundles and transported on bicycles.

Mien noodles wholesale for around US$0.50 per kg, and the average So household produces between 300 and 500kg a day.

Getting There & Away

So is in Ha Tay Province, about 25km south-west of Hanoi via Đ Nguyen Trai (National Highway 6).

BAT TRANG

Bat Trang, literally 'a place where bowls are made', is Vietnam's premier ceramics-producing community. The village dates back to the 1400s. By the 19th century merchants from Bat Trang had established retail shops on Pho Bat Su and Pho Bat Dan (both names translate to 'ceramic bowl street') in Hanoi's Old Quarter.

Pottery at Bat Trang ceramics village

Despite being busy and increasingly commercial (lots of signs in English advertising export and Visa cards), it is well worth visiting. There are over 100 kilns in Bat Trang, along the main streets and in narrow back alleys. Here you can see artisans create superb ceramic vases and other masterpieces in their kilns. It's hot, sweaty work, but the results are superb.

Kilns are coal-heated, and produce a large amount of air pollution and dusty black roads. The coal bricks are hand moulded into what looks strikingly like cow dung patties; these can be seen drying on walls all over the village.

Getting There & Away
Easily reached, Bat Trang is 13km southeast of Hanoi. Cross the Chuong Duong Bridge (motorbikes pay a US$0.04 toll) and follow National Highway 1A. Bicycle access is via the Long Bien Bridge.

MAI CHAU
One of the closest places to Hanoi where you can see an authentic Montagnard village is Mai Chau (elevation 400m) – a collection of villages, farms and huts spread out over a large area, rather than a town. Most people here are ethnic White Thai, distantly related to tribes in Thailand, Laos and China.

The most interesting things to do here are to stay overnight in one of the Thai stilt houses, and also to trek to the area's minority villages. A typical walk further afield is 7 to 8km, though longer treks of three to seven days are possible.

It is recommended that you prebook mountain treks in Hanoi, though self-propelled travellers can ask around in the villages of Lac or Pom Coong about hiring a local guide for around US$5 per day.

Places to Stay & Eat
The *Mai Chau Guesthouse* (☎ *018-867262)* has 13 basic rooms with private bath and hot showers costing US$15. Most prefer, however, to walk a few hundred metres back from the roadside and stay in the Thai *stilt*

houses of Lac village (Ban Lac) or neighbouring Pom Coong village. These are not only far more interesting, but cheaper (US$4 per person). Lac is the more busy of the two, and villagers stage a traditional song and dance performance here in the evenings. This village also attracts a growing number of young Vietnamese travellers, so if you're looking for peace and quiet, you might have better luck in Pom Coong.

Overnighting in Mai Chau's minority villages is a more 'civilised' experience than you might have expected. Local authorities (the same people who collect a 50% tax on any tourist dollars that flow into these villages) brought the villages up to 'tourist standard' before allowing in any foreigners.

Commercialisation aside, the majority of people come away pleased with the experience. The Thai villagers are exceedingly friendly and when all's said and done, even with TV and the hum of the refrigerator, it is a peaceful place and you're still sleeping in a thatched-roof house on split bamboo floors.

One traveller wrote:

There is *nothing* to do in Mai Chau. It is fantastic. Take a camera, cards, book or whatever.
Annette Low

Reservations to stay overnight are not necessary, but it's advisable to arrive by mid-afternoon. You can book meals at the house where you're staying for between US$1 to US$4. There are also some small *restaurants* near the market.

Things To Buy
Thai women are masterful weavers and there is plenty to buy in the village centre, or when strolling through the pleasant lanes. Villagers are not overly sales-aggressive, though polite bargaining is the norm.

Getting There & Away
Mai Chau is 135km south-west of Hanoi, 6km south of Highway 6 from the Tong Dau junction.

You'll be hard pressed to find any direct public transport to Mai Chau from Hanoi, but buses to Hoa Binh and nearby Tong Dau are plentiful. From either of these places you can get a local bus or hire a motorbike taxi to Mai Chau.

As you enter the town there is a barricade across the road. All foreigners must stop here and pay an admission toll of US$0.50.

Most cafés and travel agencies in Hanoi run inexpensive overnight trips to Mai Chau; also consider combining a trip to Mai Chau with sites in the Ninh Binh area.

NINH BINH AREA
☎ 030

Ninh Binh's recent transformation from sleepy backwater to tourist magnet has little to do with the city itself, and more to do with its proximity to nearby Tam Coc (9km away), Hoa Lu (12km) and Cuc Phuong National Park (45km).

Although it is possible to visit these sites as a day trip from Hanoi (which is 93km to the north), most prefer to spend the night in Ninh Binh and enjoy the scenery at a more leisurely pace.

Tam Coc
Known to travellers as 'Halong Bay without the water', 'Halong Bay on the rice paddies', 'Dry Halong Bay' etc, Tam Coc boasts breathtaking scenery. While Halong Bay (described later in this chapter) has huge rock formations jutting out of the sea, Tam Coc has them jutting out of the rice paddies.

Tam Coc means 'three caves'. Hang Ca, the first cave, is 127m long; Hang Giua, the second cave, is 70m in length; and smallest is Hang Cuoi, the third cave, at only 40m.

The way to see Tam Coc is by rowboat on the Ngo Dong River. The boats actually row into the caves; a very peaceful and scenic trip. The boat trip to all three caves takes about three hours, including the stops. Tickets are sold at the small booking office by the docks. One boat can seat only two passengers and costs US$3.50 per person (US$2 entry fee and US$1.50 boat fee). The biggest problem is that the boat owners hassle you almost constantly to buy embroidery – if you don't want it, just say no.

An even more annoying scam is the boat vendors who paddle up alongside your boat and try to sell drinks. If you don't want any, they may 'suggest' you buy a Coke for your oarsperson. Many travellers do this and then later find that the Cokes get sold back to the drink vendors for half price.

On a sunny day bring sunscreen, a hat or umbrella to protect your skin – there's no shade in the boats. Alternatively, rent an umbrella at the pier for US$0.50.

Bich Dong is another cave with a built-in temple. It's about 2km past Tam Coc and getting there is easy enough by river or road. However, many foreigners shun the place because of the very aggressive souvenir vendors (mostly children). Admission to the cave temples is US$1.50.

In the area behind the restaurant is Van Lan village, known for its embroidery. You can watch the craftspeople make napkins, tablecloths, pillowcases, T-shirts etc. It's better to buy embroidery here rather than from the boat owners because you'll find a wider selection at slightly lower prices.

There are many restaurants at Tam Coc including the excellent *Anh Dzung Restaurant* (☎ 860230).

Tam Coc is 9km south-west of Ninh Binh. Follow National Highway 1 south and then head west at the Tam Coc turn-off. Many budget cafés in Hanoi book day trips to Tam Coc.

Hoa Lu
The scenery here resembles nearby Tam Coc, though Hoa Lu has an interesting historical twist. Hoa Lu was the capital of Vietnam under the Dinh Dynasty (968-80) and the Early Le Dynasty (980-1009).

The ancient citadel of Hoa Lu, most of which has been destroyed, covered an area of about 3 sq km. The outer ramparts encompassed temples, shrines and the place where the king held court. The royal family lived in the inner citadel.

Yen Ngua mountain provides a scenic backdrop for Hoa Lu's two remaining temples. The first temple, Dinh Tien Hoang, was restored in the 17th century and is dedicated

Hoan Kiem Lake

MASON FLORENCE

MASON FLORENCE

The Turtle Pagoda in the Lake of Returned Sword (Ho Hoan Kiem)

'They say it was a big turtle.'

MASON FLORENCE

A myth tells of a giant golden turtle emerging from Hoan Kiem Lake to reclaim Le Loi's magic sword.

MASON FLORENCE

The sheer limestone cliffs of one of Halong Bay's 3,000 islands.

Sampan in Halong Bay

Basket boat in Halong Bay

to the Dinh Dynasty. Out the front is the stone pedestal of a royal throne; inside are bronze bells and a statue of Emperor Dinh Tien Hoang with his three sons. The second temple, Dai Hanh (or Dung Van Nga), commemorates the rulers of the Early Le Dynasty. Inside the main hall are all sorts of drums, gongs, incense burners, candle holders and weapons; to the left of the entrance is a sanctuary dedicated to Confucius.

You must climb about 200 steps to reach the sanctuaries, but you'll be rewarded for your efforts with great views.

There is a US$2 entrance fee to Hoa Lu. There are Vietnamese-speaking guides at the temples who work for free (but you should offer a tip). Or you can hire an English-speaking guide, which costs an outrageous US$15 per group.

Hoa Lu is 12km north of Ninh Binh. There is no public transport so most travellers get there by bicycle, motorbike or car.

Cuc Phuong National Park

Cuc Phuong National Park, established in 1962, is one of Vietnam's most important nature preserves. Ho Chi Minh personally took time off from the war in 1963 to dedicate this national park, Vietnam's first.

Though wildlife has suffered a precipitous decline in Vietnam in recent decades, the park's 222 sq km of primary tropical forest remain home to an amazing variety of animal and plant life. The elevation of the highest peak in the park is 648m. At the park's lower elevations, the climate is subtropical.

Excellent hiking opportunities abound in the park and days can be spent trekking through the forest and caves. The park office can provide you with maps to find the trailheads. For longer treks, a guide is mandatory, and it would be foolish and risky to attempt a trek alone through the dense jungle. There are three-day treks to Muong minority villages which can be also be arranged through travel agencies in Hanoi or Ninh Binh.

The best time of year to visit the park is in the dry months from October through March. April to June become increasingly hot and wet and from July to September the rains arrive and bring with them *lots* of leeches. Entry to the park is US$5.

Cuc Phuong National Park is 45km from Ninh Binh. There is no public transport to the park, so most travel by car or motorbike.

Endangered Primate Rescue Centre

One of the highlights of a visit to Cuc Phuong is the Endangered Primate Rescue Centre. The facility is run by German biologists and local Vietnamese. There are currently 13 different species of rare Gibbon and Languer monkeys here (four types of Languer exist only here).

What started out as a small scale operation in 1995 with just a handful of primates has grown into a centre where over 50 monkeys are being cared for, studied and bred. Tragically, the black market demand has driven several such species straight into extinction. All of the animals at the centre were either rescued from illegal traders (most on the way to China), or were bred in captivity.

There is currently no charge to visit the centre, but you might consider purchasing some postcards or a poster – you'll see that the money is going to a very good cause.

Places to Stay & Eat

Ninh Binh Area Kudos goes to the *Thuy Anh Mini-Hotel* (☎/fax 871602, 55A Đ Truong Han Sieu). Its clean rooms range from US$7 to US$15 and the food served at the rooftop restaurant is superb.

Another family-run backpacker favourite is *Thanh Thuy's Guesthouse* (☎ 871811, 128 Đ Le Hong Phong). The six basic rooms here cost from US$3 to US$10.

Queen Mini-Hotel (☎ 871874) is pleasant and just 30m from Ninh Binh train station. Rooms cost US$5 to US$10.

The *Star Hotel* (☎ 871522, fax 871200, 267 Đ Tran Hung Dao) has 10 rooms priced between US$6 and US$28.

Cuc Phuong National park headquarters charge US$10 for a few basic rooms in a

Muong-style house (shared toilet and cold showers). Rooms in the park *guesthouse* rent for US$35 (but at this price you are probably better off staying in Ninh Binh). Meals are available for overnight guests, and reservations can be made by contacting: Cuc Phuong National Park, Nho Quan District, Ninh Binh Province (☎ 866085), or its office in Hanoi at 1 Pho Doc Tan Ap (☎ 829 2604).

Getting There & Away

Bus Regular public buses leave hourly and make the 2½ hour run for US$1.60. Ninh Binh is also a hub for the north-south 'open tours' and it's possible to travel to/from Hanoi on these air-con buses for US$4.

Train Ninh Binh is a scheduled stop for the *Reunification Express* trains travelling between Hanoi and Saigon.

East of Hanoi

HALONG BAY
☎ 033
Magnificent Halong Bay, with its 3000-plus islands rising from the clear, emerald waters of the Gulf of Tonkin, is one of the natural marvels of Vietnam.

The bay and its numerous islands sprawl over an area of 1500 sq km. In 1994 the bay was designated as Vietnam's second UN-ESCO World Heritage site. These tiny islands are dotted with innumerable beaches and grottoes created by the wind and the waves.

Ha long means 'where the dragon descends into the sea'. Legend has it that the islands of Halong Bay were created by a great dragon who lived in the mountains. As it ran towards the coast, its flailing tail gouged out valleys and crevasses; as it plunged into the sea, the areas dug up by the tail became filled with water, leaving only bits of high land visible.

The dragon may be legend, but sailors in the Halong Bay region have often reported sightings of a mysterious marine creature

of gargantuan proportions known as the Tarasque. More paranoid elements of the military suspect it's an imperialist spy submarine, while eccentric foreigners believe they have discovered Vietnam's own version of the Loch Ness monster.

Dragons aside, the biggest threat to the bay may be from souvenir-hunting tourists. Rare corals and seashells are rapidly being stripped from the sea floor, while stalactites and stalagmites are being broken off from the caves. These items get turned into key rings, paperweights and ashtrays which are on sale in the local souvenir shops. You might consider the virtue of not buying these items and spending your cash instead on postcards and silk paintings.

Grottoes
Due to the rock type of Halong Bay's islands, the area is dotted with thousands of caves of all sizes and shapes.

Halong Warning

In the past there were stories of pirate-style robberies from small boats involving weapons – the foreign passengers lost all their money, passports etc. This has been cracked down upon. Still, be careful with your valuables. Snatch-and-run-style theft is still a possibility.

Sometimes a boat approaches and offers fish and crabs, but beware – these people may be robbers! They grabbed the bag of an English guy (with his passport, money and cheques) and disappeared. Our tourist boat was slow and couldn't catch that fast boat. Two travellers we met reported that the crew of their boat stole some small things while they were swimming.

Pat Sanders

You may be able to arrange to sleep on boats, but technically this is banned (for your own protection from robbery), so do this at your own risk.

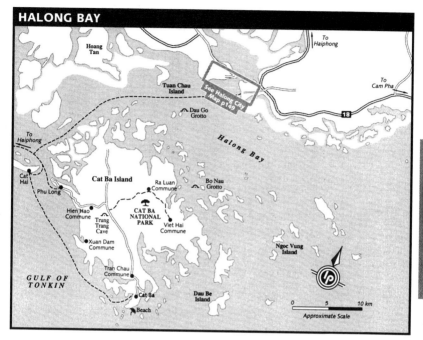

HALONG BAY

Hang Dau Go (Grotto of Wooden Stakes), known to the French as the Grotte des Merveilles (Cave of Marvels), is a huge cave consisting of three chambers which you reach via 90 steps. Among the stalactites of the first hall, scores of gnomes appear to be holding a meeting. The walls of the second chamber sparkle if bright light is shone on them. The cave derives its Vietnamese name from the third of the chambers, said to have been used during the 13th century to store the sharp bamboo stakes which Tran Hung Dao planted in the bed of the Bach Dang River to impale Kublai Khan's invasion fleet.

Drum Grotto is so named because when the wind blows through its many stalactites and stalagmites, visitors think they hear the sound of distant drumbeats. Other well known caves in Halong Bay include the Grotto of Bo Nau and the 2km-long Hang Hanh Cave.

Islands

Some tourist boats stop at Reu Dat Island, which supports an unusual species of monkeys which are distinguished by their red buttocks.

A few travellers also visit Ngoc Vung Island. It is easily identified by its red-brick lighthouse.

Tuan Chau Island (5km west of Bai Chay) is one of the few islands in Halong Bay which has seen any development. In early 1999 it was connected to the mainland by a bridge. Currently there are three state-run *villas* (☎ 842001) with rooms costing US$28 to US$38, and a restaurant. There are ambitious plans to develop the island into a multimillion dollar resort complex, complete with hotels, villas and a golf course.

Ho Chi Minh's modest former summer residence is here.

Getting Around

You won't see much unless you take a boat tour of the islands and their grottoes. Cruises, from a few hours up to a whole day, are offered by private boat owners, travel agencies and hotels; competition is fierce. Since the area to be cruised is large, it's advisable to have a fast boat in order to see more. The rare, but romantic, junks are slow but very photogenic, and can be hired as well.

All tourist boats depart from a marina about 1km west of Bai Chay. You needn't rent a whole boat for yourself. A small boat can hold up to 12 people and costs between US$5 and US$8 per hour. Mid-sized boats (the most popular ones) take around 20 passengers and should cost between US$6 to US$10 per hour.

In fact, these 'standard' prices are increasingly hard to get, so it is well worth booking Halong Bay tours in Hanoi. If you use a reliable agent you will find that it is virtually impossible to do it any cheaper on your own, and the hassle factor in Halong City for individual travellers can make your hair fall out!

Most tours sold in Hanoi are very reasonably priced, from around US$20 to US$30 per person for a two-day/one-night trip, inclusive of transport, meals, accommodation and boat tours. You are well advised to check in advance exactly what food, drink and accommodation you can expect, and you might ask to see a picture of the boat. Three-day/two-night tours typically include Cat Ba Island and cost between US$30 and US$40. It is also possible to stay longer, and arrange for pick-up in Halong City by phone.

Those with time constraints and budgetary freedom can make arrangements in Hanoi for a one day whirlwind tour of the bay. This entails a private car and boat, but buys you time enough to cruise the bay for about five hours, with lunch on board. For a group of 1 to 3 people, you'd be looking at upwards of US$100 all-inclusive.

If you're hell-bent on going solo you might consider giving the riff-raff in Halong

City a complete miss and make a beeline for Cat Ba Island (described later in this chapter). A far more pleasant alternative, from where you can also book boat trips around Halong Bay.

If you book a tour, there is always a small, but real, chance that the boat trip may be cancelled due to bad weather. This may entitle you to a partial refund, but remember that the boat trip is only a small portion of the cost of the journey (it's hotels, food and transport that really add up).

HALONG CITY
☎ 033

The majority of Halong Bay's food, accommodation and other life-support systems are found in Halong City, the capital of Quang Ninh Province. These days it is a pleasure den for domestic and foreign package tourists, and unless you're keen on the 'Thai Massage' scene, there is no good reason to visit Halong City, other than as a launch pad for boats.

If you are booked on a tour from Hanoi you will be spared dealing with the hassles and sleaze, and putting up for a night in Bai Chay should not be the end of the world.

Orientation

Halong City is bisected by a small bay and for travellers the most important district (on the western side) is called Bai Chay. Accommodation can be found on both sides of the bay, but Bai Chay is more scenic, closer to Hanoi and much better endowed with hotels and restaurants. Bai Chay is also where the majority of tourist boats are moored.

A short ferry ride (US$0.04) east across the bay takes you to Hon Gai, the main port district for coal transport. The ferry from Haiphong docks in Hon Gai.

Information

There is an office of Quang Ninh Tourist (Cong Ty Du Lich Quang Ninh; ☎ 846321, fax 846318) on the main drag in Bai Chay. This travel agency owns several hotels and can inform you about boat tours.

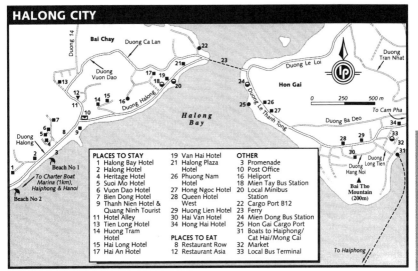

HALONG CITY

PLACES TO STAY	19 Van Hai Hotel	OTHER
1 Halong Bay Hotel	21 Halong Plaza	3 Promenade
2 Halong Hotel	Hotel	10 Post Office
4 Heritage Hotel	26 Phuong Nam	16 Heliport
5 Suoi Mo Hotel	Hotel	18 Mien Tay Bus Station
6 Vuon Dao Hotel	27 Hong Ngoc Hotel	20 Local Minibus
7 Bien Dong Hotel	28 Queen Hotel	Station
9 Thanh Nien Hotel &	West	22 Cargo Port B12
Quang Ninh Tourist	29 Huong Lien Hotel	23 Ferry
11 Hotel Alley	30 Hai Van Hotel	24 Mien Dong Bus Station
13 Tien Long Hotel	34 Hong Hai Hotel	25 Hon Gai Cargo Port
14 Huong Tram		31 Boats to Haiphong/
Hotel	PLACES TO EAT	Cat Hai/Mong Cai
15 Hai Long Hotel	8 Restaurant Row	32 Market
17 Hai An Hotel	12 Restaurant Asia	33 Local Bus Terminal

Places to Stay
The majority of travellers stay in Bai Chay, as it is more convenient to the tour boat dock. There are now more than 100 hotels in Halong. Keen competition keeps prices down, and touts hungry.

Bai Chay The hotels are found in several areas. The heaviest concentration is right in town, in the so called 'hotel alley'. Countless mini-hotels charge around US$10 to US$15 for a double with private bath and air-conditioning.

A couple of hillside hotels with views of the bay are the *Huong Tram Hotel* (☎ 846365, fax 845930), with 15 rooms at US$8/13 for fan/air-con rooms, and the 20-room all-air-con *Hai Long Hotel* (☎ 846378, fax 846171), priced at US$15.

A little farther east and high up in the hills is the 40-room *Hai An Hotel* (☎ 845514, fax 845512), a fancy place with sea views, satellite TV and rates from US$30 to US$35.

The 101-room *Heritage Hotel* (☎ 846888, fax 846718) has rooms from US$70 to US$170.

Right by the car ferry landing is the *Halong Plaza Hotel* (☎ 845810, fax 846867), a snazzy 106-room Thai-Vietnamese joint venture. Rooms here range from US$140 to US$350; 30% discounts are usually offered.

Many other hotels, mostly large and expensive, are strung out for 2km along the main road heading west of town.

Hon Gai There are fewer places to stay here, but demand is low so prices have remained cheap. Hotels are clustered mainly along Đ Le Thanh Tong.

At 11 Đ Le Thanh Tong, the *Phuong Nam Hotel* (☎ 827242, fax 828687) has twelve basic air-con rooms costing US$11 to US$13.

Closer to the Haiphong ferry dock, at 425 Đ Le Thanh Tong, the better-appointed *Hong Hai Hotel* (☎ 825179, fax 823436) costs US$25 to US$40.

Places to Eat
Except for mini-hotels, most hotels have restaurants. If you're on a tour, it's likely that meals will be included.

Central Bai Chay has a solid row of cheap restaurants offering seafood, among them the popular *Van Song Restaurant (☎ 846084)*, where the friendly owner speaks eloquent French.

We can also endorse the *Restaurant Asia (☎ 846927)* on the 'hotel alley' slope. The owner Mr Vinh speaks excellent German (he formerly ran a restaurant in East Berlin) and some English. The Vietnamese food here is very good and prices are reasonable.

Getting There & Away

Bus Buses to Halong City (Bai Chay) depart from Hanoi's Gia Lam bus station. In Halong City, you catch Hanoi-bound buses from Mien Tay bus station (Ben Xe Mien Tay) in Bai Chay. In either direction, the first bus is at 7.30 am and the last is at 2.30 pm. The fare is US$6.

Buses from Haiphong to Halong City depart Haiphong from a bus station in the Thuy Nguyen District (on the northern bank of the Cam River). The trip takes approximately two hours. The bus station in Halong City is about 1km from the Halong Hotel.

Car Halong City is 160km from Hanoi; the trip takes about three hours.

Boat There are slow boats connecting Hon Gai to Haiphong, costing US$3.50 and taking about three hours. They currently run daily, with departures from Haiphong at 6 and 11 am and 1.30 and 4 pm, and leaving Hon Gai at 6, 8.30 and 11 am and 4 pm.

A commuter boat from Hon Gai to Cat Hai Island leaves at 12.30 pm daily and offers some views of Halong Bay. It costs US$2.30 and takes about two hours. From Cat Hai you can hop on another small ferry to Cat Ba Island (see Getting There & Away in the Cat Ba Island section).

Helicopter If you've got the cash to burn, helicopters can be chartered for whirlwind tours of the bay. Of course, it's hard to imagine how you're going to get a good look at the grottoes from a helicopter unless the pilots are *really* skilled.

Helijet has a flight every Saturday departing Hanoi at 8 am and returning at 3.30 pm. The US$195 fare includes a four-hour boat trip and lunch. Bookings can be made at Hanoi's Sofitel Metropole Hotel (☎ 04-826 6919 ext 8046).

There are also chartered flights from Hanoi to Halong Bay costing US$100 per person one way. This service is offered by Vasco (☎ 04-827 1707, fax 827 2705), which operates out of Hanoi's Gia Lam airport.

A third competitor in this business, Northern Flight Service Company (☎ 04-827 4409, fax 827 2780), at 173 Pho Truong Chinh, offers helicopter charter service from Hanoi to Halong on Saturday only. The cost is $175 per person (paying an extra $20 includes transfers to Hanoi's Gia Lam airport and the harbour in Halong, a four to five hour boat ride and lunch in Halong Bay).

Getting Around

Motorbike drivers in both Bai Chay and Hon Gai can take you from the respective ferry landings into town or the tourist boat landing for about US$0.15.

CAT BA ISLAND

Cat Ba is the largest island in Halong Bay. While the vast majority of Halong Bay's islands are uninhabited vertical rocks sticking out of the sea, Cat Ba actually has a few tiny fishing villages. The terrain is too rocky for large scale agriculture and most residents earn their living from the sea.

About half of Cat Ba Island (which has a total area of 354 sq km) and 90 sq km of the adjacent inshore waters were declared a national park in 1986 in order to protect the island's diverse ecosystems. These include subtropical evergreen forests on the hills, freshwater swamp forests at the base of the hills, coastal mangrove forests, small freshwater lakes and offshore coral reefs. Most of the coastline consists of rocky cliffs, but there are a few sandy beaches tucked into small coves. The main beaches are Cai Vieng, Hong Xoai Be and Hong Xoai Lon.

There are numerous lakes, waterfalls and grottoes in the spectacular limestone hills, the highest of which rises 331m above sea level. Vegetation growth is stunted near the summits because of high winds. The largest permanent body of water on the island is Ech Lake which covers an area of 3 hectares. Almost all of the surface streams are seasonal; most of the island's rainwater flows into caves and follows underground streams to the sea, resulting in a shortage of fresh water during the dry season. Although parts of the interior of the island are below sea level, most of the island is between 50 and 200m in elevation.

The waters off Cat Ba Island are home to 200 species of fish, 500 species of molluscs and 400 species of arthropods. Larger marine animals in the area include seals and three species of dolphins.

Stone tools and bones left by human beings who lived between 6000 and 7000 years ago have been found at 17 sites on the island. The most thoroughly studied site is Cai Beo Cave, discovered by a French archaeologist in 1938, 1.5km from Cat Ba village.

Today, the island's human population of 12,000 is concentrated in the southern part of the island, including the fishing village of Cat Ba.

During February, March and April, Cat Ba's weather is often cold and drizzly, although the temperature rarely falls below 10°C. During the summer months, tropical storms are frequent.

Cat Ba National Park

Cat Ba National Park is home to 20 types of mammals – including François monkeys, wild boar, deer, squirrels and hedgehogs – and 69 species of birds have been sighted, including hawks, hornbills and cuckoos. Cat Ba lies on a major migration route for waterfowl (ducks, geese and shorebirds) who feed and roost in the mangrove forests and on the beaches. The 745 species of plants recorded on Cat Ba include 118 timber species and 160 plants with medicinal value.

You pay US$1 admission to the park; the services of a guide cost US$5 per day regardless of group size. A guide is not mandatory, but is *definitely* recommended – otherwise, all you are likely to see is a canopy of trees. The guide will take you on a walk through a cave, so bring a torch (flashlight). The walk also brings you to a mountain peak. The last part of the walk is rather hairy, but push on to the summit if you can – many say the views are worth it.

There is a hard-core 18km (five to six hour) hike through the park that many travellers like to do. You need a guide plus bus transport to the trailhead and a boat to return – all of this can be easily arranged in Cat Ba village. The hike includes a visit to Viet Hai, a remote minority village. If you're planning on doing this hike, equip yourself with a generous supply of water, plus some food, as there are no opportunities (yet) to buy things en route.

Camping is possible in the park, but you'll need to bring all of your own gear.

There are two caves in the national park that are open to visitors. One has been preserved in its natural state while the other has historical significance – it served as a secret, bomb-proof hospital during the American War. There is an additional US$1 fee to visit the Trung Tang Cave.

To reach the national park headquarters at Trung Trang, take a minibus from one of the hotels in Cat Ba; the one-way trip takes 30 minutes and should cost US$0.50. All of the various restaurants and hotels sell minibus tickets. Another way is to hire a motorbike for about US$1.60.

Beaches

The white sand Cat Co beaches (called simply Cat Co 1 and Cat Co 2) make a great place to lounge around for the day. They are about 1.5km from Cat Ba village and can be reached on foot or by motorbike (US$0.25). There is a US$0.40 entry fee to the beaches.

Places to Stay

There is an astounding number of new hotels concentrated along the bay front in

Cat Ba village, feeding both an expanding domestic and foreign tourist market. Hotels get filled up on weekends and holidays.

Room rates fluctuate greatly between high season summer months (May to September) and the slower winter months (October to April). Consider one without karaoke if you prefer peace and quiet.

The *Quang Duc Family Hotel* (☎ 888231) was one of Cat Ba's first. Twin rooms cost US$10/12 in winter/summer.

Hoang Huong Hotel (☎ 888274), near the ferry pier, has fan twin rooms for US$8 in winter and US$12 in summer. Air-con raises the price to US$10 and $US15 to 17 respectively.

The friendly *Sunflower Hotel* (☎ 888215, fax 888451) has an open-air billiards bar on the 7th floor rooftop. Winter rates are US$12/15 for fan/air-con rooms.

The *Lan Ha Hotel* (☎ 888299) is on a quiet side street (ask for a room on the 5th floor – good views). Fan twin rooms cost just US$4 in winter and US$5 in summer.

One entrepreneur was building beach bungalows on a small nearby island called Cat Da Bang; there is also talk of organised beach camping on Cat Ba Island.

Places to Eat

The friendly *Huu Dung Restaurant* offers some of the best seafood in town. Easy to spot, the 'Coka Cola Restaurant' has a red-tile roof painted like a Coke billboard.

Another excellent choice is the *Gaulois Restaurant* (☎ 888482). The owners serve delicious Vietnamese and 'backpacker' fare and are a great source of travel information.

Getting There & Away

Cat Ba Island is 40km east of Haiphong and 20km south of Halong City. A great innovation for getting there are the 108-seat Russian-built hydrofoils. These air-conditioned water rockets reduce the Haiphong-Cat Hai-Cat Ba journey to just two hours. The one-way fare for foreigners is US$6. The hydrofoil currently runs once daily in each direction; from Haiphong to Cat Ba at 9 am, and the reverse trip at 3 pm. Be aware that

this schedule is *highly* subject to change depending on the numbers of passengers.

Slow boats take about four hours and run on a slightly more dependable schedule; from Haiphong at 6.30 am and 1.30 pm, and the reverse trip at 6 am and 1 pm, but you should check on this as well.

An alternative way to reach Cat Ba is via the island of Cat Hai, which is closer to Haiphong. A boat departs Haiphong for Cat Hai, makes a brief stop and continues on to the port of Phu Long on Cat Ba Island. There is also a 12.30 pm slow boat from Hon Gai (Halong City) which takes about two hours to Cat Hai, from where it's possible to catch another boat across to Phu Long port (20 minutes, US$0.60).

From the port on Cat Ba, motorbike drivers will be waiting to whisk you away for the 30km ride to the centre of town (or about half the distance to the national park) for about US$4. There is also a public bus meeting the boats costing US$1.60, but this takes considerably more time getting you to your hotel.

Getting Around

Note – there is more than one pier on the island. One is in Cat Ba village (where most travellers want to go) and the other is at Phu Long some 30km away. At Phu Long there should be a bus waiting to take you to Cat Ba village. The high-speed tourist boat does not stop at Phu Long, but the slow local boats do.

Tours of the island and national park, plus boat trips around Halong Bay and fishing trips are peddled by nearly every hotel and restaurant in Cat Ba village. Prices depend on the number of people, but typical prices are US$8 for day trips and US$20 for a two-day/one-night trip.

We can endorse a few reliable tour operator/guides including Mr Thang at the Gaulois Restaurant, Mr Phuc at the Quang Duc Family Hotel, and the friendly folks at the Huu Dung Restaurant.

Minibuses are easily arranged. Motorbike rentals (with or without driver) are available from most of the hotels, as are some rental bicycles. Warning: if you're heading out to the beaches or national park, pay the US$0.15 parking fee to make sure your vehicle is still there when you return.

You'll have plenty of offers to take a trip around Cat Ba fishing harbour in a small rowboat for around US$1.50.

HAIPHONG
☎ 031

Haiphong is Vietnam's fourth most populous city and one of the country's most important seaports.

The French took possession of Haiphong – then a small market town – in 1874. Industrial concerns were established here in part because of its proximity to coal supplies.

In spite of its size, Haiphong today is a relatively sleepy place with little traffic and many dilapidated buildings. While it may not be worth a special trip, it could make a reasonable stopover en route to/from Cat Ba Island or Halong Bay.

Places to Stay
The *Hoa Binh Hotel (☎ 846907, 104 Pho Luong Khanh Thien)* is across from the train station and costs US$10 to US$25.

The name of the *Dien Bien Hotel (☎ 745 264, fax 754743, 67 Pho Dien Bien Phu)* will probably not enthral French travellers, but the rooms are OK and cost US$15 and US$20. Directly across the street, at No 62, is the French-era *Hotel du Commerce (☎ 842706, fax 842560)*. The tariff is US$20 to US$60. Next door is the snazzy three-star *Huu Nghi Hotel (☎ 823310, fax 823245)*, with 126 well-appointed rooms ranging from US$50 to US$300.

Places to Eat
Com Vietnam (☎ 841698, 4 Pho Hoang Van Thu) is near the post office and serves Vietnamese food for reasonable prices and has a pleasant little courtyard in front.

Getting There & Away
Bus Hanoi-Haiphong buses and minibuses depart from Hanoi's Gia Lam bus station. Departures are from approximately 5 am

until 6 pm and the journey takes around two hours. Minibuses depart only when full. In Haiphong, get these buses at the Tam Bac bus station.

Haiphong has several long distance bus stations. For Bai Chay (Halong City), the station you want is in the Thuy Nguyen district (accessed by ferry). There is only one bus scheduled daily, although minibuses will make the run when demand is sufficient. The scheduled bus departs Haiphong at 9 am for Bai Chay. Departure from Bai Chay is at 12.30 pm. The one-way fare is US$4.

Train Haiphong is not on the main line between Hanoi and Saigon, but there is a spur line connecting it to Hanoi. There is one express train daily to/from Hanoi station and several others from Long Bien station (near Hanoi on the eastern side of the Red River). Hard seats cost US$3.50.

The train from Hanoi station departs at 6 am and arrives in Haiphong at 8.05 am. Going the other way, the train departs Haiphong at 6.25 pm and arrives in Hanoi at 8.30 pm.

The trains from Long Bien station depart at 10 am, 3 pm, 5.05 pm and 8.20 pm and take about 2½ hours to Haiphong. For the return, trains depart Haiphong at 6.30 am, 10.35 am and 1.40 pm to Long Bien station.

There are two train stations within the city limits of Haiphong. The Thuong Li station is in the western part of the city, far from the centre. The Haiphong station is right in the city centre; this is the last stop for the train coming from Hanoi and this is where you should get off.

Car Haiphong is 103km from Hanoi on National Highway 5. Via this new expressway (Vietnam's first) the journey takes under 1½ hours.

Boat The two boats of interest to travellers are those going to Cat Ba Island and Hon Gai (Halong City). See the Cat Ba Island and Halong Bay sections for details.

EXCURSIONS

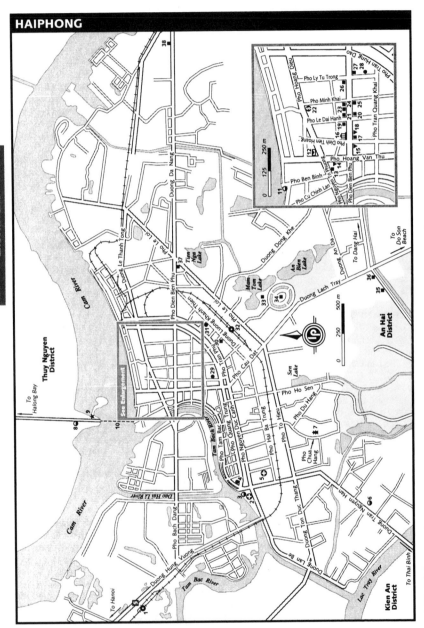

PLACES TO STAY
13 Duyen Hai Hotel
17 Transport Hotel
19 Hong Bang Hotel
20 Dien Bien Hotel
21 Hotel du Commerce
23 Huu Nghi Hotel
24 My Nghi Hotel
25 Thang Nam Hotel
26 Bach Dang Hotel
27 Navy Hotel
30 Hoa Binh Hotel
33 Bong Sen Hotel
34 Thanh Lich Hotel
35 Hong Hai Hotel
36 Cau Rao Hotel

37 Blue Star Hotel
38 Holiday Mansion Hotel

PLACES TO EAT
14 Com Vietnam
15 Saigon Cafe
18 Chie

OTHER
1   Thuong Li Train Station
2   Traditional Medicine
    Hospital
3   Tam Bac Bus Station
4   Sat Market
5   Vietnam-Czech Friendship
    Hospital

6   Bus Station
7   Du Hang Pagoda
8   Buses to Halong City
9   Police Checkpoint
10 Ferry Route
11 Boats to Halong City &
    Cat Ba Island
12 Post Office
16 Haiphong Museum
22 Vietcombank
28 Do Thanh Laundry & Dry
    Cleaning
29 Municipal Theatre
31 Vietnam Airlines
32 Haiphong
    Train Station

EXCURSIONS

Getting Around

Haiphong has metered air-conditioned taxis and there are plenty of cyclos cruising the town.

DO SON BEACH

The palm-shaded beach at Do Son, 21km south-east of central Haiphong, is a popular seaside resort. The hilly, 4km-long promontory ends with a string of islets. The peninsula's nine hills are known as the Cuu Long Son (Nine Dragons).

The town is famous for its ritual buffalo fights, held annually on the 10th day of the eighth lunar month, and for its casino, opened in 1994, the first to open in Vietnam since 1975. Foreigners are permitted to lose their fortunes here, but Vietnamese are barred from entering the casino.

North & East of Hanoi

CO LOA CITADEL

Co Loa Citadel (Co Loa Thanh) is the first fortified citadel recorded in Vietnamese history. This spiral shaped structure was built during the Kingdom of Au Lac (258-208 BC). Only vestiges of the massive concentric ramparts, which enclosed an area of about 5 sq km, are extant. Co Loa

again became the national capital under Ngo Quyen (reigned 939-44).

In the centre of the citadel there are temples dedicated to King An Duong Vuong (ruled 257-208 BC), who founded the legendary Thuc Dynasty, and his daughter My Nuong (My Chau). When My Nuong showed her father's magic crossbow trigger – which made the Vietnamese king invincible in battle – to her husband (the son of a Chinese general), he stole it and gave it to his father. With its help, the Chinese were able to defeat An Duong Vuong and his forces, depriving Vietnam of its independence.

Co Loa Citadel is 16km north of central Hanoi in Dong Anh district.

LE MAT

Le Mat is known as the 'snake village' *(Lang Ran)*. The locals here raise snakes for upmarket eateries in Hanoi and village restaurants, and for medicinal spirits.

The village itself is not much to look at; most people come in order to sample the local fare. It is very difficult to visit the snake farms, as breeding centres demand quiet. Most restaurant owners, however, will be happy to reveal your meal before it is slain, and show off their bottles of snake wine. Many of the restaurants double as mini-zoos with caged monkeys, wildcats, porcupines and other reptiles

A flagon of snake wine containing snakes and the snake-hunting Boucal bird that caught them.

in trees, which may explain their use in curing headaches. Kraids (both yellow and black ringed and black and white ringed) take over underground rat holes, so are believed to be good for foot ailments like rheumatism.

Around 25 restaurants in Le Mat specialise in reptile meat and elixir. While a large King Cobra can cost up to US$100 (feeding four to six persons), prices for most meals are not unreasonable. For about US$6 to US$8 per person you are served a set course consisting of snake meat prepared in around 10 different ways, as well as a selection of exotic snake alcohol tasters.

Highly regarded are jars of wine containing three, five, seven or nine different poisonous snakes. Some popular potions are fermented with penises (snakes have two!), testes (snakes sport around 20!), gall bladder, bile, blood curd, and – perhaps hardest to swallow – unborn snake foetus *(ruou bao tu ran)*. Other gruesome concoctions are jars of snakes fermented together with the snake-hunting Boucal bird *(Bim Bip)* – people believe this provides bodily protection.

All snake spirits are said to be a boon to male sexual potency. Also popular is a wine made with the black leaves of the *Dam Duong Hoac* (literally 'perverted black goat') bush of the same name *(herba epimedii)*. It is said that a goat which eats these leaves can service up to 20 female goats (who needs Viagra anyway?).

Though some visitors purchase bottles of wine to take home, bear in mind that most western countries will confiscate these at customs, and you could face paying a fine, or worse.

You might poke your head into a few restaurants before deciding where to eat, and beware of freelance touts who may try to lure you into an overpriced meal. Be sure to establish what you're getting, and the cost, before ordering.

Frequented by foreign tour groups, *O Sin* (☎ 04-827 2984), *Phong Do* (☎04-827 3244) and *Phong Do II* (☎04-827 1091) are all close to the turn-off; further into the village, keep an eye out for *Tran Ban* (☎04-827 2406), *Linh Linh* (☎04-827 4719) and

like salamanders and geckos on display, sometimes in quite squalid conditions.

The price of eating snake has risen significantly since 1998, when authorities placed a ban on the capture of most wild animals. Overhunted, decreasing snake populations throughout Vietnam were causing an increase in rice field rats which can quickly decimate rural crops. Snakes sold in Le Mat are supposed to be 100% farmed, though widespread poaching and smuggling (primarily over the border into China) are said to continue.

All of the snakes raised here are highly poisonous – the more venomous (hence a higher medicinal quality), the more expensive. The strong-boned King Cobra *(Ho Mang Chua)* and Copperhead *(Ho Mang Banh)* are both said to relieve back pain; the spearheaded Coluber *(Ran Rao)* and green-camouflaged Dendrophis *(Ran Luc)* live high

Quoc Trieu (☎ *04-827 2898)*. A few places have English menus, though very little English is spoken in Le Mat.

On the 23rd day of the third lunar month is the very interesting Le Mat Festival, featuring 'snake dances' and other activities.

Getting There & Away

Le Mat is just 7km east of central Hanoi and is easily reached by motorbike. Cross the Chuong Duong Bridge (motorbikes pay a US$0.04 toll) and follow National Highway 1A. The turn-off is signposted about 800m past the large roundabout which forks off to Highway 5. Bicycle access is via the Long Bien Bridge, through the town of Gia Lam.

PHU LANG

The dusty ceramics village of Phu Lang is known for the production of small earthenware coffins and unglazed jars. The village is quiet and picturesque, with giant stacks of kiln-firing wood everywhere and broken coffin fragments creatively fashioned into walls, windows and door frames.

The coffins, which can be seen for sale in Hanoi's Old Quarter, are about 50cm long and are typically adorned with the Chinese character for longevity. Though they appear to be made for babies, the coffins are where peoples' bones are transferred to three years after burial. Some, however, have discovered other creative uses for the coffins (such as for flower planters), and one artist in Hanoi built an entire house of them! Wholesale costs are as low as about US$1.50 for simple coffins, or US$3 for larger ones with a cover.

Throwing a pot in Phu Lang

Jars in Phu Lang are made in a variety of shapes and sizes and function mainly as containers for water and spirits. Prices range from about US$1 for small sticky rice steamers to US$3 for large sized water jars.

The village's brick kilns are large enough to accommodate about 1000 stacked coffins. The average firing requires about three days and consumes a massive 15 cubic metres of sandalwood *(bach dan)*, at a cost of about US$250.

If you wander around the village you should be able to catch a glimpse of all stages of the process, from throwing the coffins and jars to emptying the kilns and loading up bicycles for transport to the area's markets.

Getting There & Away

Phu Lang is 55km north of Hanoi. From the town of Bac Ninh, it is about 20km to the turn-off to the village. The road leading to

Earthenware coffin

the village is about 5km before a giant thermal electric plant, but is not signposted. The left turn-off is about 50m after a stone road marker reading H4 – 20. Head along this windy dirt road for about 5km to the centre of the village.

THO HA

Tho Ha is a delightful village active in producing spring roll rice paper and a potent local alcohol. The village is also famed for local folk songs and crooners.

Densely populated, this peaceful village is isolated from the mainland, on a peninsula wound around a bend in the Cau River, which separates the provinces of Bac Ninh and Bac Giang. Much of the village's old-world charm lies in it being completely free of motor traffic.

Most of the 1000 or so families tucked into Tho Ha's narrow streets and alleyways manufacture rice paper, and about 20% also distil alcohol. There is virtually no farming in the village – a relative rarity in Vietnam.

Notably humorous are the village's hobo pigs, which exist in a virtual state of inebriation from feeding daily on the discharged remains of the alcohol fermentation process. These lazy creatures can be seen stumbling down pathways and sleeping sprawled out in different parts of the village.

The spring roll papers are made from pure rice powder mixed with water and a touch of salt. Similar in preparation and appearance to crêpes, they are poured one by one onto a coal-heated hot plate, covered with a foot-controlled pop-top for a few seconds, removed and placed on woven bamboo racks to sun dry. The papers wholesale for US$0.40 per 100, and one person can churn out about 2000 a day.

About 90% of the alcohol made here is from cassava; the rest is from rice, which is more expensive to produce and smoother on the taste buds. The cassava fire-water can put hair on your chest. The average household in Tho Ha can produce about 70L a day, and the wine wholesales for just US$0.25 per litre, about half the price of rice wine.

Getting There & Away

Tho Ha is 35km north of Hanoi. From the town of Bach Ninh, it is about 4km to the boat landing at Ben Van. From here you must make the short crossing by river boat (US$0.80) to reach Ben Dinh Tho Ha.

DONG KY

Dong Ky, about 20km north-east of Hanoi, was at one time known as the 'firecracker village'. Prior to 1994, when the government banned firecrackers, there was always a firecracker festival in Dong Ky. A competition for the loudest firecracker once resulted in the construction of a gargantuan firecracker 16m in length!

With the firecracker industry now extinguished, the village survives by producing beautiful traditional furniture, much of it inlaid with elaborate mother-of-pearl. All along the main street are workshops where craftspeople are busy sawing, sanding, carving, inlaying, polishing and, of course, selling wares.

The most common types of wood used in Dong Ky (in order of demand) are rosewood *(trac)*, sindora *(gu)*, ebony *(mun)* and ironwood *(lim)*. Inlaying the mother-of-pearl is highly labour-intensive and it is fascinating to watch how it is delicately sawed into fine fish-bone slivers and painstakingly set into the wood. The shells are mostly imported from Singapore, and depending on the quality can cost up to thousands of dollars per kilogram.

TAM DAO HILL STATION

Tam Dao Hill Station (elevation 930m), known to the French as the Cascade d'Argent (Silver Cascade), was founded by the French in 1907 as an escape from the heat of the Red River Delta. Hanoi residents still retreat to the high elevation and cool climate of Tam Dao, in particular from May to August.

The three summits of Tam Dao Mountain, all about 1400m in height, are visible from the hill station to the north-east. Many hill tribe people live in the Tam Dao region, though they are largely assimilated. The best times of the year to visit Tam Dao are generally from late May to mid-September and from mid-December to February.

Dampness makes the Tam Dao area particularly rich in flora and fauna. However, logging (both legal and otherwise) has severely affected the environment.

Remember that it is cool up in Tam Dao and that this part of Vietnam has a distinct winter. Don't be caught unprepared.

Places to Stay & Eat

There are many hotels, mostly charging from US$10 to US$15. One such place is the *Tam Dao Hotel* (Khach San Tam Dao).

There are heaps of *restaurants*, but they are generally expensive – ask prices first. The chief items are fried or grilled deer, roast squirrel and roast silver pheasant. The latter delicacy is not yet considered an endangered species, but is soon likely to be one, so please don't order it!

Getting There & Away

Tam Dao Hill Station is 85km north-west of Hanoi. Public transport is a problem. First, you must take a bus from Kim Ma bus station (west of Hanoi's city centre) to Vinh Yen – the last one leaves at 1 pm. From there you must hire a motorbike (about US$2) or taxi for the 24km single-lane track that leads up to Tam Dao. There is a toll for using this road – about US$0.25 for motorbikes or US$1.60 for cars.

Probably the easiest way to reach Tam Dao is to simply rent your own motorbike in Hanoi and drive yourself. The road getting there is very picturesque.

Budget tour operators typically ask around US$50 for a three passenger vehicle to bring you to Tam Dao from Hanoi, and return you the following day. They can also advise you on hotels and help with reservations.

EXCURSIONS

Appendix – Motorbiking in Northern Vietnam

Vietnam's northern mountains hide some of the most spectacular scenery in all of Asia. A long distance motorbike journey from Hanoi into the mountainous hinterland, though risky in terms of traffic accidents and definitely tiring, offers unprecedented opportunities to interact with hill tribe people and reach areas that cars – no matter how-many-wheel-drive they are – simply cannot navigate.

The roads might be rough and the motorbikes a little primitive, but the experience of passing through frontier areas practically untouched by foreign passage will more than compensate for any discomfort thrown up by the road or the weather. You might not want to do it during the coldest months (January and February), and in mid-summer you have to contend with occasionally heavy rains, but despite such annoyances many travellers prefer motorbike trekking to all other forms of transport.

Motorbike wrecks are the number one cause of death in Vietnam, so don't become a statistic. Read the Motorbike section in the Getting Around chapter before you embark on your motorbiking tour.

THE CLASSIC RIDES

Expect to be able to cover an average of 100-150km a day, with plenty of breaks. Only if you drive without stopping for 12 hours will you get more than 300km a day.

The Dien Bien Phu to Sapa Loop (Hanoi – Mai Chau – Son La – Dien Bien Phu – Lai Chau – Tam Duong – Sapa – Hanoi) If you give yourself six days then expect five/six hours driving time per day, allowing enough free time to mingle with local people and photograph the amazing scenery along the way. The entire loop is sealed, except for the 50km stretch between Dien Bien Phu and Binh Lu.

The Northern Loop (Hanoi – Lang Son – Cao Bang – Ba Be Lakes – Hanoi) A minimum four day ride on sealed road all the way (except for a few rocky bits between Lang Son and Cao Bang). Give yourself extra time to explore around Cao Bang and to relax in Ba Be National Park.

THE BIKES
Minsk

Short of bringing your own, the best overall bike to take into the mountains is the two-stroke, 125cc Belarussian Minsk. Minsks pack the kind of power you'll need for the mountainous regions, plus they're light enough to be carried by two people across rivers and over rocky terrain. The Russian-made Minsk is pre-WWII in design, just like a Volkswagon. This means the bike is simple and robust, and does not require a rocket scientist to repair it. The bike's wiring is very basic, parts are cheap and you don't need special tools to open it up.

The Minsk manual proudly says: 'These motorcycles are especially suitable for service in the countryside with bad or no roads'. But perhaps the sweetest thing about Minsks is that for only US$50 you can completely refit the bike out with new parts (including the entire electrical system, cables, brakes, lights, filters etc), so you can be fairly sure that any problems on the road will be minor in nature. In the mountains of Vietnam, the Minsk rules supreme; every mechanic knows how to fix one, and places everywhere sell Minsk parts.

Buying a Minsk Minsks can't be rented, so expect to pay US$350 to US$450 for a second-hand bike that will get about the same at resale. Check the message boards in the travellers' cafés and expat watering holes like Bar Le Maquis and the Pear Tree

Pub, or Hoa Sua Restaurant. There are Minsk agents on Pho Lo Duc (nos 47, 67, 87 and 113) and on Pho Anh Thach (down the alley between 25D Pho Nguyen Bieu and St Joseph's Cathedral), but expect to be sold a bike in need of fixing. Perhaps the best bet is to email the Minsk Club directly (minskclub@geocities.com); they run a trading post for second-hand Minsks.

Minsk Mania Most members of Hanoi's free-wheelin' Minsk Motorcycle Club never even heard of a Minsk before coming to Vietnam. These days, however, owning the Russian wonderbike is the latest craze among the city's eclectic expat community, and the Minsk Club roster continues to expand. The hipness of riding a Minsk has grown to cult-like proportions as converts leave their reverence for Hondas and Harleys in the dust.

The Minsk Club is a social group with the simple aim of getting people up into the mountains for fun on two wheels. It holds monthly meetings and parties, and a couple of rallies a year. Two die-hard members recently set out from Hanoi to Bombay, while one Russian bloke sold his return ticket home so he could ride a Minsk! The club has a web page, loads of Minsk merchandise, repair manuals and tips about the backroads of Vietnam. Check it out at www.geocities.com/TheTropics/8799/.

Bonus

The four-stroke, single cylinder 125cc Bonus is a Taiwanese bike assembled in Vietnam. It is biggest and most commonly available bike for rent, and extremely fuel efficient and easy to drive. So long as you make sure it's not a dud, then a rented Bonus should get you there hassle free. You'll want to spend a long morning casing the rental shops to find a good one. Do get the spark plug cleaned, get them to tighten the chain if needed and fill the engine with new oil. Bonus seats are uncomfortable on long drives as they are sloped and have distinct edges. The suspension is nothing to rave about and the tread on the tyres is very smooth compared to a Minsk.

Bentley

No relation to the luxury car company, the four stroke, twin cylinder 125cc Honda Bentley is more comfortable and stronger than the Bonus, but normally costs more to rent. As it's a Honda, you don't need to worry too much about breakdowns and countryside mechanics are mostly familiar with them. Like the Bonus, the bike is fine for good and medium-quality roads, but not well suited for poor road conditions. It's very low and heavy and the twin exhaust pipes ride close to the ground.

Dream

There are more 110cc Honda Dream scooters in Vietnam's cities than any other bike. They are very well made, strong and surprisingly fast for a four stroke scooter. Dreams are exceptionally reliable and fuel efficient – something like 50km per litre. These bikes will get you anywhere sealed roads go, and are popular for the treacherous Hanoi – Ho Chi Minh City journey along National Highway 1. They can take a bit of dirt, but not too much as the suspension is light. Seats are hard so your rear end will suffer on a long haul.

Yamaha Dirt Bike

In 1996 Yamaha introduced two dirt bikes – a 125cc two stoke and a 175cc two-stroke – to Vietnam. Like the Honda bikes and the Bonus, you can buy these direct from the showroom, though they are not cheap. If you take this bike your experience will be like back home – the bike won't go wrong, and you won't learn anything about bikes. You will have fun, however, but don't drop the bike and break a lever – no spares outside of Hanoi. Yamahas can be rented at the Memory Café, 33 Pho Tran Hung Dao.

WHO TO GO WITH

Some cafés in Hanoi have motorbike rentals and can also arrange guides, drivers and itinerary planning. Inquire at TF Handspan (☎ 04-828 1996, tfhandspn@hn.vnn.vn), 116 Pho Hang Bac, in the Old Quarter.

Also well worth considering is Bourlingue Association (☎/fax 04-828 4402, mobile 091-207986, fredo-binh@hn.vnn.vn), the 'Ramblers Association' run by Fredo (or Binh in Vietnamese), an adventure-loving French-Vietnamese expat. Fredo is Hanoi's motorbike guide extraordinaire AND he and his guides know the wild northern territory inside out. Rates for expat guides are considerably higher than for local Vietnamese one, but those who have travelled with this outfit (especially photographers) say it's worth every dong. Bourlingue Association can be contacted at Bar Le Maquis, consequently a hang-out of the notorious Minsk Club (see the Minsk section earlier).

It is always a good idea to register with your embassy before heading out of Hanoi on a motorbike. Give them your itinerary, and details of your travel/health insurance (a must!). Also be sure to take with you the relevant contact numbers for your embassy (and swap this info with your companions). Should you need immediate medical attention (including airlift emergencies), call Dr Rafi Kot in Hanoi (☎ 04-843 0748, fax 846 1750, mobile 090-401919). Alternatively, try AEA International (☎ 04-934 0555, fax 934 0556).

WHAT TO BRING

Be sure you have all the basics: your papers, a first aid kit, Swiss Army knife, sunglasses, toilet paper, mosquito repellent, sunscreen lotion and small denominations of Vietnamese dong.

You can pick up a bottle of western eye drops in most pharmacies as your eyes will take a beating. Some good pipe tobacco (Con Ga is a popular Hanoi brand) will be well appreciated in the mountains, as well as cigarettes. Other things to consider are multivitamins, fizzy codeine, ear plugs (Vietnamese love late night karaoke) and some instant 'three-in-one' coffee packets for neurological disorders.

Try to wear as many clothes as possible – jeans and boots are standard equipment, regardless of how hot it is. Don't be like the half-witted backpackers in Thailand who ride motorbikes with nothing but shorts and sandals to protect against road burn in the event of a crash.

Apart from a Goretex rain jacket, you can buy just about any type of clothing in Hanoi inexpensively. Factory outlets at 37-40 Pho Ngo Quyen sell quality fleece and bike jackets, and Đ Le Duan (running south from the train station) is a good place to find army surplus clothes. If you have a pair of hiking gaiters, bring 'em.

There are dozens of motorbike shops along Pho Hué and this is the place to pick up biker knick-knacks. These shops also sell decent-quality helmets in the US$20 to US$40 range.

Language

The Vietnamese language (Kinh) is a fusion of Mon-Khmer, Tai and Chinese elements. From the non-tonal Mon-Khmer languages, Vietnamese derived a significant percentage of its basic words. From the Tai languages, it adopted certain grammatical elements and tonality. Chinese gave Vietnamese most of its philosophical, literary, technical and governmental vocabulary, as well as its traditional writing system.

Written Vietnamese

For centuries, the Vietnamese language was written in standard Chinese characters *(chu nho)*. Around the 13th century, the Vietnamese devised their own system of writing *(chu nom* or just *nom)*, which was derived by combining Chinese characters or using them for their phonetic significance only. Both writing systems were used simultaneously until the 20th century – official business and scholarship was conducted in chu nho, while chu nom was used for popular literature.

The Latin-based *quoc ngu* script, in wide use since WWI, was developed in the 17th century by Alexandre de Rhodes, a brilliant French Jesuit scholar who first preached in Vietnamese only six months after arriving in the country in 1627. By replacing nom characters with quoc ngu, Rhodes facilitated the propagation of the gospel to a wide audience. The use of quoc ngu served to undermine the position of mandarin officials, whose power was based on traditional scholarship written in chu nho and chu nom, scripts largely inaccessible to the masses.

The Vietnamese treat every syllable as an independent word, so 'Saigon' is spelled 'Sai Gon' and 'Vietnam' is written as 'Viet Nam'. Foreigners aren't too comfortable with this system – we prefer to read 'London' rather than 'Lon Don'. This leads to the notion that Vietnamese is a 'monosyllabic language', where every syllable represents an independent word. This idea appears to be a hangover from the Chinese writing system, where every syllable was represented by an independent character and each character was treated as a meaningful word. In reality, Vietnamese appears to be polysyllabic, like English. However, writing systems do influence people's perceptions of their own language, so the Vietnamese themselves will insist that their language is monosyllabic – it's a debate probably not worth pursuing.

Pronunciation

Most of the names of the letters of the quoc ngu alphabet are pronounced like the letters of the French alphabet. Dictionaries are alphabetised as in English except that each vowel/tone combination is treated as a different letter. The consonants of the Romanised Vietnamese alphabet are pronounced more or less as they are in English with a few exceptions, and Vietnamese makes no use of the Roman letters 'f', 'j', 'w' and 'z'.

c	as an unaspirated 'k'
đ	(with crossbar) a hard 'd' as in 'do'
d	(without crossbar) as the 'z' in 'zoo'
gi-	as the 'z' in 'zoo'
kh-	as the 'ch' in Scottish *loch*
ng-	as the '-nga-' in 'long ago'
nh-	as the 'ni' in 'onion'
ph-	as the 'f' in 'far'
r	as the 'z' in 'zoo'
s	as the 's' in 'so'
tr-	as the 'ch' in 'church'
th-	a strongly aspirated 't'
x	like an 's'
-ch	like a 'k'
-ng	as the 'ng' in 'long' but with the lips closed
-nh	as the 'ng' in 'sing'

Tones

The hardest part of studying Vietnamese for westerners is learning to differentiate between the tones. There are six tones in spoken Vietnamese. Thus, every syllable in Vietnamese can be pronounced six different ways. For example, depending on the tones, the word *ma* can be read to mean 'phantom', 'but', 'mother', 'rice seedling', 'tomb' or 'horse'.

The six tones of spoken Vietnamese are indicated with five diacritical marks in written form (the first tone is left unmarked). These should not be confused with the four other diacritical marks used to indicate special consonants, such as the crossbar in **d**.

The following examples show the six different tone representations:

Tone Name	Example	
dấu ngang	*ma*	'ghost'
dấu sắc	*má*	'mother'
dấu huyền	*mà*	'which'
dấu nặng	*mạ*	'rice seedling'
dấu hỏi	*mả*	'tomb'
dấu ngã	*mã*	'horse'

A visual representation looks something like this:

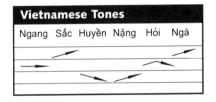

Vietnamese Tones

Ngang Sắc Huyền Nặng Hỏi Ngã

Grammar

Vietnamese grammar is fairly straightforward, with a wide variety of possible sentence structures. Nouns have no masculine/feminine or plural forms and verbs have only one form regardless of gender, person or tense. Instead, tool words and classifiers are used to show a word's relationship to its neighbours. For example, in the expression *con mèo (của) tôi* (my cat), *con* is the classifier, *mèo* is the noun, *của* means 'belong to' (and can be omitted), and *tôi* is the possessive adjective 'my'.

Questions are asked in the negative, as with *n'est-ce pas?* in French. To ask 'Is it OK?' the Vietnamese say 'It is OK, is it not?'. The answer 'No' means 'Not OK it is not,' which is the double-negative form of 'Yes, it is OK'. The answer 'Yes', on the other hand, means 'Yes, it is not OK' or as we would say in English 'No, it is not OK'. The result is that when negative questions ('It's not OK, is it?') are posed to Vietnamese, great confusion often results.

Proper Names

Most Vietnamese names consist of a family name, a middle name and a given name, in that order. Thus, if Henry David Thoreau had been Vietnamese, he would have been named Thoreau David Henry. He would have been addressed as Mr Henry – people are called by their given name, but to do so without the title Mr, Mrs or Miss is considered as expressing either great intimacy or arrogance of the sort a superior would use with his or her inferior.

In Vietnamese, Mr is *Ong* if the man is of your grandparents' generation, *Bac* if he is of your parents' age, *Chu* if he is younger than your parents and *Anh* if he is in his teens or early 20s. Mrs is *Ba* if the woman is of your grandparents' age and *Bac* if she is of your parents' generation or younger. Miss is *Chi* or *Em* unless the woman is very young, in which case *Co* might be more appropriate. Other titles of respect are *Thay* (Buddhist monk), *Ba* (Buddhist nun), *Cha* (Catholic priest) and *Co* (Catholic nun).

There are 300 or so family names in use in Vietnam, the most common of which is Nguyen (which is pronounced something like 'nwyen'). About half of all Vietnamese have the surname Nguyen! When women marry, they usually (but not always) take their husband's family name. The middle name may be purely ornamental, may indicate the sex of its bearer or may be used by all the male members of a given family. A person's given name is carefully chosen to form a harmonious and meaningful ensemble with their family and middle names and with the names of other family members.

For a more comprehensive guide to the language get a copy of Lonely Planet's *Vietnamese Phrasebook*. The following list of words and phrases will help get you started. Some variation exists between the Vietnamese of the north and the south. Foreign students who learn Vietnamese in Hanoi and then move to Saigon to find work (or vice versa) have been dismayed to find that they cannot communicate. The language spoken in the north is considered 'Queen's Vietnamese', while central and southern dialects have a harsher sound to them.

Pronouns

I	*tôi*
you (polite; to older man)	*ông/các ông* (sg/pl)
you (polite; to older woman)	*bà/các bà* (sg/pl)
you (informal; to man own age)	*anh/các anh* (sg/pl)
you (informal; to woman own age)	*chi/các chi* (sg/pl)
he	*ông ấy/anh ấy* (pol/inf)
she	*bà ấy/chị ấy* (pol/inf)
we	*chúng tôi*
they	*họ*

Greetings & Civilities

Hello.	*Xin chào.*
How are you?	*Có khoẻ không?*
Fine, thank you.	*Khoẻ, cám ưn.*
Good night.	*Chúc ngủ ngon.*
Excuse me. (often used before questions)	*Xin lỗi.*
Thank you (very much).	*Cám ưn (rất nhiều).*
Yes.	*Vâng.*
No.	*Không.*

Useful Words & Phrases

change money	*đổi tiền*
come	*đến*
give	*cho*
fast	*nhanh*
slow	*chậm*
man	*nam*
woman	*nữ*
understand	*hiểu*

I don't understand.	*Tôi không hiểu.*
I need ...	*Tôi cần ...*

Small Talk

What's your name?	*Tên là gì?*
My name is ...	*Tên tôi là ...*
I like ...	*Tôi thích ...*
I don't like ...	*Tôi không thích ...*
I want ...	*Tôi muốn ...*
I don't want ...	*Tôi không muốn ...*

Getting Around

What time does the first bus depart?	*Chuyến xe buýt sớm nhất chạy lúc mấy giờ?*
What time does the last bus depart?	*Chuyến xe buýt cuối cùng sẽ chạy lúc mấy giờ?*
How many kilometres to ...?	*Cách xa bao nhiêu ki-lô-mét ...?*
How long does the journey take?	*Chuyến đi sẽ mất bao lâu?*
I want to go to ...	*Tôi muốn đi ...*
What time does it arrive?	*Mấy giờ đến?*
Go.	*Đi.*

hire a car	*thuê xe hưi*
bus	*xe buýt*
bus station	*bến xe*
cyclo (pedicab)	*xe xích lô*
map	*bản đồ*
railway station	*ga xe lửa*
receipt	*biên lai*
sleeping berth	*giường ngủ*
timetable	*thời biểu*
train	*xe lửa*

Around Town

office	*văn phòng*
post office	*bưu điện*
restaurant	*nhà hàng*
telephone	*điện thoại*
tourism	*du lịch*
boulevard	*đại lộ*
bridge	*cầu*
highway	*xa lộ*
island	*đảo*
mountain	*núi*
National Hwy 1	*Quốc Lộ 1*

river	sông
square (in a city)	công viên
street	đường/phố

north	bắc
south	nam
east	đông
west	tây

Accommodation

hotel	khách sạn
guest house	nhà khách

Where is there a (cheap) hotel?	Ở đâu có khách sạn (rẻ tiền)?
How much does a room cost?	Giá một phòng là bao nhiêu?
I'd like a cheap room.	Tôi thích một phòng loại rẻ.
I need to leave at (5) o'clock tomorrow morning.	Tôi phải đi lúc (năm) giờ sáng mai.

air-conditioning	máy lạnh
bathroom	phòng tắm
blanket	mền
fan	quạt máy
hot water	nước nóng
laundry	giặt ủi
mosquito net	mùng
reception	tiếp tân
room	phòng
room key	chìa khóa phòng
1st-class room	phòng loại 1
2nd-class room	phòng loại 2
sheet	ra trãi giường
toilet	nhà vệ sinh
toilet paper	giấy vệ sinh
towel	khăn tắm

Shopping

I'd like to buy ...	Tôi muốn mua ...
How much is this?	Cái này giá bao nhiêu?
I want to pay in dong.	Tôi muốn trả bằng tiền Việt Nam.

buy	mua
sell	bán
cheap	rẻ tiền
expensive	đắt tiền
very expensive	rất đắt
market	chợ

mosquito coils	hương đốt chống muỗi
insect repellent	thuốc chống muỗi
sanitary pads	băng vệ sinh

Time, Days & Numbers

evening	chiều
now	bây giờ
today	hôm nay
tomorrow	ngày mai

Monday	Thứ hai
Tuesday	Thứ ba
Wednesday	Thứ tư
Thursday	Thứ năm
Friday	Thứ sáu
Saturday	Thứ bảy
Sunday	Chủ nhật

1	một
2	hai
3	ba
4	bốn
5	năm
6	sáu
7	bảy
8	tám
9	chín
10	mười
11	mười một
19	mười chín
20	hai mươi
21	hai mươi mốt
22	hai mươi hai
30	ba mươi
90	chín mươi
100	một trăm
200	hai trăm
900	chín trăm
1000	một ngàn
10,000	mười ngàn
one million	một triệu
two million	hai triệu

first	thứ nhất
second	thứ hai

Health

dentist	nha sĩ
doctor	bác sĩ
hospital	bệnh viện
pharmacy	nhà thuốc tây

Emergencies

Help!	*Cứu tôi với!*
I'm sick.	*Tôi bị ốm.*
Please call a doctor.	*Làm ơn gọi bác sĩ.*
Please take me to the hospital.	*Làm ơn đưa tôi bệnh viện.*
Thief!	*Cướp, cắp!*
Pickpocket!	*Móc túi!*
police	*công an*
immigration police station	*phòng quản lý người nước ngoài*

backache	*đau lưng*
diarrhoea	*tiêu chảy*
dizziness	*chóng mặt*
fever	*cảm/cúm*
headache	*nhức đầu*
malaria	*sốt rét*
stomachache	*đau bụng*
toothache	*nhức răng*
vomiting	*ói/mửa*

FOOD
Breakfast

pancake	*bánh xèo ngọt*
banana pancake	*bánh chuối*
pineapple pancake	*bánh dứa*
papaya pancake	*bánh đu đủ*
orange pancake	*bánh cam*
plain pancake	*bánh không nhân*

bread with ...	*bánh mì ...*
omelette	*trứng rán*
fried eggs	*trứng ốp la*
butter	*bơ*
butter & jam	*bơ mứt*
jam	*mứt*
cheese	*phomá*
butter & cheese	*bơ phomát*
butter & honey	*bơ mật ong*
combination sandwich	*săn huýt*

Lunch & Dinner

noodles & rice noodles	*mì, hủ tíu*
chicken noodle soup	*mì gà/phở gà*

vegetarian noodle soup	*mì rau/mì chay*
duck & bamboo shoot noodle soup	*bún măng*
beef noodle soup	*mì bò/phở bò*

potatoes	*khoai tây*
french fries	*khoai rán*
fried potato & tomato	*khoai xào cà chua*
fried potato & butter	*khoai chiên bơ*
fried dishes	*các món xào*
fried noodle with chicken	*mì xào gà/hủ tíu xào gà*
fried noodle with beef	*mì xào bò/hủ tíu xào bò*
mixed fried noodle	*mì xào thập cẩm*

chicken	*gà*
roast chicken	*gà quay/gà rô-ti*
chicken salad	*gà xeù phay*
fried chicken in mushroom sauce	*gà sốt nấm*
batter fried chicken	*gà tẩm bột rán/chiên*
fried chicken with lemon sauce	*gà rán/chiên sốt chanh*
curried chicken	*gà cà-ri*

pork	*lợn/heo*
skewered-grilled pork	*chả lợn xiên nướng/ chả heo nướng*
sweet & sour fried pork	*lợn xào chua ngọt/ heo xào chua ngọt*
roasted pork	*thịt lợn quay*
grilled pork	*thịt lợn nướng xả/ heo nướng xả*

beef	*thịt bò*
beefsteak	*bít tết*
skewered grilled beef	*bò xiên nướng*
spicy beef	*bò xào sả ớt*
fried beef with pineapple	*bò xào dứa*
fried beef with garlic	*bò xào tỏi*
grilled beef with ginger	*bò nướng gừng*
rare beef with vinegar	*bò nhúng giấm*

hot pot (hot & sour soup)	*lẩu*
beef hot pot	*lẩu bò*
eel hot pot	*lẩu lươn*
fish hot pot	*lẩu cá*
combination hot pot	*lẩu thập cẩm*
spring roll	*nem*
meat spring rolls	*nem thịt*
vegetarian spring rolls	*nem rau*
sour spring rolls	*nem chua*
pigeon	*chim bồ câu*
roast pigeon	*bồ câu quay*
fried pigeon in mushroom sauce	*bồ câu xào nấm sốt*
soup	*súp*
chicken soup	*súp gà*
eel soup	*súp lươn*
combination soup	*súp thập cẩm*
maize soup	*súp ngô*
vegetarian soup	*súp rau*
fish	*cá*
grilled fish with sugarcane	*chả cá bao mía*
fried fish in tomato sauce	*cá rán/chiên sốt cà*
sweet & sour fried fish	*cá sốt chua ngọt*
fried fish with lemon	*cá rán/chiên chanh*
fried fish with mushrooms	*cá xào hành nấm rơm*
steamed fish with ginger	*cá hấp gừng*
boiled fish	*cá luộc*
grilled fish	*cá nướng*
steamed fish in beer	*cá hấp bia*
shrimp/prawns	*tôm*
sweet & sour fried shrimp	*tôm xào chua ngọt*
fried shrimp with mushrooms	*tôm xào nấm*
grilled shrimp with sugarcane	*tôm bao mía*

batter fried shrimp	*tôm tẩm bột/ tôm hỏa tiễn*
steamed shrimp in beer	*tôm hấp bia*
crab	*cua*
salted fried crab	*cua rang muối*
crab with chopped meat	*cua nhồi thịt*
steamed crab in beer	*cua hấp bia*
squid	*mực*
fried squid	*mực chiên*
fried squid with mushrooms	*mực xào nấm*
fried squid with pineapple	*mực xào dứa*
squid in sweet & sour sauce	*mực xào chua ngọt*
eel	*lươn*
fried eel with chopped meat	*lươn cuốn thịt rán/chiên*
simmered eel	*lươn om*
fried eel with mushrooms	*lươn xào nấm*
snail	*ốc*
spicy snail	*ốc xào sả ớt*
fried snail with pineapple	*ốc xào dứa*
fried snail with tofu & bananas	*ốc xào đậu phu (đậu hủ) chuối xanh*
vegetarian	*các món chay*
I'm a vegetarian.	*Tôi là người ăn lạt.*
vegetables	*rau*
fried noodles with vegetables	*mì/hủ tíu xào rau*
vegetarian noodle soup	*mì/hủ tíu nấu rau*
fried vegetables	*rau xào*
boiled vegetables	*rau luộc*
fried vegetables	*rau xào*
boiled vegetables	*rau luộc*
sour vegetables	*dưa góp*
fried bean sprouts	*giá xào*

vegetable soup (large bowl)	canh rau
salad	rau sa lát
fried vegetable with mushrooms	rau cải xào nấm

tofu	đậu phụ/đậu hủ
fried tofu with chopped meat	thòt nhồi đậu phụ/ đậu hủ
fried tofu with tomato sauce	đậu phụ/đậu hủ sốt cà
fried tofu with vegetable	đậu phụ/đậu hủ xào

rice	cơm
steamed rice	cơm trắng
mixed fried rice	cơm rang thập cẩm
rice porridge	cháo

specialities	đặc sản
lobster	con tôm hùm
frog	con ếch
oyster	con sò
bat	con dơi
cobra	rắn hổ
gecko	con tắc kè/kỳ nhông/ kỳ đà
goat	con dê
pangolin	con trúc/tê tê
porcupine	con nhím
python	con trăn
small hornless deer	con nai tơ
turtle	con rùa
venison	thịt nai
wild pig	con heo rừng

Fruit

fruit	trái cây
apple	trái táo
apricot	trái lê
avocado	trái bư
banana	trái chuối
coconut	trái dừa
custard apple	trái măng cầu
durian	trái sầu riêng
grapes	trái nho
green dragon fruit	trái thanh long
guava	trái ổi
jackfruit	trái mít
jujube (Chinese date)	trái táo ta

lemon	trái chanh
longan	trái nhãn
lychee	trái vải
mandarin orange	trái quýt
mangosteen	trái măng cụt
orange	trái cam
papaya	trái đu đủ
peach	trái đào
persimmon	trái hồng xiêm
pineapple	trái khóm/trái dứa
plum	trái mận/trái mơ
pomelo	trái bưởi
rambutan	trái chôm chôm
starfruit	trái khế
strawberry	trái dâu
tangerine	trái quýt
three seed cherry	trái sê-ri
water apple	trái roi đường
watermelon	trái dưa hấu

fruit salad	sa lát hoa quả
yoghurt	sữa chua
mixed fruit cocktail	cốc-tai hoa quả

Condiments

pepper	tiêu xay
salt	muối
sugar	đường
ice	đá
hot pepper	ớt trái
fresh chillis	ớt
soy sauce	xì dấu
fish sauce	nước mắm

DRINKS

coffee	cà phê
hot black coffee	cà phê đen nóng
hot milk coffee	nâu nóng
iced black coffee	cà phê đá
iced milk coffee	nâu đá

tea	chè
hot black tea	chè đen nóng
hot milk black tea	chè đen sữa
hot honey black tea	chè mật ong

chocolate milk	cacao sữa
hot chocolate	cacao nóng
iced chocolate	cacao đá
hot milk	sữa nóng
iced milk	sữa đá

fruit juice	*nước quả/nước trái cây*	tinned soft drinks	*thức uống đóng hộp*
hot lemon juice	*chanh nóng*	Coke	*Coca Cola*
iced lemon juice	*chanh đá*	Pepsi	*Pepsi Cola*
hot orange juice	*cam nóng*	7 Up	*7 Up*
iced orange juice	*cam đá*	tinned orange	*cam hộp*
pure orange juice	*cam vắt*	juice	
fruit shake	*sinh tố/trái cây xay*	soda water &	*soda chanh*
banana shake	*nước chuối xay*	lemon	
milk & banana	*nước chuối sữa xay*	soda water, lemon	*soda chanh đường*
shake		& sugar	
orange-banana	*nước cam/chuối xay*		
shake		beer	*bia*
papaya shake	*nước đu đủ xay*	333 beer	*bia 333*
pineapple shake	*nước dứa*	BGI beer	*bia BGI*
mixed fruit shake	*sinh tố tổng hợp/*	Carlsberg beer	*bia Carlsberg*
	nước thập cẩm xay	Chinese beer	*bia Trung Quốc*
mango shake	*nước xoài xay*	Halida beer	*bia Halida*
mineral water	*nước khoáng*	Heineken beer	*bia Heineken*
lemon mineral	*khoáng chanh*	Mastel beer	*bia Amstel*
water		San Miguel beer	*bia San Miguel*
spring water	*nước suối chai*	Tiger beer	*bia Tiger (chai to)*
(large/small)	*(lớn/nhỏ)*	(large bottle)	

Glossary

A Di Da – Buddha of the Past
am & duong – Vietnamese equivalent of yin and yang
Amerasians – half white or half black children borne of unions between Asian women and American servicemen during the *American War*
American War – Vietnamese name for what most other nations call the 'Vietnam War'
Annam – old Chinese name for Vietnam meaning 'Pacified South'
ao dai – national dress of Vietnamese women (and men)
arhat – monk who has attained nirvana

ban – village
bang – congregation (in the Chinese community)
binh dinh vo – traditional martial art performed with a bamboo stick
bonze – Vietnamese Buddhist monk
buu dien – post office

can – 10 year cycle
Caodaism – indigenous Vietnamese religion
cay son – tree from whose resin lacquer is made
Cham – ethnic minority descended from the people of Champa
Champa – Hindu kingdom dating from the late 2nd century AD
Charlie – American soldiers nickname for the *VC*
cheo – comedy
Chuan De – Buddhist 'Goddess of Mercy' (Chinese: Guanyin)
chu nho – standard Chinese characters (script)
chu nom – also *nom*, Vietnamese script
Cochinchina – southern part of Vietnam during the French colonial era
cowboys – motorbike-borne thieves
crachin – fine drizzle
cu ly – fern stems used to stop bleeding

cyclo – pedicab or bicycle rickshaw

danh de – illegal numbers game
dau – oil
den – black
Di Lac Buddha – Buddha of the Future
dinh – communal meeting hall
doi moi – economic restructuring or reform
dong – natural caves
dong chi – comrade
DRV – Democratic Republic of Vietnam (the old North Vietnam)

fengshui – see *phong thuy*
fu – talisman

garuda – Sanskrit term for griffin-like sky beings who feed on *naga*
ghe – long, narrow rowboat
giay phep di lai – internal travel permit
gom – ceramics

hai dang – lighthouse
han viet – Sino-Vietnamese literature
hat tuong – classical theatre in the north
Hoa – ethnic-Chinese, the largest single minority group in Vietnam
ho ca – aquarium
Ho Chi Minh Trail – route used by the *NVA* and *VC* to move supplies to guerrillas in the south
hoi – 60 year period (used in calendar)
hoi quan – Chinese congregational assembly halls
ho khau – residence permit needed for everything: to attend school, seek employment, own land, register a vehicle, buy a home, start a business etc
Honda om – motorbike taxi
huyen – rural district

Indochina – Vietnam, Cambodia and Laos. The name derives from Indian and Chinese influences.

kala-makara – sea-monster god

kalan – religious sanctuary
Khong Tu – Confucius
khach san – hotel
Khmer – ethnic-Cambodians
kich noi – spoken drama
Kinh – Vietnamese language
ky – 12 year cycle (used in calendars)

lang – hereditary noble family who rules the communal land and collects the benefits of labour and tax through its use by locals
lang tam – tombs
Liberation – 1975 takeover of the South by the North; what most foreigners call 're-unification'
Lien Xo – literally, Soviet Union; used to call attention to a foreigner
linga – stylised phallus which represents the Hindu god Shiva
li xi – lucky money

mandapa – meditation hall
manushi-buddha – Buddha who appeared in human form
mat cua – 'watchful eyes', supposed to protect the residents of the house from any harm
MIA – missing in action
Moi – derogatory word meaning 'savages', mostly used to describe hill tribe people
Montagnards – term meaning highlanders or mountain people, still used to refer to the ethnic minorities who inhabit remote areas of Vietnam
muong – large village unit made up of *quels*

naga – Sanskrit term for a giant snake, often depicted forming a kind of shelter over the Buddha
nam phai – for men
napalm – jellied petrol (gasoline) dropped and lit from aircraft, with devastating effect
NGO – nongovernment organisation
nha hang – restaurant
nha khach – hotel or guesthouse
nha nghi – guesthouse
nha rong – large stilt house, used by hill tribes as a kind of community centre
nha tro – dormitory

NLF – National Liberation Front; official name for the *VC*
nom – see *chu nom*
nui – mountain
nu phai – for women
nuoc dua – coconut juice
nuoc mam – fish sauce, added to almost every dish in Vietnam
nuoc suoi – mineral water
NVA – North Vietnamese Army

ODP – Orderly Departure Program; carried out under the auspices of the *UNHCR*, designed to allow orderly resettlement of Vietnamese political refugees

pagoda – traditionally an eight sided Buddhist tower, but in Vietnam the word is commonly used to denote a temple
phong thuy – literally, wind water; used to describe geomancy; also known by its Chinese name, *fengshui*
Politburo – Political Bureau; about a dozen members overseeing the Party's day-to-day functioning with the power to issue directives to the government
POW – prisoner of war
PRG – Provisional Revolutionary Government, the temporary Communist government set up by the *VC* in the South. It existed from 1969 to 1976.

quan – urban district
quel – small stilt-house hamlets
quoc am – modern Vietnamese literature
quoc ngu – Latin-based phonetic alphabet in which Vietnamese is written

rap – cinema
Revolutionary Youth League – first Marxist group in Vietnam and predecessor of the Communist Party
roi can – conventional puppetry
roi nuoc – water puppetry
ruou – wine
RVN – Republic of Vietnam (the old South Vietnam)

social evils – campaign to prevent evil ideas from the west 'polluting' Vietnamese society

song – river
SRV – Socialist Republic of Vietnam (Vietnam's current official name)
stele – carved stone slab or column

Tam Giao – triple religion, the fusion of Confucian, Buddhist, Taoist, Chinese beliefs and Vietnamese animism
Tao – the Way; the essence of which all things are made
Tet – Vietnamese Lunar New Year
thanh long – dragon fruit
Thich Ca – historical Buddha (Sakyamuni)
thung chai – gigantic round wicket| baskets sealed with pitch; used as rowboats
thuoc bac – Chinese medicine
toc hanh – express bus
Tonkin – northern part of Vietnam during the French colonial era; also name of a body of water in the north (Tonkin Gulf)
truyen khau – traditional oral literature

VC – Viet Cong or Vietnamese Communists; considered a derogatory term until recently
Viet Kieu – Overseas Vietnamese
Viet Minh – League for the Independence of Vietnam, a nationalistic movement which fought the Japanese and French but later became fully Communist-dominated

xang – petrol
xe dap loi – wagon pulled by bicycle
xe Honda loi – wagon pulled by a motorbike
xe Lam – three wheeled motorised vehicle

yang – genie

Lonely Planet On-line
www.lonelyplanet.com *or* **AOL keyword: lp**

Whether you've just begun planning your next trip, or you're chasing down specific info on currency regulations or visa requirements, check out Lonely Planet On-line for up-to-the minute travel information.

As well as mini guides to more than 250 destinations, you'll find maps, photos, travel news, health and visa updates, travel advisories, and discussion of the ecological and political issues you need to be aware of as you travel. You'll also find timely upgrades to popular guidebooks which you can print out and stick in the back of your book.

There's also an on-line travellers' forum where you can share your experience of life on the road, meet travel companions and ask other travellers for their recommendations and advice.

And of course we have a complete and up-to-date list of all Lonely Planet travel products including travel guides, diving and snorkeling guides, phrasebooks, atlases, travel literature and videos, and a simple on-line ordering facility if you can't find the book you want elsewhere.

Lonely Planet Diving & Snorkeling Guides

Known for indispensible guidebooks to destinations all over the world, Lonely Planet's Pisces Books are the most popular series of diving and snorkeling titles available.

There are three series: **Diving & Snorkeling Guides**, **Shipwreck Diving** series and **Dive Into History**. Full colour throughout, the **Diving & Snorkeling Guides** combine quality photographs with detailed descriptions of the best dive sites for each location, giving divers a glimpse of what they can expect both on land and in water. The **Dive Into History** series is perfect for the adventure diver or armchair traveller. The **Shipwreck Diving** series provides all the details for exploring the most interesting wrecks in the Atlantic and Pacific oceans. The list also includes underwater nature and technical guides.

LONELY PLANET

Guides by Region

Lonely Planet is known worldwide for publishing practical, reliable and no-nonsense travel information in our guides and on our Web site. The Lonely Planet list covers just about every accessible part of the world. Currently there are nine series: travel guides, shoestring guides, walking guides, city guides, phrasebooks, audio packs, travel atlases, diving and snorkeling guides and travel literature.

AFRICA Africa – the South • Africa on a shoestring • Arabic (Egyptian) phrasebook • Arabic (Moroccan) phrasebook • Cairo • Cape Town • Central Africa • East Africa • Egypt • Egypt travel atlas • Ethiopian (Amharic) phrasebook • The Gambia & Senegal • Kenya • Kenya travel atlas • Malawi, Mozambique & Zambia • Morocco • North Africa • South Africa, Lesotho & Swaziland • South Africa, Lesotho & Swaziland travel atlas • Swahili phrasebook • Tanzania, Zanzibar & Pemba • Trekking in East Africa • Tunisia • West Africa • Zimbabwe, Botswana & Namibia • Zimbabwe, Botswana & Namibia travel atlas
Travel Literature: The Rainbird: A Central African Journey • Songs to an African Sunset: A Zimbabwean Story • Mali Blues: Traveling to an African Beat

AUSTRALIA & THE PACIFIC Australia • Australian phrasebook • Bushwalking in Australia • Bushwalking in Papua New Guinea • Fiji • Fijian phrasebook • Islands of Australia's Great Barrier Reef • Melbourne • Micronesia • New Caledonia • New South Wales & the ACT • New Zealand • Northern Territory • Outback Australia • Papua New Guinea • Papua New Guinea (Pidgin) phrasebook • Queensland • Rarotonga & the Cook Islands • Samoa • Solomon Islands • South Australia • Sydney • Tahiti & French Polynesia • Tasmania • Tonga • Tramping in New Zealand • Vanuatu • Victoria • Western Australia
Travel Literature: Islands in the Clouds • Sean & David's Long Drive

CENTRAL AMERICA & THE CARIBBEAN Bahamas and Turks & Caicos • Barcelona • Bermuda • Central America on a shoestring • Costa Rica • Cuba • Dominican Republic & Haiti • Eastern Caribbean • Guatemala, Belize & Yucatán: La Ruta Maya • Jamaica • Mexico • Mexico City • Panama
Travel Literature: Green Dreams: Travels in Central America

EUROPE Amsterdam • Andalucía • Austria • Baltic States phrasebook • Barcelona • Berlin • Britain • British phrasebook • Canary Islands • Central Europe • Central Europe phrasebook • Corsica • Croatia • Czech & Slovak Republics • Denmark • Dublin • Eastern Europe • Eastern Europe phrasebook • Edinburgh • Estonia, Latvia & Lithuania • Europe • Finland • France • French phrasebook • Germany • German phrasebook • Greece • Greek phrasebook • Hungary • Iceland, Greenland & the Faroe Islands • Ireland • Italian phrasebook • Italy • Lisbon • London • Mediterranean Europe • Mediterranean Europe phrasebook • Norway • Paris • Poland • Portugal • Portugal travel atlas • Prague • Provence & the Côte d'Azur • Romania & Moldova • Rome • Russia, Ukraine & Belarus • Russian phrasebook • Scandinavian & Baltic Europe • Scandinavian Europe phrasebook • Scotland • Slovenia • Spain • Spanish phrasebook • St Petersburg • Switzerland • Trekking in Spain • Ukrainian phrasebook • Vienna • Walking in Britain • Walking in Italy • Walking in Ireland • Walking in Switzerland • Western Europe • Western Europe phrasebook
Travel Literature: The Olive Grove: Travels in Greece

INDIAN SUBCONTINENT Bangladesh • Bengali phrasebook • Bhutan • Delhi • Goa • Hindi/Urdu phrasebook • India • India & Bangladesh travel atlas • Indian Himalaya • Karakoram Highway • Nepal • Nepali phrasebook • Pakistan • Rajasthan • South India • Sri Lanka • Sri Lanka phrasebook • Trekking in the Indian Himalaya • Trekking in the Karakoram & Hindukush • Trekking in the Nepal Himalaya
Travel Literature: In Rajasthan • Shopping for Buddhas

LONELY PLANET

Mail Order

L onely Planet products are distributed worldwide.They are also available by mail order from Lonely Planet, so if you have difficulty finding a title please write to us. North and South American residents should write to 150 Linden St, Oakland, CA 94607, USA; European and African residents should write to 10a Spring Place, London NW5 3BH, UK; and residents of other countries to PO Box 617, Hawthorn, Victoria 3122, Australia.

ISLANDS OF THE INDIAN OCEAN Madagascar & Comoros • Maldives • Mauritius, Réunion & Seychelles

MIDDLE EAST & CENTRAL ASIA Arab Gulf States • Central Asia • Central Asia phrasebook • Iran • Israel & the Palestinian Territories • Israel & the Palestinian Territories travel atlas • Istanbul • Jerusalem • Jordan & Syria • Jordan, Syria & Lebanon travel atlas • Lebanon • Middle East on a shoestring • Turkey • Turkish phrasebook • Turkey travel atlas • Yemen
Travel Literature: The Gates of Damascus • Kingdom of the Film Stars: Journey into Jordan

NORTH AMERICA Alaska • Backpacking in Alaska • Baja California • California & Nevada • Canada • Chicago • Florida • Hawaii • Honolulu • Los Angeles • Louisiana • Miami • New England USA • New Orleans • New York City • New York, New Jersey & Pennsylvania • Pacific Northwest USA • Rocky Mountain States • San Francisco • Seattle • Southwest USA • USA • USA phrasebook • Vancouver • Washington, DC & the Capital Region
Travel Literature: Drive Thru America

NORTH-EAST ASIA Beijing • Cantonese phrasebook • China • Hong Kong • Hong Kong, Macau & Guangzhou • Japan • Japanese phrasebook • Japanese audio pack • Korea • Korean phrasebook • Kyoto • Mandarin phrasebook • Mongolia • Mongolian phrasebook • North-East Asia on a shoestring • Seoul • South-West China • Taiwan • Tibet • Tibetan phrasebook • Tokyo
Travel Literature: Lost Japan

SOUTH AMERICA Argentina, Uruguay & Paraguay • Bolivia • Brazil • Brazilian phrasebook • Buenos Aires • Chile & Easter Island • Chile & Easter Island travel atlas • Colombia • Ecuador & the Galapagos Islands • Latin American Spanish phrasebook • Peru • Quechua phrasebook • Rio de Janeiro • South America on a shoestring • Trekking in the Patagonian Andes • Venezuela
Travel Literature: Full Circle: A South American Journey

SOUTH-EAST ASIA Bali & Lombok • Bangkok • Burmese phrasebook • Cambodia • Hill Tribes phrasebook • Ho Chi Minh City • Indonesia • Indonesia's Eastern Islands • Indonesian phrasebook • Indonesian audio pack • Jakarta • Java • Laos • Lao phrasebook • Laos travel atlas • Malay phrasebook • Malaysia, Singapore & Brunei • Myanmar (Burma) • Philippines • Pilipino (Tagalog) phrasebook • Singapore • South-East Asia on a shoestring • South-East Asia phrasebook • Thailand • Thailand's Islands & Beaches • Thailand travel atlas • Thai phrasebook • Thai audio pack • Vietnam • Vietnamese phrasebook • Vietnam travel atlas

ALSO AVAILABLE: Antarctica • Brief Encounters: Stories of Love, Sex & Travel • Chasing Rickshaws • Not the Only Planet: Travel Stories from Science Fiction • Travel with Children • Traveller's Tales

Index

Text

Bold indicates maps.

Boxed Text

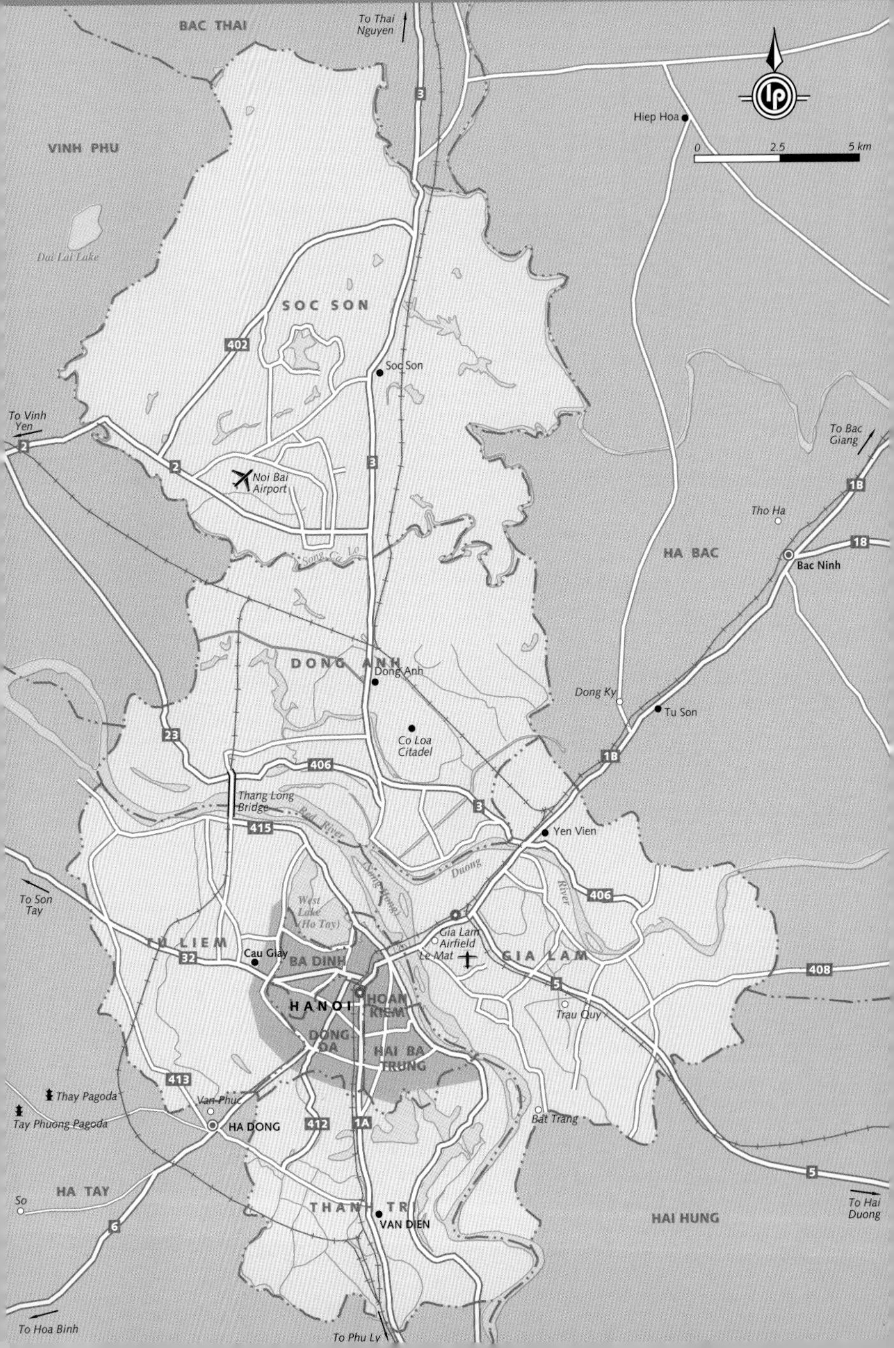

BAC THAI

To Thai
Nguyen

VINH PHU

Dai Lai Lake

SOC SON

402

Soc Son

To Vinh
Yen

2

2

Noi Bai
Airport

3

Hiep Hoa

0   2.5   5 km

To Bac
Giang

1B

Tho Ha

HA BAC

Bac Ninh

18

DONG ANH

Dong Anh

23

Co Loa
Citadel

Dong Ky

Tu Son

406

1B

Thang Long
Bridge

415

Red River

Duong

Yen Vien

River

406

To Son
Tay

West
Lake
(Ho Tay)

TU LIEM

32

Cau Giay

BA DINH

Gia Lam
Airfield
Le Mat

GIA LAM

Trau Quy

408

HANOI

HOAN
KIEM

5

DONG
DA

HAI BA
TRUNG

Thay Pagoda

413

Van Phuc

Tay Phuong Pagoda

HA DONG

412

1A

Bat Trang

5

So

HA TAY

6

THANH TRI

VAN DIEN

HAI HUNG

To Hai
Duong

To Hoa Binh

To Phu Ly

MAP 2 – GREATER HANOI

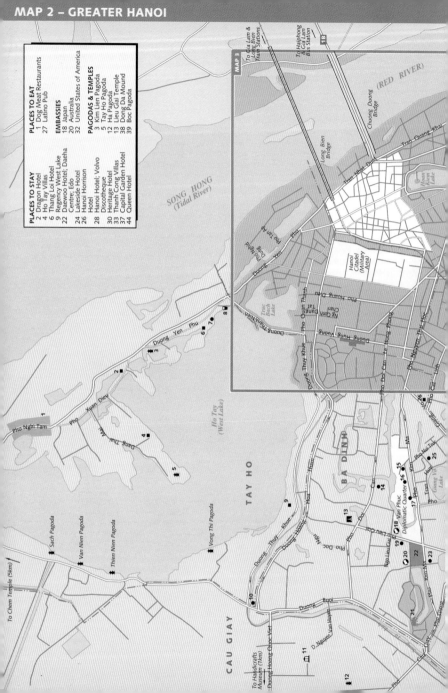

PLACES TO STAY
2   Dragon Hotel
4   Ho Tay Villas
6   Thang Loi Hotel
9   Regency West Lake
22 Daewoo Hotel; Daeha
    Centre; Edo
24 Lakeside Hotel
26 Hanoi Horrison
    Hotel
28 Hanoi Hotel; Volvo
    Discotheque
30 Heritage Hotel
33 Thanh Cong Villas
37 Capital Garden Hotel
44 Queen Hotel

PLACES TO EAT
1   Dog Meat Restaurants
27 Latino Pub

EMBASSIES
18 Japan
20 Australia
32 United States of America

PAGODAS & TEMPLES
3   Kim Lien Pagoda
5   Tay Ho Pagoda
5   Ha Pagoda
13 Lieu Giai Temple
38 Dong Da Mound
39 Boc Pagoda

MAP 2 – GREATER HANOI

MAP 4

HOAN KIEM

HAI BA TRUNG

DONG DA

THANH XUAN

CAU GIAY

Duong Tran Khanh Du
Duong Nguyen Khoai
Pho Lac Trung
Pho Kim Nguu
Pho Lo Duc
Pho To Lich
Thanh Nhan Lake
Pho Thanh Nhan
Pho Hue
Pho Bach Mai
Pho Minh Khai
Pho Tran Hung Dao
Duong Dai Co Viet
Dieu Nam Temple
Pho Dai La
Thuyen Quang Lake
Kinh Luong Park
Bay Mau Lake
Duong Le Duan
Duong Giai Phong
Ba Mau Lake
Pho Kim Lien
Pho Phuong Mai
Pho Kham Thien
Pho Ton Duc Thang
Pho Tran Trung
Duong Truong Dinh
1A
To Phap Van Temple (800m)
0 400 800 m
42
43
44
45
46

Pho Nguyen Bang
Pho Chua Boc
39
38
Ho Dong Da
Thai Ha
Pho Tay Son
Industrial Area
To Hanoi City Cemetery and Crematorium (5km)
40
41
Pho Khuong Trung
Industrial Area
Duong La Thanh
28
27
Khanh
29
32
31
31
33
34
36 35
37
30
Pho Thanh Cong
Pho Lang
Thai
Thinh
Duong Vu Trong Phung
47
48
Duong Nguyen Tuan
Pho Lang Trung
Industrial Area
Duong Thanh Xuan
To Ha Dong Bus Station (1km)
Duong Luong The Vinh
49

OTHER
7 Hanoi Club
8 C & W Bar
10 Buoi Market
11 Museum of Ethnology
14 NGO Resource Centre;
   La Thanh Hotel
15 The Dental Clinic
16 Hanoi Family Medical
   Practice
17 United Nations School
19 Hanoi International
   School
23 Ngoc Khanh Cinema
25 Amsterdam School
29 Cosmos Bowling Centre

31 Hanoi Superbowl;
   Fortuna Hotel
34 Lang Ha Golf Club
35 Vuon Dien Anh
   Cinema Complex
36 Queen Bee Nightclub
40 Institute of Acupuncture
41 Magic Nightclub
42 VMS Mobi-Fone
43 Mo Market
45 Giap Bat Bus Station
46 Giap Bat Train Station
47 Son La Bus Station
48 Hanoi National
   University
49 Hanoi Foreign Languages
   College

MAP 3 – CENTRAL HANOI (NORTH)

Ho Tay
(West Lake)

BA DINH

Truc Bach
Lake

TAY HO

0   200   400 m

Bach Thao Park &
Botanical Garden

Ba
Dinh
Square

BA DINH

Hanoi Citadel
(Military Area)

Chi Lang
Park

DONG DA

MAP 4

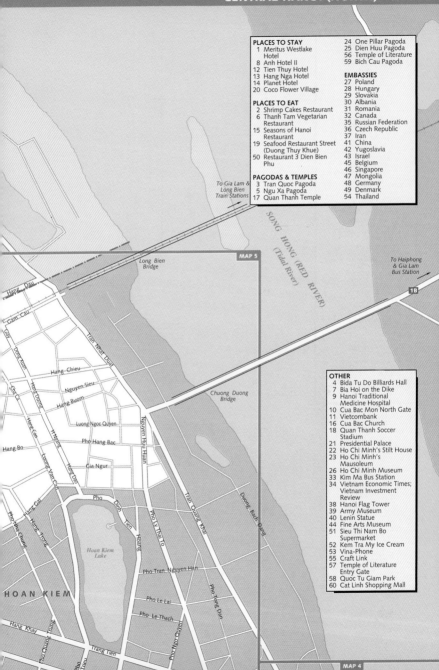

PLACES TO STAY
1 Meritus Westlake Hotel
8 Anh Hotel II
12 Tien Thuy Hotel
13 Hang Nga Hotel
14 Planet Hotel
20 Coco Flower Village

PLACES TO EAT
2 Shrimp Cakes Restaurant
6 Thanh Tam Vegetarian Restaurant
15 Seasons of Hanoi Restaurant
19 Seafood Restaurant Street (Duong Thuy Khue)
50 Restaurant 3 Dien Bien Phu

PAGODAS & TEMPLES
3 Tran Quoc Pagoda
5 Ngu Xa Pagoda
17 Quan Thanh Temple
24 One Pillar Pagoda
25 Dien Huu Pagoda
56 Temple of Literature
59 Bich Cau Pagoda

EMBASSIES
27 Poland
28 Hungary
29 Slovakia
30 Albania
31 Romania
32 Canada
35 Russian Federation
36 Czech Republic
37 Iran
41 China
42 Yugoslavia
43 Israel
45 Belgium
46 Singapore
47 Mongolia
48 Germany
49 Denmark
54 Thailand

OTHER
4 Bida Tu Do Billiards Hall
7 Bia Hoi on the Dike
9 Hanoi Traditional Medicine Hospital
10 Cua Bac Mon North Gate
11 Vietcombank
16 Cua Bac Church
18 Quan Thanh Soccer Stadium
21 Presidential Palace
22 Ho Chi Minh's Stilt House
23 Ho Chi Minh's Mausoleum
26 Ho Chi Minh Museum
33 Kim Ma Bus Station
34 Vietnam Economic Times; Vietnam Investment Review
38 Hanoi Flag Tower
39 Army Museum
40 Lenin Statue
44 Fine Arts Museum
51 Sieu Thi Nam Bo Supermarket
52 Kem Tra My Ice Cream
53 Vina-Phone
55 Craft Link
57 Temple of Literature Entry Gate
58 Quoc Tu Giam Park
60 Cat Linh Shopping Mall

To Gia Lam & Long Bien Train Stations

SONG HONG (RED RIVER) (Tidal River)

MAP 5

Long Bien Bridge

To Haiphong & Gia Lam Bus Station

1B

Hang Dau

Cam Cau

Tran Nhat Duat

Hang Chieu

Nguyen Sieu

Hang Buom

Luong Ngoc Quyen

Pho Hang Bac

Hang Bo

Gia Ngur

Pho

Dinh Tien

Hoang

Nguyen Huu Huan

Tran Quang Khai

Chuong Duong Bridge

Duong Bach Dang

Pho Ly Thai To

Hoan Kiem Lake

Pho Tran Nguyen Han

HOAN KIEM

Pho Le Lai

Pho Le Thach

Hang Khay

Trang Tien

Pho Tong Dan

MAP 4

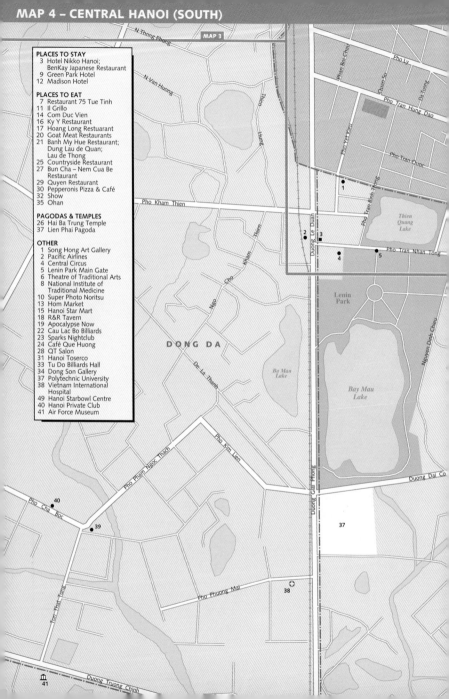

MAP 4 – CENTRAL HANOI (SOUTH)

MAP 3

PLACES TO STAY
3 Hotel Nikko Hanoi;
   BenKay Japanese Restaurant
9 Green Park Hotel
12 Madison Hotel

PLACES TO EAT
7 Restaurant 75 Tue Tinh
11 Il Grillo
14 Com Duc Vien
16 Ky Y Restaurant
17 Hoang Long Restuarant
20 Goat Meat Restaurants
21 Banh My Hue Restaurant;
   Dung Lau de Quan;
   Lau de Thong
25 Countryside Restaurant
27 Bun Cha – Nem Cua Be
   Restaurant
29 Quyen Restaurant
30 Pepperonis Pizza & Café
32 Show
35 Ohan

PAGODAS & TEMPLES
26 Hai Ba Trung Temple
37 Lien Phai Pagoda

OTHER
1 Song Hong Art Gallery
2 Pacific Airlines
4 Central Circus
5 Lenin Park Main Gate
6 Theatre of Traditional Arts
8 National Institute of
   Traditional Medicine
10 Super Photo Noritsu
13 Hom Market
15 Hanoi Star Mart
18 R&R Tavern
19 Apocalypse Now
22 Cau Lac Bo Billiards
23 Sparks Nightclub
24 Café Que Huong
28 QT Salon
31 Hanoi Toserco
33 Tu Do Billiards Hall
34 Dong Son Gallery
37 Polytechnic University
38 Vietnam International
   Hospital
49 Hanoi Starbowl Centre
40 Hanoi Private Club
41 Air Force Museum

N Thong Phong

N-Van Huong

Thien

Hung

Pho Kham Thien

Pho Cho

Ngo

Khanh Thien

Duong Le Duan

Pho Bai Chat

Pho Ly

Quan Su

Da Tuong

Pho Tran Hung Dao

Pho Ly Thong Kiet

Pho Tran-Binh-Trong

Pho Tran Quor

Thien
Quang
Lake

Pho Tran Nhan Tong

D O N G   D A

De La Thanh

Lenin
Park

Nguyen Dinh Chieu

Bu Man
Lake

Bay Mau
Lake

Pho Pham Ngoc Thach

Pho Kim Lien

Duong Giai Phong

Duong Dai Co

37

Pho Chat Boc

40

39

38

Pho Phuong Mai

Ton That Tung

41

Duong Truong Chinh

MAP 3

0   200   400 m

SONG HONG (RED RIVER)
(Tidal River)

MAP 5

Trang Tien

Pho Hai Ba Trung

Thuong Kiet

Pho Tho Nhuom

Nhuom

Pho Ba Trieu

Pho Hang Bai

Pho Nguyen Khac Can

Pho Ngu Quyen

Pho Phan Chu Trinh

Pho Le Thanh Tong

Pham Ngu Lao

D. Thai Than

Duong Tran

Chuong Duong

Pho Toan

Pho Ham Long

Pho Ngo Quyen

Phan Huy Chu

Khan Du

HOAN KIEM

Pho Nguyen Du

Pho Le Van Huu

Pho Han Thuyen

Nhiem

▼ 12

11

Vuong

Pho Ha Ng Chuoi

Pho Tran Thanh Tong

Duong

Bach Dang

10
● 9

▼ 14

Hai

13

Pho Tang Bat Ho

● 6

Binh

Tran Xuan Soan

● 7

Trieu

Xuan

Viet

De

15

Bach

Pho Ngo Hau

● 18

24

▼ 8

17

16

Pho Hoa Ma

Pho Hue

Pho Tu Duc

Pho Tu Tue

Tinh

Chan Tien Pagoda

Pho Tho Nham

19   20 21   22

23

27

28   29

25 ▼

32

Bui Thi

Trieu

30

33

31

Pho Nguyen Cong Tru

Pho To Hien Thanh

Nguyen Cao

Pho Dong Nhan

Nguyen

Pho

Pho

Pho

Mai

Yen Bai

26

Duong Nguyen Khoai

Doan Tran Nghiep

● 4

Pho Le Dai Hanh

Pho Hue

35

Thai Phien

Pho Thinh Yen

HAI BA TRUNG

Viet

Pho Tran

Khat Chan

Thanh Nhan Lake

Pho Bach Mai

36

Pho Kim Nguu

Pho Thanh Nhan

Pho Lac Trung

MAP 5 – HOAN KIEM & OLD QUARTER

MAP 5 – HOAN KIEM & OLD QUARTER

PLACES TO STAY

2 Galaxy Hotel
3 Chains First Eden Hotel
13 Dong Xuan Hotel
16 Anh Dao Hotel
19 My Kinh Hotel
25 Thuy Lam Hotel
26 Thanh Ha Hotel
27 Nam Hoa Hotel
28 Prince Hotel
29 Asia Hotel
31 Hung Hiep Hotel
33 Quoc Hoa Hotel
44 Hoa Linh Hotel
46 Fortuan (Phu Do) Hotel
49 TF Handspan Hotel & Tour
   Office; The Whole Earth
   Vegetarian Restaurant
53 Van Xuan Hotel
55 Camilla Hotel
58 Kim Tin Hotel
64 Mai Phuong Hotel
67 Binh Minh Hotel; Queen Café 2
69 Anh Sinh Hotel
70 Royal Hotel
72 Phu Long Hotel
73 Time Hotel
81 Trang An Hotel
86 Win Hotel
93 Hong Ngoc Hotel
104 Nam Phuong Hotel
122 Especen Hotel & Tour Office;
   Café de Paris
124 Phu Gia Hotel; Rendevoux Café
127 Energy Hotel; Hanoi Star Mart
128 Binh Minh Hotel; China
   Southern Airlines; Standard
   Chartered Bank
132 Tong Dan Hotel
146 Nam Phuong Hotel
155 Thuy Nga Hotel
161 Bodega Café
165 Trang Tien Hotel
167 Dan Chu Hotel
172 Sofitel Metropole Hotel; Le
   Beaulieu Restaurant; Met Pub
182 Army Hotel
183 Hanoi Opera Hilton
195 Melia Hanoi Hotel; Thai
   Airways International
200 Prince Hotel
203 Cuu Long II Hotel

205 Cuu Long I Hotel
209 Mango Hotel
210 Dong Loi Hotel
214 Saigon Hotel
215 Guoman Hotel
222 The Eden Hotel; Pear Tree Pub;
   A Little Italian Restaurant
226 Lotus Café & Guesthouse
234 Hoa Binh Hotel
241 ATS Hotel
245 De Syloia Hotel; Cay Cau
   Restaurant
260 Thu Do Hotel
261 Hotel 30/4

PLACES TO EAT

5 Lau De Nhat Ly
6 Van Xuan
7 Thanh Thuy
10 Thang Long Restaurant
22 Baan Thai Restaurant
23 Tuyet Nhung Restaurant
24 Cha Ca La Vong
32 La Dolce Vita Restaurant
   (Bat Dan Café)
35 Cha Ca 66
37 Café Quyen
38 Pho Gia Truyen Noodle Shop
41 Bun Bo Nam Bo
42 Tin Tin Bar & Café
48 Old Darling Café
52 Gallery Café
54 Sinh Café
57 A to Z Queen Café & Tours
60 Pho Cuong Noodle Shop
61 Café Lam
62 Love Planet Café & Tours;
   Lovely Pub
63 Tandoor Indian Restaurant
65 Lonely Planet Café
66 Pho Ga
68 Sinh Café
71 Les Flamboyants
78 Smiling Café
80 Real Darling Café
82 No Noodles
87 Old Quarter (Pho Co) Café
88 Dinh Lang Restaurant;
   Thuy Ta Café
89 Mama Rosa
90 Le Café des Arts
91 Café Nhan

99 Pho Bo Dac Biet Noodle Shop
103 Sukiyaki
105 Kangaroo Café
106 Thu Huong Chinese Restaurant
107 Hoa Long Hotel
111 Five Royal Fish Restaurant
114 Moca Café
118 Mediterraneo Restaurant
129 Khazana Indian Restaurant;
   Bangkok Bank
130 Quan Cay Da Café; Children's
   Theatre
133 President Garden Restaurant
136 Trong Dong Restaurant
141 Dak Linh Café
143 Café Lac Viet
144 Il Padrino
145 Green Ho Guom; Carvel Ice
   Cream
154 Saigon Sakura Restaurant
156 Friend Café
158 Ciao Café
174 Mai La Café
175 Au Lac Café
176 The Press Club
186 Gustave Eiffel Restaurant
187 Seafood Restaurant
188 The Deli
192 Al Fresco's
199 Indochine Restaurant
202 Kinh Do Café
206 Khoa Goose Restaurant
211 Tam Tu Thai Restaurant
213 Wild Horse Saloon
217 San Ho Restaurant
218 Emotion Cybernet Café
220 Lan Anh Restaurant; Mekki's Bar
221 Hoa Sua Restaurant & Bakery
233 Le Splendide
237 Quan Hué Restaurant
238 Café Pho
239 Huong Giang Restaurant
253 Thu Thuy Asian Food
256 Com Chay Nang Tam
257 Orient Café
258 Chau Giang Restaurant
267 Soho Café
268 Meeting Café
269 Cung Dinh Quan
270 Tiem Pho Noodle Shop
272 Mai Anh Noodle Shop
274 Hanoi Gourmet

HOAN KIEM & OLD QUARTER – MAP 5

EMBASSIES
173 Italy
194 UK Embassy; AEA International; Hong Kong Bank
223 Laos Consulate
224 India
229 New Zealand
246 Philippines
247 Indonesia
250 Cambodia
252 France
263 Laos

PAGODAS & TEMPLES
20 Bach Ma Temple
43 Dau Temple
76 Ngoc Son Temple
109 Le Thai To Temple & Statue
115 Ly Quoc Su Temple
120 Ba Da Temple
125 Thap Rua (Tortoise Pagoda)
219 Ambassadors' Pagoda

OTHER
1 Long Bien Bus Station
4 TNT
8 Chua An Do Islamic Mosque
9 Dai Dong Centropell
11 Dong Xuan Post Office
12 Dong Xuan Market
14 Cua O Quan Chuong (Old East Gate)
15 Exotissimo Travel
17 Trang An Gallery
18 Bar Le Maquis
21 Goethe Institue
30 The Culture of Vietnam Ethnic Groups Shop
34 Bat Dan Post Office
36 Bia Hoi Ha Chau Quan
39 Bach Ma Community House
40 Loc Tai Bakery
45 Red River Tours & Café
47 Memorial House at 48 Pho Hang Ngang
50 Kim Café
51 Chuong Vang Theatre
56 The Pan Flute Shop
59 Buffalo Tours
74 Municipal Water Puppet Theatre
75 Martyrs' Monument
77 The Huc Bridge
79 Vietnamese Craft Guild
83 Luong Van Can Post Office
84 Co Xanh Gallery
85 Khai Silk
92 Kim Dung Embroidery Shop
94 Hang Da Market
95 Cyclo Bar & Restaurant
96 Apricot Gallery
97 Salon Natasha
98 Tu Lap CD Shop
100 WOW CD Shop
101 Golden Cock Bar
102 Polite Pub
108 ANZ Bank
110 Central Cultural House
112 Gallerie L'Atelier
113 Deltadeco; Nha Quay
116 Lan
117 St Joseph Cathedral
119 Indochine House
121 Vietcombank
123 Quan Nhac Jazz Club
126 Hanoi Peoples' Committee Building
131 Vietcombank
134 Vietcombank (Main Branch)
135 Indira Gandhi Park
137 DHL
138 Main Post Office (GPO)
139 Federal Express; UPS
140 Hoa Phong Tower
142 Fanny's Ice Cream
147 Hoan Kiem Cultural House
148 Credit Lyonnais Bank
149 Green Bamboo Tours
150 Aeroflot Airlines
151 National Library and Archives
152 Vietnam Airlines
153 Ecomtour Tours
157 Air France; Japan Airlines
159 Librairie Vietnamienne Francophone
160 Hanoi Optic Shop
162 Thang Long Bookshop
163 Trang Tien Bookshop
164 Nam Son Gallery
166 Kem Trang Tien
168 Opera Fine Art Gallery; The New Factory Gallery
169 Hanoi Bookstore; Foreign Language Bookshop
170 Citibank; ING Bank; Singapore Airlines
171 Malaysia Airlines
177 Bia Hoi Viet Ha
178 Co Tan Park
179 Revolutionary Museum
180 History Museum; Foreign Languages College
181 Geological Museum
184 Hanoi Opera House
185 Mini Mart Trang Tien
189 Baskin Robbins Ice Cream
190 Xunhasaba Bookshop
191 The Spotted Cow
193 Culturimex Furniture Shop
196 Maison Centrale
197 Hanoi Towers; The Red Onion Bistro; Fat Jacks Bar; Cathay Pacific Airways
198 Cua Hang Thuc Pham 17 Food Shop
201 Metal Night Club
204 Cua Nam Market
207 Tran Quy Cap Train 'B' Station
208 Main Hanoi Train Station
212 Fanslands Cinema
216 Relax Bar
225 ECCO Voyages
227 Vietnamese Women's Museum
228 Kem Kiwi
230 Vietnamtourism
231 Science Library
232 Bank of America
235 Hanoi Tourism
236 Verandah Bar & Café
240 Mai Gallery
242 Border Guard Museum
243 China Airlines
244 World Conservation Union
248 The Gioi Publishers
249 Thang 8 & New Age Cinemas
251 Hanoi Library
254 Western Canned Goods
255 Best Service Travel
259 Ann Tours
262 Alliance Française de Hanoi
264 Hanoi Studio
265 Lao Aviation
266 Chinfon Commercial Bank
271 Ham Long Catholic Church
273 Memorial House at 5D Pho Ham Long

MAP LEGEND

BOUNDARIES

- ━ ━ ━ ━ .... International
- ━ ━ ·· .... State
- ━ ━ ━ ━ .... Disputed

HYDROGRAPHY

- .... Coastline
- .... River, Creek
- .... Lake
- ...... Intermittent Lake
- .... Salt Lake
- .... Canal
- .... Spring, Rapids
- .... Waterfalls
- .... Swamp

ROUTES & TRANSPORT

- .... Freeway
- .... Highway
- .... Major Road
- .... Minor Road
- .... Unsealed Road
- .... City Freeway
- ...... City Highway
- .... City Road
- ..... City Street, Lane

- ...... Pedestrian Mall
- ⊃ ═ ═ .... Tunnel
- ⊶◎⊶ .. Train Route & Station
- ⊶Ⓜ⊶ ...... Metro & Station
- ▬▬▬▬▬ .... Tramway
- ⊢⊢⊢⊢⊢ .. Cable Car or Chairlift
- ─ ─ ─ ─ ...... Walking Track
- ─────── ...... Walking Tour
- ─ ─ ─ ─ .... Ferry Route

AREA FEATURES

- .... Building
- ✿ .... Park, Gardens
- .... Cemetery
- .... Market
- .... Beach, Desert
- .... Urban Area

MAP SYMBOLS

✈ .... Airport	← ...... One Way Street	
∿ ...Ancient or City Wall	‡ .... Pagoda	
⊖ .... Bank	Ⓟ .... Parking	
🏖 .... Beach	)(................ Pass	
⌒ .... Cave	★ .... Police Station	
🚻 ✝ .... Church	✉ .... Post Office	
⌒ ....Cliff or Escarpment	❖ ...... Shopping Centre	
☉ .... Embassy	🏛 .... Stately Home	
✪ .... Hospital	🏊 ...... Swimming Pool	
⚱ .... Monument	☎ .... Telephone	
◪ .... Mosque	🏯 .... Temple	
▲ ...... Mountain or Hill	❶ ....Tourist Information	
🏛 .... Museum	⊖ .... Transport	
⛲ .... National Park	🐘 .... Zoo	

- ✪ **CAPITAL** ...... National Capital
- ◉ **CAPITAL** .... State Capital
- ● **CITY** .... City
- ● **Town** .... Town
- ● Village .... Village
- ○ ...... Point of Interest

- ■ .... Place to Stay
- ⚐ ...... Camping Ground
- ⊞ .... Caravan Park
- ⌂ .... Hut or Chalet

- ▼ .... Place to Eat
- 🍺 .... Pub or Bar

Note: not all symbols displayed above appear in this book

LONELY PLANET OFFICES

Australia
PO Box 617, Hawthorn, Victoria 3122
☎ (03) 9819 1877 fax (03) 9819 6459
email: talk2us@lonelyplanet.com.au

USA
150 Linden St, Oakland, CA 94607
☎ (510) 893 8555 TOLL FREE: 800 275 8555
fax (510) 893 8572
email: info@lonelyplanet.com

UK
10a Spring Place, London, NW5 3BH
☎ (0171) 428 4800 fax (0171) 428 4828
email: go@lonelyplanet.co.uk

France
1 rue du Dahomey, 75011 Paris
☎ 01 55 25 33 00 fax 01 55 25 33 01
email: bip@lonelyplanet.fr
3615 lonelyplanet *(1,29 F TTC/min)*

World Wide Web: www.lonelyplanet.com *or* AOL keyword: lp
Lonely Planet Images: lpi@lonelyplanet.com.au

Contents – Text